DECENT CAPITALISM

'The authors present a highly stimulating and thoughtful proposal on how to stabilise the world economy and how to make financial crises less likely and less lethal in the future. It is comforting to see such a constructive contribution to this debate coming from Europe.'
Nouriel Roubini, Professor of Economics and International Business, Stern School of Business, New York University

'Dullien, Herr and Kellermann have written an important contribution to the post-crisis economic literature by offering sensible, practical and distinctly non-utopian policy options. The proposals in Decent Capitalism rest on three overriding principles – that balanced and sustainable economic growth remains desirable and necessary, that the global financial and monetary system must be stabilised, and that income inequality needs to addressed through active policies. Whatever policy agenda is likely to emerge from the current financial mess, I would bet it will be based on the principles outlined in this book.'
Wolfgang Münchau, associate editor of the *Financial Times*

'The authors go far far beyond the parameters of neoliberalism in providing the grounds for an egalitarian, partially regulated, green market economy. This book is definitely part of a new generation of economic thinking for the left that takes us forward.'
Colin Crouch, Professor of Governance and Public Management, University of Warwick Business School

'An outstanding book that gives a comprehensive, sensitive and thoughtful account of the crisis and presents a feasible model for a better world economy to benefit all the people. It should be compulsory reading for scholars and lay persons alike.'
Yaga Venugopal Reddy, Emeritus Professor of Economics at the University of Hyderabad and Former Governor of the Reserve Bank of India

'Dullien, Herr and Kellermann's engaging argument is worth reflecting upon. This is the kind of bold thinking we need today, if we are to match the challenges of our times.'
Poul Nyrup Rasmussen, President, Party of European Socialists

Decent Capitalism
A Blueprint for Reforming our Economies

Sebastian Dullien,

Hansjörg Herr

and Christian Kellermann

PlutoPress
www.plutobooks.com

First published 2011 by Pluto Press
345 Archway Road, London N6 5AA

Distributed in the United States of America exclusively by
Palgrave Macmillan, a division of St. Martin's Press LLC,
175 Fifth Avenue, New York, NY 10010

www.plutobooks.com

British Library Cataloguing in Publication Data
A catalogue record for this book is available from the British Library

ISBN   978 0 7453 3110 2   Hardback
ISBN   978 0 7453 3109 6   Paperback

Library of Congress Cataloging in Publication Data applied for

10 9 8 7 6 5 4 3 2 1

Designed and produced for Pluto Press by
Curran Publishing Services, Norwich

Printed and bound in the European Union by
CPI Antony Rowe, Chippenham and Eastbourne

CONTENTS

FIGURES

PREFACE

'Decent' describes something which is not obscene or immodest, something respectable. The International Labour Organisation for example stresses 'decent work'. Capitalism, many argue, is by definition indecent. Finance capitalism's excesses of the last decade were obviously the opposite of decency. The growth model of that period was built on financial and housing bubbles, unsustainable credit expansion of almost all economic sectors and major global imbalances. We all know the result. In the end the bill was passed on to the public, leaving governments' capabilities to care for those in our society who need support or to counterbalance economic recessions even weaker than before.

It was at the climax of this financial crisis, in early 2009, that we met a range of high-level experts from banking, finance and economics in Frankfurt, Germany's financial centre. We wanted to know more about the various perspectives on that crisis, which was unfolding in front of our eyes with dramatic speed and reach. There has always been a divide between the perspective of a single investor or investment firm and the more systemic macroeconomic perspective, but as our seminar showed, that gulf has never been greater. There was no awareness at all among the finance specialists of the need of a higher level of regulation of their own business from the systemic perspective. And there was not the least suspicion that there could be something wrong with income distribution, corporate governance or unstable international capital flows. It was very clear that finance just wanted to continue with business as usual: taking excessive risks, keeping activities as opaque as possible, and having someone else pay for the damage if things go wrong – a perfect world, from one special perspective at least.

The Friedrich Ebert Foundation, which organised this seminar, took that depressing insight as a call to action, and reinforced its activities in building up knowledge of and support for a more fundamental correction of capitalism's excesses. The foundation, set up in 1925, has a vast institutional memory of financial crises and the misery they have caused for many workers and families throughout history. However, the foundation also has the memory of how things can be changed to engender more decent economic systems. This happened for example after the Second World War, when out of the devastation of the Great Depression and the terrible war that followed, highly egalitarian societies were constructed in Europe which provided the vast population with breathtaking improvements in their living standards for decades to come. In the light of this, sitting on the sidelines and watching global stalemate was simply not an option.

For that reason we were asked to write this book. It is conceived as a blueprint for a better economic system (still) based on capitalist principles. Our *Decent Capitalism* tries to dig deep and reveal the structural problems of our economic system as a whole. In doing this, we have to give disturbing news and send out a number of distress calls to those who have the technical resources to save the system. When the book was first published in Germany, the discussions were consequently rather heated and controversial, not only because we criticised the German export model and its role in fuelling global and regional imbalances, but also because we brought other markets into the context of the financial market's dominating power. At the same time, we (rather anti-cyclically) did not attack capitalism as such, but offered a framework to allow markets to add to productive, social and ecological dynamics while minimising their associated risks. We do not offer a radical blueprint for an artificially constructed society based on utopian ideas of giving up markets or globalisation. For us such an option is not plausible in the foreseeable future. Nonetheless, we believe the present system has to be reformed in a radical social, ecological and democratic way. We thought and still think that such an economic model is not only theoretically possible, but also politically feasible. However, it needs a substantially different balance of various markets as well as of markets and society as such. The last time a capitalist system was remoulded and embedded in society in this way, that change was framed by the aftermath of war and by the rising surge of communism.

Naturally, we were also criticised. The two main criticisms were that we paid too little attention to two features that were crucial for a decent economic system: the issue of growth in general and the issue of 'what growth?' in particular. We therefore spent another summer discussing and thinking together in Berlin and revised the book substantially in order to elaborate a concept of growth, which then even became the core of our 'decent capitalism'. Public interest in the topic of growth could hardly be higher at the moment: global warming, stagnant global development, growing cross-border competition and the question of how to secure social and ecological security and equality in our societies seem to present an unsolvable dilemma. We have tried to approach this complex task and develop a blueprint for a growth path that resolves some of the contradictions by combining global needs and national capabilities in a realistic arrangement.

Against the background of these vast questions, current political reactions are tentative and constricted by national or even more bigoted interests of global finance. Nevertheless, many recent regulatory corrections have tended to go into the right direction, but at best they treat the symptoms of the problems, not the underlying causes; they remain cosmetic and opaque even in their limited focus on increasing financial stability. Serious comprehensive approaches to rebalance the global web of economic interdependencies and reduce globalisation's current dysfunctions are hard to find.

We want to provide such material for any political actor or individual who is not willing to settle for cosmetic approaches to the economic deficiencies of our times and systems. There is no explicit political bias in our writing, although the Friedrich Ebert Foundation works mainly with the global labour movement in order to strengthen global social democracy. We look critically into the Green New Deal in the same way that we analyse Basel III or Barack Obama's regulatory initiatives. However, we deliberately argue for a more structural approach. This goes beyond the flood of snapshot literature on economic reform which tends to focus on single dysfunctions.

At the time of writing, the crisis of financial markets has been shifted onto sovereign balance sheets. It remains totally unclear, however, who will rescue the rescuers. Nationalism is flourishing again, the European Union is blocked by its own intrinsic institutional shortcomings, global governance institutions lack the necessary legitimacy, and the world economy is deadlocked over global imbalances. At the end of the day we are witnessing a global game of 'beggar my neighbour' again with the outcome unknown. Our economic system is in deep waters, and it needs just as deep a set of reforms.

Sebastian Dullien, Hansjörg Herr and Christian Kellermann
Berlin/Stockholm, January 2011

INTRODUCTION

This is not a book about 'the Crisis'. At least, not only. This is a book about our economic life as a whole and how we can construct a 'decent capitalism' which delivers to all people and is a lot less crisis-ridden and more sustainable than the current variants of capitalism. It goes without saying that there is something deeply wrong with our economic system as we know it. The most recent crises are just a symptom of the underlying failures of the latest stage of finance capitalism. Misconduct rooted in hubris and greed, both bred by deregulated markets, nearly brought the system down in ruins. It was only because governments stepped in and bailed out what were declared to be systemically relevant financial institutions that our economies did not collapse completely. We all know 'the crisis story' by now and many of us ask whether all that was inevitable after all. Couldn't we have stepped in a lot earlier and make the system more crisis-proof? And what will follow now with the debts of households, firms and countries still high even after shifting parts of those debts onto governments? Will changes to the system be merely cosmetic or will there be a significant reform in the financial and other sectors and finally of capitalism as a whole? Can capitalism actually be made better?

'Capitalism' as a term is back on Main Street. Crashing, dismantling, reforming, repairing, restoring – all kinds of approaches to capitalism are discussed in the wake of the recent crisis. The debate has gained far more momentum today than it had during the past decade, though we had already witnessed a number of such crises. In contrast to the debates of the first decade of our century, policy alternatives to a wholesale freeing up of markets are suddenly being seriously discussed again. However in practice, the gap between regulatory rhetoric and actual reform of our economies is still considerable. Our systems remain at risk of ongoing instability. Crises will continue to be the norm rather than the exception, if we keep on working with the dysfunctions of current capitalism. Many of us will be unable to live a decent life under conditions of increased insecurity, inequalities and pressure in terms of wages, jobs, raising children and providing for old age. An excessive degree of unequal income distribution and personal insecurity is not only detrimental to a good life, it is also economically dangerous and inefficient. The reasons for economic crises and increasing inequality, which are symptom and root of personal and systemic insecurity and inefficiency alike, are manifold.

Most of today's mainstream economics books concentrate on the most obvious crisis factor, financial markets (see for example Wolf 2008, Posner 2009, Rajan 2010, Paul Krugman 2009). The sheer amount of books published in the wake of the crisis suggests a major shortcoming in this sphere of capitalism. And in fact finance has played a crucial role in most of the economic crises we have experienced since the 1990s. Financial markets are both gigantic amplifiers of imbalances within and between our economies and a root of imbalances themselves. Illuminating the cracks in finance is therefore the logical starting point for fixing or overcoming our capitalistic system. However, one has to be very careful not to fall for the argument that the cracks are not that dramatic after all. Behind fancy finance talk of controlling credit default swaps and asset backed securities is sometimes the hidden agenda of scapegoating single financial instruments or actors in order to be able to leave the basic structure of the system untouched. Like the US economist Nouriel Roubini and historian Stephen Mihm, we think that a broader look at capitalism is necessary. We also agree that sticking to ideologies and taboos like the simple belief that free markets will always solve economic problems best unduly narrow our perspective of what is wrong with today's capitalism. As Roubini and Mihm (2010: 6) put it: 'It's necessary to check ideology at the door and look at matters more dispassionately.'

A sober and encompassing approach to today's economic dysfunctions is necessary, because the excesses of finance are only one part of the fundamental problems economies and societies are facing and which have contributed to the recent crisis. There are at least two dimensions of instability which are related to finance but go beyond the narrow instabilities of the financial system. First, imbalances between different sectors within economies have escalated. One expression of this is highly indebted private households as well as governments, as a consequence of real-estate and other bubbles, which were fuelled by the financial system. Second, international imbalances have never been as big as today – take for example the most prominent cases, the current account deficit of the United States and current account surpluses of China, Germany or Japan.

Besides such instabilities, the market-liberal globalisation of the last decades led to income and wage disparities which had not been seen since the early times of brutal capitalism before the First World War. Without doubt a certain degree of inequality based on hard work or innovative entrepreneurship is the fuel of capitalism. When the degree of inequality – as it is today – becomes very high and the level of incomes loses all sensible relationship to an individual's effort or performance, however, the system begins to crack.

It is not surprising that 'equality' is back on the agenda when discussing the successes and the future of market societies. Influential books in that matter include *The Spirit Level* by Richard Wilkinson and Kate Pickett (2009) and *Animal Spirits* by George Akerlof and Robert Shiller (2010). Increasing inequality is a phenomenon which can be found in almost every country. High inequality does not only provoke a feeling of 'unfairness' in and between societies; it also hinders social mobility, has negative impacts on health and also on productivity. Hungry wolves do not hunt best – in fact, the very opposite is true for our today's economies. The American Dream of high social mobility within a society and the opportunity for anyone to become rich if they work hard enough is in fact little more than a mirage. Today, mobility within society is more of a reality in the Nordic countries of Scandinavia, where equality is higher than in the Anglo-Saxon world of capitalism (Lind 2010). This is an important insight for redesigning capitalism.

Capitalism has other problems: in the past, it has led to a very special type of technology, production and consumption growth which is blind to ecological problems and the fact that natural resources are limited. Prices systematically fail to incorporate ecological dimensions and the deterioration of nature in an adequate way, and give the wrong signals for the direction of innovation as well as of production, consumption and the way we live. After experiencing a number of regional ecological disasters in the past century, the world is now heading for a global ecological disaster, unless fundamental changes take place very soon. This makes the search for solutions very complicated. The present crisis is not only a deep crisis of traditional capitalism, but it has emerged at a time when a deep ecological crisis is also evolving. To solve only one of the two crises is not enough to provide humanity with sustainable and acceptable living conditions.

This is where 'decent capitalism' is relevant. Based on the analysis of what has gone wrong in recent years – both globally and in national contexts – we outline a new approach. In this book we develop a proposal for an economic model whose fundamental orientation is to ensure social justice and environmental sustainability at a high level of prosperity. We start by looking at two key problems with the existing economic model which has formed in many industrialised countries since the 1970s, problems which can and must be solved.

First, the reforms of the past 40 years were based on a naïve market radicalism. Markets were conceived as self-regulating mechanisms which automatically led to stability, including high employment and a reasonably acceptable distribution of income. Since the unleashing of markets did not, generally speaking, deliver the desired results, economic policy persistently prescribed yet one more dose of freedom. As early as 1944, the Austrian-Hungarian economist and philosopher Karl Polanyi noted that, although markets play an important role in economic and social development, land, labour and money must be subject to strict rules. Otherwise, labour markets, financial markets and environmental processes can turn into 'satanic mills', as he put it. The Indian socio-economics philosopher Amartya Sen (1999) has expressed similar views, emphasising that markets are a source of freedom, but can deliver its fruits only if, on the one hand, institutions and regulations exist which ensure they function properly and, on the other hand, market actors have the material prerequisites for participation. It is vital to jettison the delusion that markets can function properly without the framework provided by government. We need a new balance between state, market and society – and it is clear that both state and society must be given more weight.

Second, since the 1970s markets have become global, while attempts to regulate them have often remained at the national level, or at best at the level of a group of countries. Until this asymmetry is resolved it will be difficult to ensure stable and sustainable global economic and ecological development. Without effective and global institutions and regulation, economic, social and environmental problems may intensify in such a way that globalisation will be rolled back, a process which will be accompanied by crisis-ridden upheavals. For a region such as the European Union that means either further integration or disintegration. A European currency without a proper European federal governance structure will just not work, leading to permanent economic problems and even the threat of ultimate failure, as has been shown by the recent euro debt crisis. At the same time, individual states must espouse global rules which are binding for all, and not rely on the discretionary 'codes of conduct' developed by financial experts and multinational companies themselves. At the global level, there will be no such thing as a global state in the foreseeable future. Global institutions are needed, however, which can organise global coordination and impose sanctions.

One of the key issues for a new economic model is clearly what role should be assigned to the financial markets. The financial sector and its dynamism in the creation of credit should not be condemned. Although profligate lending practices were one of the main causes of the bubble in the US real-estate market and thus of the following crisis, it should not be forgotten that credit and credit growth are not bad in themselves. Rather, credit provides the fuel for innovation and growth. In our view, the financial sector has an important role in a 'decent capitalism'. In contrast to recent years, however, when financial transactions were often an end in itself, this sector should once more become a service provider for the rest of the economy, especially the enterprise sector. Financial markets must provide the economy with sufficient funds to ensure a level of production which allows full employment. Of course, in mature (post-)industrial societies working time reductions must also become an important element to guarantee high employment, but this does not change the basic fact that economic growth will remain the necessary condition for social progress in the medium term. Financial markets must finance the ecological restructuring of production and furnish venture capital to enable innovations, above all in the 'green economy', within the framework provided by the state. But they must also make available 'patient' capital which enables enterprises to develop long-term strategies and plan on the basis of a longer time horizon. The framework for financial markets must be shaped in such a way that the sector as a whole performs these tasks.

Similarly to the approach of Joseph Stiglitz (2010), who looks beyond the epicentre of the recent crises, we follow a global view to explain crisis capitalism. International economic imbalances must be reduced as well as volatile exchange rate movements. Selective international capital controls and the reduction of some types of capital flows seem necessary to achieve this goal.

Better international and national financial market regulation might be a necessary condition for a stable capitalism, but it is not sufficient. The rest of the economic framework must also be shaped in such a way that sufficient and sustainable aggregate demand growth can be generated without permanently rising indebtedness within countries and between countries. This means that the generation of demand via wages and salaries should again be given greater weight. The key instrument for managing this demand should be an active wage policy, which provides decent wages for all. A reduction in wage dispersion is needed in almost all countries. Also income inequality in general, which depends among other factors on how much income is transferred to the financial sector and groups benefiting from such transfers, has to be reduced substantially. The economic rationale behind a more equal income distribution in respect to demand creation is simple: high-income earners consume relatively less than those living on low incomes. As a result, a greater demand effect can be generated from raising low incomes than from bestowing tax cuts on millionaires, quite apart from considerations of fairness.

How to achieve 'decent capitalism' is a systemic question. Decent capitalism aims at a proper balance between markets, the government and society. At many points we once again need more state intervention. However, that in no sense means a return to the models of the 1950s and 1960s. Neither does 'more state' mean a rolling back of liberalisation in the social sphere. The old models often reinforced dubious power structures, which had to be overcome. Many groups were excluded from the labour market or at least from certain positions. For women, for example, due to more gender discrimination, career opportunities in the 1950s and 1960s were much more scarce than today. A return is therefore neither desirable nor possible.

After the recent crisis, however, it should be clear that the unreformed Anglo-Saxon model which has long been seen as something to strive for cannot be a model for all industrial countries or for emerging markets. In fact, the subprime crisis and its impact in the United States and the United Kingdom have shown the weakness of an economic model which is based on short-term increases in 'shareholder value' and which grants an excessive role to financial markets beyond the commercial banking system. We believe that in developed countries, different types of 'decent capitalism' based on different traditions and political constellation will and should exist – not to speak about developing countries which may and should look for their own type of capitalism.

There are a number of capitalist models today, which compete to become predominant. From the global perspective they all have strengths and shortcomings; in concert they are all rather dissonant. Quite pragmatically we want to point to different problems in different countries in order to understand different perspectives and discuss different options. In this book we take the examples of the United States, China and Europe and examine their situation. In this way, we include a large share of the world economy measured by GDP weight in our analysis. Moreover, we include both developing and developed countries, both current account surplus and deficit countries, and countries with different relations between state and market.

Axiomatically, any book about capitalism must confront a discussion about economic growth: Do we want growth, do we need it, and how should growth look like? Our 'decent capitalism' needs growth, however of a very different quality from what we know today. Many rich economies have grown to enormous 'heights', but growth as it happened in the past is simply not possible from the ecological point of view. Even zero growth without changing the quality of economic output would destroy our planet and thus ourselves in the long run. Fundamental restructuring in the way we produce and consume is unavoidable. To achieve this aim even in developed countries, growth will be needed for at least for some time. In a global 'Green New Deal' governments will set incentives for 'decent growth' which allows for a globally balanced level of prosperity. A global Green New Deal does not exclude developed countries from undertaking such restructuring. In fact, although it is very unlikely that restructuring can be successful if it does not occur in developed countries, the developed world also has to increase its efforts to promote innovations and transfer them as part of development aid without restrictions to developing countries. Of course, redistribution is key to balancing prosperity levels within societies and globally. This approach, however, is not compatible with the political reality of today's power relations. We are convinced that fundamentally changing technologies and the way we consume and produce will allow further growth for the foreseeable future. Therefore we need 'decent growth' based on incentive structures, direct prohibitions of harmful behaviour, effective taxation and also more public and other forms of ownership.

A new economic model, like the one developed in this book, is an extremely ambitious goal. Many elements in such a model are beyond the reach of single countries, especially if they are integrated in regional blocs, such as the European Union, and are thus closely interconnected with their neighbours, both economically and legally. Furthermore, for many steps, the supranational level is the appropriate one. This applies in particular to ecological problems, but also to financial markets, taxes and the correction of global imbalances. However, in many areas a transition to a new economic model can also begin at home. A start could be made on reducing current account surpluses or deficits, wage inequalities and the number of precarious jobs. Also greater domestic redistribution via the tax system and provision of public goods such as decent education, health, public transport or research facilities is a task which can be tackled unilaterally. Fundamental measures to prevent global warming and to save natural resources must start at home. For all of this, however, the goal must be known and very clear. This book provides such a blueprint, a goal towards which policy can navigate. The aim of this book, therefore, is to initiate the project of a better global economic system – a decent capitalism, no more, no less.

PART I

THE ROOTS OF CRISIS CAPITALISM

1

THE RISE OF MARKET LIBERALISM

The world economy's plunge into the Great Depression of the 1930s resulted in major losses in terms of growth and employment, not to mention deflationary tendencies in virtually every corner of the globe. However, it also smoothed the way for a specific model of regulated capitalism. The world economic crisis engendered the conviction, among people of almost every political stripe, that only a regulated capitalism could have any chance of surviving. In contrast to the period after the First World War, at the end of the Second World War the United States actively developed a global hegemony in order to support economic development in Western Europe, as well as in other countries in the Western bloc.

One of the cornerstones of the regulatory model created at that time was the Bretton Woods Agreement. It was negotiated, first and foremost, by the United States and the United Kingdom at a conference in the small American town of Bretton Woods. Concluded in July 1944, while the Second World War was still raging, it was adopted in 1947. Every country in the developed Western world was included in the agreement, which was characterised by fixed exchange rates which, however, could be adapted in response to fundamental imbalances. The rates were permitted to fluctuate on foreign exchange markets only within a narrow range of plus or minus 1 per cent around the institutionally fixed central rate. If need be, central banks were called upon to stabilise the exchange rate by means of interest rates, foreign exchange market interventions or interventions in capital movements. In practice the agreement meant that only central banks outside the United States were responsible for defending exchange rates, while the US Federal Reserve (the Fed) was able to remain completely passive. Such asymmetrical burden sharing in exchange rate stabilisation can be explained by the absolute dominance of the United States during the closing stages of the Second World War and in its aftermath. In order to boost confidence in the US dollar the United States committed itself, apart from the Bretton Woods Agreement, to convert dollar credits from central banks into gold, for which a conversion rate of US$35 per ounce was laid down. For central banks outside the United States, therefore, holding dollar reserves was tantamount to holding gold.

The International Monetary Fund (IMF) and the World Bank were also created at the Bretton Woods Conference. The IMF was tasked with providing loans to support countries which encountered difficulties in defending their exchange rate. The World Bank, by contrast, assumed development-policy functions. Besides fixed exchange rates, the international financial system was subjected to a whole range of regulations. Capital movements in developing countries were very modest and there were practically no private loans, but there were international capital movements between the developed countries, and these were extensively regulated. It was taken for granted that countries could employ capital movement regulations to defend exchange rates and to limit current account imbalances. This right remains inscribed in the statutes of the IMF even today.

The Bretton Woods system conferred on the world economy a stable monetary framework. Although, in some countries, incessant current account surpluses developed – for example, in Germany – the imbalances, as a percentage of gross domestic product (GDP), were modest in comparison with the world economic situation of previous years. Since currency crises were few and far between, the IMF largely had little to do and, in comparison with the decades after the collapse of the Bretton Woods system, did not play a central role.

National financial systems were also strictly regulated, and different spheres were often separated from one another. Real-estate financing, for instance, was, as a rule, disconnected from the rest of the system or tightly controlled by the state. Consumer credit played a subordinate role: credit expansion was focused on the business sector. Dynamic consumer demand was based on income growth. In many countries, such as the United States, upper limits were imposed on interest rates. Even in countries such as the United States and the United Kingdom, which traditionally had capital-market-based financial systems, the stock market did not play an exceptional role. In continental Europe, Japan and the developing countries, bank-centred systems dominated, with so-called 'house banks' acting as the most important sources of external finance for enterprises.

The capitalist model of the post-war period took a number of different forms. In Asia – for example, in Japan and many other market-oriented countries – state intervention was extensive and included a far-reaching industrial policy, which in turn incorporated political allocation of loans. Foreign trade was characterised by protectionist intervention. In addition, in countries such as Japan, employees were bound to their companies and were at almost no risk of losing their jobs, based on a model in which employment was for life and exhibited a number of features that were openly paternalistic. Similarly, income distribution in these countries was markedly egalitarian. Although in Europe the role of the state was less all-encompassing than in Asia, there was industrial policy intervention on a massive scale there too.

Europe also featured a compromise between the classes that took the form of a strong welfare state. In Germany, for example, opportunities for workers' participation in enterprise management were created. So-called 'economic democracy' made it possible in Germany for employees to be represented in the supervisory boards and even the boards of directors of large companies. Wage development in Europe was, as a rule, regulated by collective agreements which were negotiated by strong trade unions and employers' organisations and applied to whole industries or even the whole economy. In Europe, too, in comparison with the situation today, income distribution was fairly balanced.

Even the United States, during the post-war period, was characterised by more or less the same basic model. As late as the end of the 1960s, J.K. Galbraith (1967) was able to characterise American managers as 'state bureaucrats committed to public welfare' – there was then no sign of the gamblers engaged in a ruinous capitalism with whom we have become all too familiar. Like Japan and Europe, the United States was a middle-class society, in which both absolute poverty and extreme wealth manifested themselves only occasionally.

This model, established after the Second World War, bestowed on the global economy a whole series of economic miracles like those in Germany and Japan. However, all Western countries were able to notch up positive development in terms of real growth. Unemployment was comparatively low during this period, and some countries – including the Federal Republic of Germany – even experienced labour shortages in the 1960s, which were made good by bringing in guest-workers.

The economic model that emerged from the Great Depression in the 1930s and managed to establish itself in the Western world – as it was constituted at the time – after the Second World War, can be contrasted with the current situation not only in its high growth and low unemployment, but also in a fair distribution of income. Welfare state provisions and labour market regulation guaranteed a high level of social security and of living standards to the overwhelming majority of the population. The model, which in these terms can be described as a 'golden age of capitalism', fell into a deep crisis in the 1970s which prepared the way for the market-liberal globalisation project.

THE END OF BRETTON WOODS AND ITS CONSEQUENCES

Not least because of the considerable privileges which Bretton Woods system afforded the United States, the system collapsed in February 1973 after a crisis which had lasted since the end of the 1960s. The United States had taken particular advantage of the privilege of not having to look after the stability of its currency itself but rather, as already mentioned, being able to pass the burden onto other countries. As a result, from the end of the 1960s, lack of confidence in the US dollar led to capital outflows in the United States, which the US central bank did nothing about. Triggering this falling confidence and the high capital outflows were the expansionary monetary and fiscal policy and the overheating of the US economy in the second half of the 1960s caused by the Vietnam War and domestic efforts to combat poverty. The loss of confidence in the dollar was intensified by President Nixon's announcement, in August 1971, that the dollar credits of foreign central banks would no longer be converted into gold. Clearly, the US government of the time feared that the weakness of the dollar would lead to massive outflows of gold from the United States. The so-called 'Nixon shock' caused the system of fixed exchange rates to totter. The Smithsonian Agreement of December 1971 was an attempt to rescue the system under modified conditions. Further capital outflows from the United States provoked increasingly drastic foreign exchange market interventions by central banks in order to prevent a devaluation of the dollar. This again impeded monetary policy in the countries affected. The Fed remained on the sidelines. The German Bundesbank, in particular, was forced into intervening since the deutschmark had begun to establish itself as the second reserve currency next to the US dollar. The Bundesbank was then one of the leading central banks which refused to keep on buying US dollars on 12 February 1973, permitting the drastic devaluation of the dollar.

The instability of international capital flows which characterised the Bretton Woods system in its final stage must be seen against the background of a gradual liberalisation of international capital movements, which in turn clearly hindered the defence of the system. In the end, fixed exchange rates found diminishing support, both politically and academically. In the academic sphere, the naïve view took hold that flexible exchange rates were a suitable way of allowing each country an autonomous economic policy, even with liberalised goods and capital movements. It was also believed that flexible exchange rates would lead to balanced current accounts.[1] If a different economic policy had been adopted, particularly on the part of the United States, and if reform had been undertaken – for example, retaining certain regulations on capital movements that could have curtailed US privileges – the Bretton Woods system could have been saved. However, the political will was lacking and the collapse of the system was regretted by few at the time.

The case of Europe

It was also not realised at the time that the transition to flexible exchange rates would destabilise foreign exchange markets. Figure 1.1 shows that exchange rates between the yen, the mark and the dollar remained stable until the end of Bretton Woods (apart from the one-off revaluation of the mark in 1961). The ensuing period of weakness of the US dollar caused it to lose half its value in relation to the mark – the dollar's main rival at the time – by the end of the 1970s. Up to 1985 there was another period of dollar revaluation – by around 100 per cent – followed by another halving of the external value of the dollar against the mark. The euro did not bring stability, either. After its introduction at the beginning of 1999, it was devalued against the dollar by around 20 per cent, only to increase in value against the dollar by around two-thirds from 2003. The development of the dollar–yen rate witnessed similar somersaults. The exchange rates of the French franc, the UK pound, the Italian lira and other European currencies were also extremely unstable against the dollar and amongst themselves. Such crass exchange rate fluctuations transformed the global currency system into a shock generator in which countries' competitive positions could change rapidly and fundamentally, while fluctuating import prices could trigger welfare and price shocks. It soon emerged that

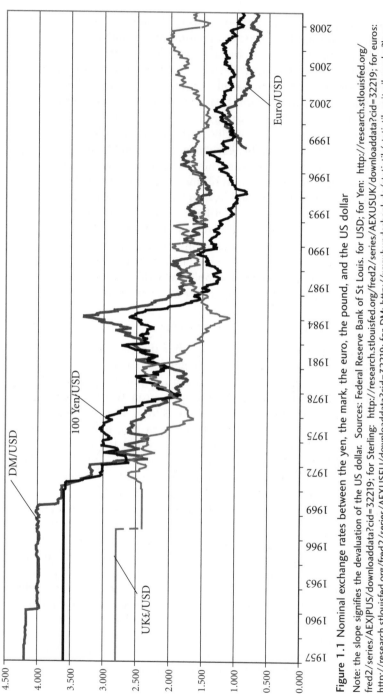

Figure 1.1 Nominal exchange rates between the yen, the mark, the euro, the pound, and the US dollar. Sources: Federal Reserve Bank of St Louis. for USD; for Yen: http://research.stlouisfed.org/fred2/series/AEXJPUS/downloaddata?cid=32219; for Sterling: http://research.stlouisfed.org/fred2/series/AEXUSUK/downloaddata?cid=32219; for euros: http://research.stlouisfed.org/fred2/series/AEXUSEU/downloaddata?cid=32219; for DM: http://www.bundesbank.de/statistik/statistik_zeitreihen.php?lang=de&open=&func=row&tr=WJ5009

exchange rate movements were not to be explained by differences in inflation rates, interest rates, real GDP growth rates or other fundamentals. Economists are, quite simply, unable to deliver reliable prognoses on the development of exchange rates between the leading currencies of the world.

Flexible exchange rates were established, after the collapse of the Bretton Woods system, between the world's leading currencies: the dominant US dollar was at the top of the currency hierarchy, followed by the mark and the yen, with a markedly lower international circulation, and some other currencies, such as the Swiss franc and the British pound. It would be incorrect to assume from this, however, that since 1973 exchange rates have been completely determined by the market between all the currencies in the world. Rather a large US dollar bloc emerged, in which many weaker currencies – above all in Asia and Latin America – were pegged to the dollar. In Europe the so-called European 'currency snake' developed, since different currencies had begun to gather around the mark. The yen, by contrast, was unable to form its own currency bloc, and other currencies are simply too insignificant to be a major trading or reserve currency.

Turning to a more detailed analysis of monetary integration in Europe, some currencies underwent chaotic fluctuations after the collapse of the Bretton Woods system; the Italian lira and the British pound, for example, experienced profound currency crises. This exchange rate turbulence inflicted considerable harm on European integration and further steps in that direction ran into difficulties. This was one of the main reasons why German Chancellor Helmut Schmidt and French President Valéry Giscard d'Estaing launched an initiative for the stabilisation of exchange rates in Europe. In 1979, the European Monetary System (EMS) succeeded the informal 'currency snake' and created a system of fixed exchange rates between France, the Federal Republic of Germany, Italy and the Benelux countries, although the rates could be modified if necessary, as was indeed the case from time to time during the lifetime of the EMS. As a number of other countries joined the system, the EMS grew, while currencies – such as the Austrian schilling – linked up with the deutschmark without joining the EMS. The crucial difference between the Bretton Woods system and the EMS was the fact that no reserve currency was established in the EMS. All currencies in the system were linked to the European currency unit (ECU), which represented a basket currency related to all the currencies in the system and functioned as the unit of account for fixing exchange rates. The EMS was so constructed that one of the currencies would emerge as a de facto reserve currency. As a result of its prestige among international investors, the mark immediately assumed this role, which to a considerable extent afforded the Bundesbank the privilege of setting interest rates in the EMS.

At the end of the 1980s, accelerated politically by German reunification, a new wave of deeper European integration began. In 1992, the Maastricht Treaty was signed, which foresaw the introduction of a European Monetary Union (EMU) for 1999.

At that time it was assumed that the transition from the EMS to the EMU could be accomplished without great problems. However, the EMS experienced its greatest turbulence in 1992 and 1993. In September 1992, the United Kingdom left the EMS, having entered the exchange rate mechanism (ERM) only in 1990. In 1993, the margin in relation to the institutionally fixed central rate had to be increased from plus or minus 2.5 per cent to plus or minus 15 per cent; devaluation pressures on some currencies in the EMS had become so great that this seemed unavoidable. The problem during this period was that, in order to combat modest inflationary tendencies which accompanied strong growth in West Germany after German unification, the Bundesbank imposed a tight monetary policy with high interest rates. At the same time, the other European countries found themselves in an economic downturn and wanted to lower interest rates. On top of that, the Bundesbank increased interest rates again in summer 1993, although a significant economic downturn had already been forecast in Germany, too. For a number of countries in the EMS the interest rate policy imposed on them by the Bundesbank was simply too much to bear, both economically and politically. Certainly, this was what international investors suspected, leading them to speculate against the pound and the French franc. The very restrictive monetary policy was justified by the Bundesbank as necessary to fight inflation. However, the EMS was not much liked by the Bundesbank, and nor was the EMU, which had been agreed upon in 1990. It is likely that the Bundesbank wanted to sabotage both the EMS and the EMU.

The EMU was launched on 1 January 1999, confronting the US dollar with a stronger opponent than the mark: the euro. In contrast to initial expectations that it would be only a small currency union, Austria, Belgium, Finland, France, Germany, Ireland, Italy, Luxembourg, the Netherlands, Portugal and Spain were all founding members of the EMU. Other countries, such as Sweden and Denmark, were offered the opportunity to join but turned it down.

In 2001, Greece joined the EMU, Cyprus and Malta entered in 2008 and Slovakia in 2009. For a number of European countries which did not belong to the Eurozone, the so-called European Monetary System II (EMS II) was created, which in principle functioned entirely in accordance with the rules of the original EMS. Currencies were also linked to the euro independently of EMS II. Nevertheless, even today there are currencies in the European Union which belong neither to the EMU nor to EMS II, for example the British pound.

Why is it surprising that so many countries entered the EMU and that others are likely to do so in the future? What is surprising is that the current group of EMU countries is extremely heterogeneous and that the Maastricht criteria on budget and debt levels, which were supposed to regulate entry to EMU, have in fact enabled every country either to enter or link up with the EMU. Clearly, the Maastricht criteria were not capable of ensuring a proper selection of the countries to participate in the EMU. As a consequence, the EMU countries are characterised, among other things, by extremely varied productivity levels, social, tax and financial systems, fiscal traditions and, not least, wage mechanisms. EMU integration, which consisted of the introduction of a common currency and monetary policy, lacked corresponding integration steps in other areas. These differences have led within the EMU to considerable regional upheaval. We shall discuss this situation in more detail below.

Inflation and the conservative revolution

Turning to domestic economic problems, it is clear that almost every developed Western country was affected by inflationary developments from the end of the 1960s. These contributed decisively, not only to the collapse of the Bretton Woods system, but also to the decline of the post-war economic model (see Figure 1.2). Only in the 1980s was it possible in the OECD countries to lower the inflation rate. It is remarkable that both the United States and The United Kingdom had to contend with comparatively strong inflationary processes, which began to escalate towards the end of the 1970s. Eventually, it was from these two countries that the conservative revolution would emerge.

At the end of the 1960s, unemployment rates fell to historically low levels in almost all Western industrialised countries. The resulting labour shortages bolstered the market power of employees, which in turn boosted nominal wages. That was, on the one hand, because of rising wages agreed in collective agreements, but also due to payments above the agreed rate. When wage costs rise, costs

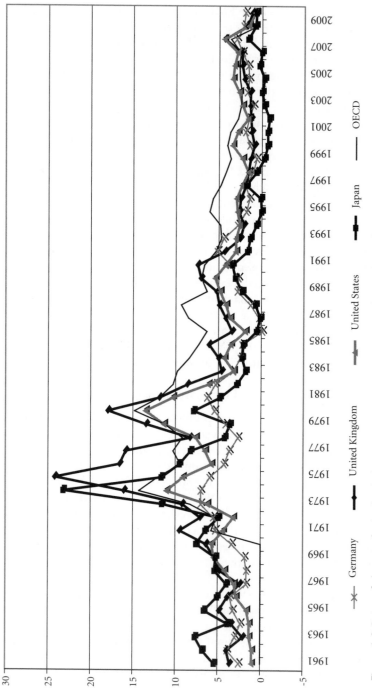

Figure 1.2 Rates of change of price levels (consumer price index, compared with previous year, %)
Source: Ameco 2010, for data on OECD: OECD StatExtracts URL.

go with them and so do price levels. The problem from the end of the 1960s, however, was deeper than a shortage of labour, which may arise periodically without necessarily undermining an economic regime. With the exception of Japan, a multitude of reform movements seemed to gain ground in the Western world at this time, some of a social democratic character, others of a socialist bent and as a rule accompanied by an active left-oriented student movement. These movements spoke up for a reinforcement of democratic rights, greater equality of opportunity, support for workers, changes in the education system, fairer income distribution, the emancipation of women and other issues connected to the notion of a more liberal society. The reform movements led, almost as a by-product, to a more aggressive wage policy.

In many countries, there was a radicalisation of established trade unions, or the founding of oppositional ones which organised so-called wildcat strikes and made radical wage demands.

Two oil price shocks, in 1973 and 1979, aggravated the situation in Western countries. The oil price increased dramatically due to high demand during the global economic upswing in the second half of the 1960s and the beginning of the 1970s. The weakness of the US dollar must also be taken into account here; oil was and still is traded, like all important raw materials, in US dollars. The dramatic fall in the external value of the dollar in the 1970s reduced the real revenues of oil exporting countries, because goods outside the dollar area became more expensive. Political events in OPEC's sphere of influence also drove the oil price upwards.[2] In the 1980s, the oil price fell back again sharply, only to positively explode after 2003 and then to collapse once again (see Figure 1.3).

The two oil price shocks led, in countries which had to pay a higher price for oil, to rising prices and corresponding falls in real wages. Accepting lower wages was clearly at odds with the ideas and expectations of the reform movements which had established themselves and asserted their demands. In particular, when the first oil shock struck in 1973 employment levels were still high, so that it was easy to force through wage increases to compensate for (real) wage losses. As a consequence, a wage–price spiral set in: higher wages increased the cost pressure on enterprises, which in turn increased prices.

The collapse of the Bretton Woods system had a similar effect. After the lifting of exchange rate controls a number of countries were hit by devaluations. Devaluations lead to import price increases and, like oil price increases, to an upward shift in price levels and

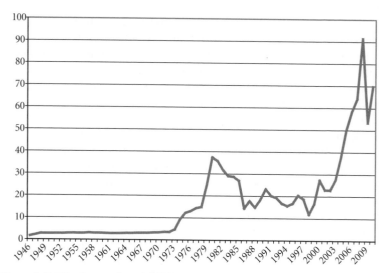

Figure 1.3 Oil price per barrel (US$), 1946–2009
Source: www.inflationdata.com/inflation/Inflation_Rate/Historical_Oil_Prices_Table.asp

a reduction in real wages. The situation was particularly difficult for countries subject to cumulative effects: for example, those hit, besides oil price increases, by a wage–price spiral and devaluation.

The development of The United Kingdom and the United States is significant with regard to the birth of the market-liberal globalisation model. In the 1970s, their economies were extremely frail. Both countries were hit by oil price rises, devaluations and inflationary wage increases. There was also political instability. The United Kingdom, during this period, saw a rapid succession of governments – Labour under Harold Wilson (1964–69), the Conservatives under Edward Heath (1970–74), Labour again under Wilson (1974–76) and then under James Callaghan (1976–79). In 1979, Margaret Thatcher came to power as leader of the Conservatives and remained in office until 1990. The governments of Wilson and Callaghan and even Heath had sought cooperation with the trade unions. The right to strike was to be reformed to a moderate extent, but the unions were willing to cooperate only up to a point. Generally speaking, wage increases were much too high and led to continuous inflation problems (see Figure 1.2 above). In 1976, the pound was caught up in a currency crisis which, because of the effects of devaluation, caused inflation rates in the United Kingdom to rise further. The United Kingdom called for assistance from the IMF, which helped out with a loan, albeit linked to a number of conditions. In the summer of 1976 Wilson resigned and Callaghan became prime minister. Callaghan was convinced of the need to rein in inflation. After a number of failed attempts to get the trade unions on board with a stabilisation policy, he eventually decided to take them on. In the so-called 'winter of discontent' a huge wave of strikes hit the entire economy in the United Kingdom and practically brought it to a standstill. Against this background, it is not surprising that Margaret Thatcher – who has gone down in history as the 'Iron Lady' – won the election in May 1979. Immediately after her victory, Mrs Thatcher began to implement her conservative project, the crux of which was made up of liberalisation, deregulation and privatisation, and declared unconditional war on inflation and the trade unions at the cost of major reductions in growth and employment.

In the United States, developments were equally turbulent, although the government was much more concerned with the international role of the dollar. Republican Richard Nixon was President in 1969, but had to resign in 1974 as a result of the Watergate scandal, ceding office to fellow Republican, Vice President Gerald Ford. In 1977, Democrat Jimmy Carter was elected President. The United States experienced a foreign and domestic policy crisis of confidence in the 1970s.

The United States seemed enfeebled as a world power. To make matters worse, in 1979 there was renewed weakness of the dollar. The sharp devaluation triggered inflation, while the US trade unions would not agree to falling wages or to modest wage development. Particularly serious for the United States was the fact that the dollar's status as world reserve currency was increasingly being called into question. The oil-exporting states openly discussed whether they should partly dissociate themselves from the dollar and allow themselves to be paid in different currencies. Carter had to do something. In August 1979, Chairman of the Federal Reserve William Miller was replaced by Paul Volcker, a monetarist hardliner, who was noted for fighting inflation unconditionally, without consideration for the effects on the real economy.

During this period, Carter pressed in particular the Federal Republic of Germany and Japan to stimulate their economies, within the framework of the so-called 'locomotive discussions', in order to boost the stability of the dollar and so relieve the strain on the United States. As a result, Japan adopted a more expansionary economic policy. Although, under Chancellor Helmut Schmidt, Germany pursued a moderately expansionary fiscal policy, the independent Bundesbank refused to cooperate with the Fed. Shortly after

Paul Volcker assumed office, in October 1979 came the so-called
Hamburg Meeting, in which Volcker again asked the Bundesbank
for more drastic (currency) market intervention to strengthen the
dollar, a request which the Bundesbank curtly dismissed. A few
days later, the Fed began to sharply raise interest rates. This highly
restrictive monetary policy led the United States, in 1980–81, into
its deepest economic crisis since the Second World War. The whole
Western world was compelled to follow US monetary policy and was
hard hit by the fall in growth. Latin America, which had dismantled
its controls on capital movements in the 1970s and incurred considerable external debt, slid into a serious debt crisis. Rising interest
rates and the fall in export revenues due to the worldwide economic
downturn led to a 'lost decade' of stagnation. In the US election at
the end of 1980, Republican Ronald Reagan won the election and
took office at the beginning of 1981, which he held until 1989. Just
like Margaret Thatcher, Reagan immediately took up the sword
against the trade unions and launched the conservative market-
liberal revolution.

WEAK LEFT AND STRONG RIGHT

Capitalist economies are always money economies. If money
loses its capacities due to inflationary developments, a money
economy cannot function over the longer term. It can be endlessly
argued whether the fight against inflation in the Federal Republic
of Germany, the United States, The United Kingdom or other
countries was too severe. What cannot be denied is that central
banks were compelled, sooner or later, to take action against the
erosion of their domestic monetary systems, particularly if the
country found itself in a currency crisis. The inflationary development of the 1970s ultimately forced all Western central banks to
adopt a restrictive monetary policy which, in turn, led to slumps in
growth and a general rise in unemployment. Governments which
had been elected by reform movements were faced with an economic
policy shambles since they had no means at their disposal with
which they could guarantee a high level of employment. Certainly,
there were a number of options for development in the 1970s.
However, the social democratic and, to some extent, socialist-ori-
ented governments and the social movements of the time lacked clear
macroeconomic ideas or were not in a position to implement them.
It would have been necessary, first, to get to grips with the escalating
inflationary processes by reducing wage increases. In almost every

country attempts were made via incomes policies to prevent inflationary wage developments. Most such attempts failed. The fact that the social movements which gained strength at the end of the 1960s linked – or even confused – their reform programmes with wage demands seems, in hindsight, to have been their biggest mistake. The collapse of the Bretton Woods system exacerbated the situation since international capital flows increased instability in a number of countries, for example, the United States and the United Kingdom.

In general, the events from the end of the 1960s can be interpreted as showing that the reform movements of the time were unable to achieve a stable economic system at national and international level. This was not the expression of a fundamental crisis of capitalism. The contradictions of capitalism did not intensify as a result of fundamental laws, nor did new production technology or the advent of mass production lead to the problems of the 1970s. The 'golden age of capitalism' fell apart because the left-wing political movements of the time, of all stripes, were not in a position to reform traditional institutions in a way that was compatible with economic stability. The breakdown of the Bretton Woods system had already prepared the way for market-liberal changes. The actual market-liberal turn, however, came with the election victories of Margaret Thatcher and Ronald Reagan. Both stood for a policy which was based wholeheartedly on low inflation rates and, in particular, profound market-liberal reforms.

Decisive for the implementation of their conservative programmes was the fact that both Thatcher and Reagan were able to draw on ideas worked out in academia which not only brought about the conservative swing but also helped to structure its implementation. The conservatives were well prepared academically and convinced that their approach was the right one, since market-liberal ideas had been developed in conservative think tanks since the end of the Second World War. Last but not least, the famous economists of the so-called neoclassical school, Friedrich von Hayek and Milton Friedman played an important role. In universities and research institutes in the 1970s neoclassical thought was able to assert itself in economics, while the economic advisers on the Left foundered on inflation.

The realisation that the model of the post-war decades was shattered by a combination of political and institutional problems holds out the hope that a regulated capitalism can succeed which is more socially acceptable, humane and stable than the market-liberal project. When one considers the global changes of recent decades, as well as the new challenge of having to take action against a looming environmental catastrophe, it is necessary to learn from the economic system of the 1950s and 1960s, although of course without wishing to copy it.

Before we go into the individual elements from which a new economic system could be constructed, however, the market-liberal revolution should be discussed in more detail. The market-liberal agenda encompassed a series of restructurings which involved both deep interventions in the financial sector, labour markets and corporate culture on the one hand, and the privatisation of previously public areas of responsibility on the other. Deregulation and enhancing the role of financial markets went hand in hand with changes in management concepts. There was also further deregulation of international financial markets for developing countries, and an extensive free-trade regime was created. Alongside the deregulation of labour markets, aimed at weakening the trade unions, state companies were privatised, including those providing public services. Finally, the dismantling of allegedly harmful elements of the welfare state commenced. This agenda was not only enthusiastically pursued in the United States and the United Kingdom, but also implemented in many other countries which had social democratic governments. Just as even conservative governments in the 1950s and 1960s had social democratic leanings, so from the 1980s most social democratic governments became market-liberal. As a result of profound changes from the 1970s, which intensified throughout the 1980s, a specific globalisation project developed, built on largely unregulated markets. It is not possible to go into all the facets of this radical market model, but in the following chapters the most important areas of market-liberal globalisation will be addressed, concentrating on developments in the industrialised countries.

2

UNLEASHING FINANCIAL MARKETS

A central element of the market-liberal globalisation project was the deregulation of financial markets at both the national and the international levels. While the financial markets developed more dynamically than all other markets, at the same time, from the 1980s they became subject to constant instability. For many years adverse effects of this instability were felt primarily in the developing countries, which were hit by deep and expensive currency and financial crises. With Japan's stock-market and real-estate bubble in the second half of the 1980s and the stagnation which followed – which continues to the present day – the volatility of the financial markets reached the advanced industrialised countries. After the dotcom bubble in the 1990s, the effects of which were handled comparatively well, the subprime crisis plunged world financial centres into a systemic crisis of proportions unknown since the 1930s, resulting in a profound worldwide crisis in the real economy. It was quite by chance that the systemic financial market crisis, which followed the onset of the subprime crisis in 2007, was sparked off by a relatively insignificant segment of the world financial system, namely the dubious financing of private real estate in the United States. The problems besetting the financial system go much deeper than real estate. Developments over recent decades had rendered the financial system increasingly susceptible to disruption, so that it was only a matter of time before the whole house of cards came tumbling down.

The destabilising deregulation of the financial system can be explained partly by the lobbying of financial market actors who wanted more and more room to manoeuvre. However, it would never have been possible if the majority of economists, managers, politicians, journalists and regulators had not allowed themselves to be convinced by the market liberals' promise that unfettered financial markets would promote efficiency and growth across the globe.

Since financial markets play such an important – albeit often obscure – role in today's debate, we have to go a bit further back and into detail in order to make our point. We start out rather briefly with the subprime crisis, as it is not only the trigger of today's reform efforts, but also so well known to many that it serves as good reference point to what went wrong with our financial system on a more fundamental level. After that, we look at the broader political context and the breaking points of financial unleashing in the past: that is, the developments which enabled subprime to develop. Then we have to become a little bit more technical, first by scrutinising the mechanics of 'financialisation' and the way in which, by impelling management to concentrate on short-term 'shareholder value' at the expense of all other considerations, it impacted on enterprises that were not necessarily even part of the financial system. The last part of this chapter is then even slightly more abstract, when we deal with the 'illusion of rationality' as the organic kernel of finance capitalism's triumphal procession. We have tried to write the technical sections as accessibly as possible, but some parts may still be a little bit laborious to read. We think it is worth the struggle, especially if one wants to understand the ongoing political debates on financial regulation and the role of financial markets in our everyday life in a way that allows for more substantial criticism or, of course, approval of the debates that tend to be concentrated in the narrow professional world of the *Financial Times*, the *Economist* or the *Wall Street Journal*. So, let's start with subprime.

Subprime and the triple-A crisis

The subprime crisis, which broke in the United States in 2007, expanded into a systemic financial market crisis and has led to the deepest crisis in the real economy since the Second World War, can be understood only in connection with the preceding deregulation of the financial markets.

Real-estate prices in the United States were remarkably stable between the 1940s and the mid-1990s.[1] With the economic upturn in the United States which gained momentum in 2003, however, they increased enormously. In fact, the upturn was mainly supported by the emerging real-estate bubble. On the one hand, rising house prices boosted house building, while on the other hand, many Americans remortgaged their property on a wave of rising real-estate prices in order to finance further consumption (so-called mortgage equity withdrawal). In 2006, real-estate prices reached their peak, only to fall back sharply from that point onwards (see Figure 2.1).

The long period of stable real-estate prices before the boom was preceded by a reorganisation of the real-estate market after the economic crisis of the 1930s within the framework of President Roosevelt's New Deal.[2] In 1938, the state Federal National Mortgage Association (known more familiarly as Fannie Mae) was founded in order to boost private house building. Fannie Mae bought real-estate loans from the banks which issued them, financing itself by issuing its own, usually long-term, bonds. This securitisation transaction was the American way of boosting house building, since it led to the availability of credit on reasonable terms for the purchase of real estate. Fannie Mae regulated the quantity and quality of real-estate loans centrally, thereby contributing to the stability of the real-estate market. For example, the banks were only permitted to resell first-class real-estate loans (prime loans) to Fannie Mae; real-estate loans with a high risk of default (subprime loans) played a minor role. At the end of the 1960s Fannie Mae was privatised and in 1970 the Federal National Mortgage Corporation (Freddie Mac) was founded in order to prevent Fannie Mae from monopolising the market. However, both institutions remained subject to strict regulatory oversight. In 1970, the first mortgage-backed securities were issued. This involved the packaging together of a number of real-estate

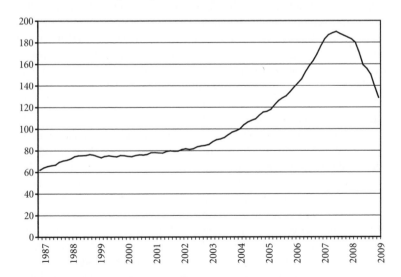

Figure 2.1 Development of real-estate prices in the United States
First quarter of each year, January 2000 = 100. Data up to April 2009.
Sourc: S&P/Case-Shiller Home Price Indices (Composite-10 CSXR).

loans, whose cash flow served as the basis of the mortgage-backed securities. Mortgage-backed securities are a subclass of asset-backed securities, which are backed by many different kinds of securities. At first, there was nothing disreputable about these securities, which in many ways resembled the mortgage bonds long known in Europe.

The situation changed fundamentally only after the recession in 2001–02. In 2003, 57.6 per cent (US$52 billion) of mortgage-backed securities were traded as prime loans, 37.4 per cent (US$34 billion) were subprime loans and 15.8 per cent (US$14 billion) were somewhere in between and counted as so-called Alt-A loans. In contrast, in the first half of 2006, only 26 per cent (US$67.2 billion) of mortgage-backed securities were issued as prime loans, while 44 per cent (US$114.3 billion) counted as subprime loans, the other 30 per cent (US$76.5 billion) being Alt-A loans.[3]

The central innovation which made possible the mass sale of subprime and Alt-A credits was the so-called 'waterfall principle'. Asset-backed securities and collateralised debt obligations were subdivided into separate tranches, typically known as the equity tranche, the mezzanine tranche and the senior tranche. If borrowers could not service their debt, at first only the so-called equity tranche (the first loss piece) was affected, and had to bear the whole loss. Then came the mezzanine tranche and only when the equity and the mezzanine tranches were completely exhausted due to losses did the purchasers of senior tranches have to take a hit. Senior tranches, therefore, seemed secure, even in the case of subprime loans, and received the highest valuations from rating agencies ('Triple A'). As a result, it was an attractive proposition for institutional investors or even conservative German regional banks to buy US subprime loans in the form of senior or mezzanine tranches. The equity tranche, because of its high yield, was bought by hedge funds and other aggressively speculative investors.

The quality of real-estate loans progressively diminished in the course of the US real-estate bubble. Among other things, this was due to increasing competition in real-estate financing, which mani-fested itself in the establishment of a multitude of mortgage financiers which were not subject to normal banking regulation. Wall Street investment banks, at the same time, ensured the refinancing of these companies through the placement of mortgage-backed securities and collateralised debt obligations. Due to the abovementioned specific risk models and accounting principles, credit expansion ballooned enormously. The dominant belief during the asset bubble that real-estate prices would continue to climb for a long time or even forever must also have played an important role. Real-estate loans were made more appetising for American households by means of all kinds of incentives, including initially low interest rates or the commencement of repayment only at a later date. Own capital and security were not required. There was a clear problem of moral hazard, since the originators of the real-estate loans paid no attention to the quality of the loans, having no trouble selling them.

The subprime crisis hit in summer 2007 – around one year after real-estate prices had stopped climbing. The end of the real-estate bubble was triggered by rising interest rates in the United States and by changing expectations in relation to future real-estate price development. The Fed set interest rates higher because it feared goods-market inflation; expectations changed, among other things because the construction boom had increased the supply of real estate. The crisis erupted when the rating agencies downgraded the value of mortgage-backed securities, to the surprise of many in the market. The immediate effect of this downgrading was that it became impossible for the special-purpose vehicles to refinance. Institutional investors and aggressive investors such as hedge funds stopped buying mortgage-backed securities and securitisations with a real-estate loan component, as well as the unsecured short-term bonds of special-purpose vehicles. The first – brutal – repercussion was that the banks had to take over their special-purpose vehicles which, in turn, plunged the banks into liquidity and even solvency problems. At this point, the fact that the special-purpose vehicles did not have equity capital began to have dire consequences and instigated an, at times, extreme maturity transformation. In combination, these factors suddenly put financial institutions which had established special-purpose vehicles under considerable pressure.

Since there was no transparency concerning which banks had to go in to bat for which special-purpose vehicles, and which banks had which risk-encumbered securities in their balance sheets, the inter-bank money market collapsed. Central banks around the world were forced to commit massive resources to guarantee the liquidity of the financial system. As the crisis proceeded, the money market could hardly be revitalised – the lack of confidence between the banks was too great. But confidence also collapsed between investment banks and other institutions in the shadow banking system.

The crisis then developed in textbook fashion. Direct write-offs of real-estate loans in the United States were estimated by the IMF as amounting to between US$500 and 600 billion.[4] That is a considerable sum, but not enough to account for the global financial and economic crisis. The decisive factor was the negative feedback mechanisms of the subprime crisis, which affected a generally unstable financial system. Financial institutions were hit by a lack of equity capital caused by the drain on their resources as they struggled to support their special-purpose vehicles. For example, as a result of their low capital ratio, commercial banks could no longer meet the legally prescribed level of equity capital reserves and had to curb their lending. Now the banking system's resort to special-purpose vehicles in order to avoid capital provisions proved devastating. Real-estate prices fell, and mortgage-backed securities, collateralised debt obligations and other securitised assets had to swallow considerable discounts. Negative expectations were transmitted to stock markets and share prices also began to fall. Falling asset prices first of all shrank the assets of the financial institutions, whose equity capital and lending capacity had already been hit by loan defaults and support for the special-purpose vehicles. Some hedge funds collapsed and so put a further strain on the financial system. Financial institutions starved of liquidity had to resort to distress sales to procure liquid assets, thereby forcing down asset prices still further. Private borrowers and heavily indebted companies were forced to take similar action. The result was a developing asset-market deflation which harboured strong endogenous reinforcement mechanisms (cf. Irving Fisher's classic article from 1933).

These processes took place against the background of extremely unfavourable institutional conditions which had already developed and which now intensified the systemic crisis: the financial system had recklessly reduced its capital ratios, and in particular, the non-legally binding capital buffers, through risky strategies and the pursuit of high returns on capital. As a result, small shocks could have big effects. Fair-value accounting, in addition, destroyed the equity capital of financial institutions, which had already been diminished, not least by generous dividends. Risk models now backfired on the downside, making matters much worse. Finally, due to the shadow banking system, the market lacked any kind of transparency, so that trust in other market participants evaporated easily.

It was only a matter of time before the asset-market deflation led to massive solvency problems. One year after the outbreak of the crisis the situation was that a large number of financial institutions had got themselves into serious solvency problems, which could only be contained by massive state guarantees, not excluding the nationalisation of individual institutions.

As a result of the lack of available capital and low expectations about the future, the banking system curbed its credit expansion. Strict credit rationing ensued, which is one of the reasons for the spillover of the financial crisis into the real economy. But other factors led to recession in 2008. For example, the negative-asset effects directly reduced consumer demand and the borrowing opportunities of enterprises and households. The developing crisis in the real economy, which brought unemployment and problems in the enterprise sector in its wake, caused further credit defaults and, together with the general pessimism about future prospects which was becoming established, a further intensification of the crisis in the real economy.

In the next section we contextualise this crisis in what we call the general breaking points of finance capitalism. This step is necessary to get a grip on the systemic dimension of what went wrong in the case of subprime. For that we have to look further back into finance history and gradually abstract the underlying dynamics of today's financial markets.

BREAKING POINTS IN FINANCE CAPITALISM

Immediately after Margaret Thatcher and Ronald Reagan came to power, the financial markets in the United Kingdom and the United States were deregulated. A process of 'financialisation' ensued: financial markets played a greater role in the economy, people and institutions in the financial markets became more powerful, the aims of the financial markets became important in all areas of society, and the national financial markets of the major industrialised countries and, to some extent, of the developing countries began to become more integrated. The accelerated unleashing of the financial markets from the 1980s made the financial system overall more susceptible to fluctuations and intensified systemic risks. The most important trends need to be mentioned here.

At the national and international levels, first of all, different segments of the financial system became more integrated. For example, in the post-war period, in almost every country, the world real-estate markets formed a distinct sector with few – or strictly regulated – relations with the rest of the financial system. Before the 1980s, real-estate loans were issued by special institutions which were subject to little competition. Typically, the amounts of real-estate loans were restricted and there were rules about the repayment period. With the beginning of deregulation of financial markets in the early 1980s this pattern changed significantly. First, new loan providers crowded into the market and intensified competition. Financial institutions outside the traditional banking system were able to double their market share as a proportion of all loans to private households, for example in the United States, Canada and Australia between the end of the 1980s and 2005. Countries with interest rate restrictions lifted their interest rate controls. Finally, financial markets for real-estate loans developed on a large scale, which made it possible to sell these loans on. That led, in particular, to the closer linking of the real-estate market to national and even international financial markets, because investors around the world could buy real-estate loans on secondary markets. Germany, France and Italy constitute an exception because in these countries changes in real-estate financing were relatively modest.[5] But even share and other asset markets were increasingly linked worldwide. International investors, from investment banks to wealthy individuals, now hold international portfolios. Cross-border capital movements and interlocking loans between countries grew enormously.

Second, so-called securitisation activities rocketed in the course of the unfettering of the financial markets and made possible a multitude of financial innovations – the very products which were partly responsible for the subprime crisis. The securitisation of obligations simplifies trade in debt obligations and, in principle, is welcome. Securitisation is a very old practice; commercial papers of exchange are one example. Nevertheless, the securitisation wave of recent decades has brought a whole series of negative developments in its train. The long-term 'buy and hold' business model of the banking system, in which loans remained with the original lender (their originator), has given way to a much more short-term-oriented 'buy and sell' business model, in which issued loans are sold on. In many countries, banks hold only a small proportion of the loans which they issued themselves. As a consequence, the ultimate holder of a loan has no knowledge of its own concerning the quality of its claim, while the originators of the loan scarcely concern themselves with the quality of the debtors. If one is in possession of complex securitised claims, one can at best turn to rating agencies, which may have just as little information on the actual debtors. From these informational shortcomings an intractable moral hazard problem arises.

A further problem with securitisation is that the liquidity of individuals increases, because even long-term loans – disregarding crisis periods – can always be sold on the markets. If in the securitisation of credit market debts long-term credit claims are financed by short-term borrowing, individual liquidity rises even further. The securitisation tendencies of the past few decades have therefore led to the accumulation of a huge mass of securities at financial institutions, companies or wealthy households, which can be sold at any time on secondary markets and so give economic actors the sense of high liquidity. But the situation calls for considerable caution: from the point of view of the economy as a whole, liquidity does not increase as a result of securitisation; if all holders of debt obligations wish to sell their securities at the same time, the value of those securities will fall off a cliff and the securitised claim will cease to function as a store of value. During the subprime crisis it turned out that the central banks had to pump billions into the markets in order to maintain the liquidity of national economies.

Third, as a result of securitisation the rating agencies increased in significance, since the buyers of securities, in the absence of direct information, had to rely on specialists in the evaluation of those securities. In addition, banks which did not have their own risk models were dependent on rating agencies to evaluate the quality of bank debtors. The so-called Basel II provisions on capital adequacy reinforced this position of power even further, since the judgements of rating agencies for banks without internal risk models determined the amount of capital that had to be held. As a result, rating agencies have become so powerful that they influence both the ability of debtors to obtain loans, and the portfolios of investors across the world. In practical terms, these agencies operate in a legal vacuum and are not subject to any state oversight. Since there are only a few important rating companies worldwide, they constitute an oligopoly, in which Standard & Poor's, Moody's and Fitch divide up the world market between them. In addition, these rating agencies in many cases advise the very companies whose financial standing and creditworthiness, or whose products, they are supposed to be evaluating.

Fourth, the traditional commercial banking system has diminished in significance. Investment banks, insurance companies and funds of every kind have taken over more and more activities which were previously the province of traditional banks. As a direct consequence of this, ever larger parts of the financial market have shifted from the comparatively strictly regulated commercial banks into less or even unregulated realms. As a result, a veritable race to the bottom commenced, aimed at avoiding regulation in order to maximise profits: banks transferred securitised real-estate loans to special-purpose companies which had no equity capital. Such special-purpose vehicles – as they are also called – are legal entities set up by banks or other financial institutions. They purchase long-term claims from banks and package them into specific short-term financial products which they then sell on in order to refinance themselves. Sometimes the financial institutions were liable for their special-purpose vehicles and granted them credit in case the constant refinancing or packaging of loans should fail. This structure of special-purpose vehicles made it possible to deliberately circumvent the capital-adequacy requirements of the commercial banking system on a large scale. Offshore centres function in a similar way, sucking enormous financial assets out of the more strictly regulated financial sector by means of more lax banking regulation, the possibility of tax evasion and money laundering. The shadow banking system which has developed in this way, with its low level of regulation, low transparency and low capital-adequacy requirements, is like a parallel world in the financial sphere.

For a multitude of reasons the fundamental systemic risks of the financial system have increased.[6] First, institutions in the shadow banking system are less regulated and, at the same time, more risk oriented. Hedge funds, investment banks and other aggressive investors take on greater risks than traditional banks. That also applies to a large proportion of small investors, who have increased in significance and, in particular, engage in speculation. Previously, the vast majority of people took no interest in shares and exchange rates. Today, we are constantly bombarded with the latest developments in almost every news bulletin, on special financial channels and in financial publications, and by a whole horde of financial advisers. Second, the danger of systemic risks also increased in the traditional banking system, because the relatively well-regulated commercial banks are closely interwoven with the shadow banking system. So, the commercial banks had to step in financially after the outbreak of the subprime crisis for their special-purpose vehicles, which they had established in order to avoid capital-adequacy requirements. Third, the banks were driven by a frenzy for returns. Symptomatic of this is the declaration by Deutsche Bank that returns on equity of 25 per cent should be the norm, because that is what the market expects. In fact, expectations with regard to returns in the shadow banking system were sometimes even higher. In particular, in periods of lower interest rates, investors' willingness to take risks also increased since they sought to stabilise their cash flow through risky investments. With the emergence of the shadow banking system and fired up by their 'returns frenzy', own capital positions in the financial system fell strongly and, at the same time, the credit leverage of many institutions increased. Fourth, the liberalisation of international capital movements and the deregulation of national financial markets have dramatically increased the pressure of competition in the financial system. Oligopolistic structures, which dominated the financial markets in many countries, are one means of curbing a destabilising appetite for risk in the financial system. This support for financial market stability was lost. Stronger regulation on the part of the financial market supervisory authorities would have been able to counter this development, but the density of regulation has diminished, not increased. A fifth aspect is the increasing procyclical functioning and dynamics of the financial markets as a consequence of the regulation of the banks through the banking supervisory system of Basel II and the new role of fair-value accounting.

Finally, national financial systems cannot be understood without considering developments in the world currency and financial system. The unfettering of international financial markets has led to a gigantic increase in international capital flows, which began in the 1970s and had lost nothing of its dynamism by the outbreak of the subprime crisis in 2007.

Since the collapse of the Bretton Woods system, exchange rates between the world's main currencies have been subject to the logic of asset markets. Exchange rate developments depend on capital flows, which in turn are based on expectations. Since the latter do not have a stable anchor, flexible exchange rates experience violent fluctuations. None of the various fundamentals could explain the sometimes extreme medium-term exchange rate fluctuations, for example, between the US dollar and the euro (and previously the deutschmark), which are analogous to the fluctuations on stock markets. The global currency system has become a shock mechanism for the global economy which dramatically increases the level of uncertainty, leads to gigantic misallocations and generates price-level shocks.

But it is not only capital flows between the world's financial centres that have lost their anchor. Capital flows between the advanced industrialised Western countries and the rest of the world, the peripheral countries, are characterised by enormous instability. Typical in this respect are periods of high capital inflows into peripheral countries, which give way to sudden capital outflows. These are often referred to as 'boom-and-bust' cycles.[7] In boom periods, capital flows into peripheral countries, which gives rise to current account deficits there and a build up of foreign debt which, given the perceived 'low quality' of their currencies, can only be incurred in foreign currency. For all sorts of internal and external reasons, capital inflows suddenly turn into capital outflows and typically give rise to simultaneous currency and domestic financial market crises, which have their origins in the increase in real foreign debts as a result of the devaluation of the domestic currency and a domestic asset market deflation.

Since the collapse of the Bretton Woods system there have been three major boom-and-bust cycles. In the 1970s, the first wave of capital inflows developed in developing and emerging countries, at that time chiefly going to Latin America, since most Asian countries had not yet liberalised capital movements. The Soviet block was, in any case, isolated from the world market, and virtually no private capital flowed into Africa because of the political and economic situation. Capital began to flow out of the Latin American countries from the end of the 1970s due to the United States' high interest rate policy, falling confidence in the US dollar after Ronald Reagan's election and the falling export revenues of the indebted developing countries. Mexico became insolvent in 1982, followed by almost all other Latin American countries. The German-American economist Rudiger Dornbusch (1990) spoke of Latin America's 'lost decade', which followed the boom period of the 1970s.

At the beginning of the 1990s, the second great wave of capital flows into developing and now also into transition countries commenced. Asian and former Soviet bloc countries in particular had dismantled their capital controls. This boom phase was only briefly interrupted by the Mexican crisis in 1994, only to give way later on to the bust phase, with the Asian crisis in 1997, followed by the Russian crisis in 1998 and the crises in Argentina and Turkey in 2001, to mention only the biggest. The biggest boom period so far began after 2003, coming to an end with the outbreak of the subprime crisis in 2007. Since 2007, the bust phase has already plunged a whole series of countries into currency crises (the Baltic states, Ukraine, Hungary, Pakistan, Iceland). Among the countries at serious risk of a currency crisis after 2007 are Russia, South Africa, Turkey and Vietnam. In light of this volatility of international capital flows and the resulting shocks for developing and emerging countries, it is not surprising that the growth performance of countries which have liberalised capital movements is no better than that of countries which regulate their international capital movements.[8]

SHAREHOLDER CAPITALISM'S FLAWED LOGIC

If in the decades after the Second World War a form of stakeholder capitalism prevailed, which sought a compromise between the different interest groups – owners, managers, employees represented by trade unions, creditors, suppliers, consumers and the regional authorities – it has been superseded by shareholder-value capitalism, and corporate governance has changed fundamentally.

In the United States, and also in the European Union, the role of the capital and financial markets in the areas of company financing and asset management, as well as social insurance, had been deliberately strengthened. The key idea was 'shareholder value', meaning that companies and banks concentrated on the value of shares, with a whole range of consequences for business structures and market and investment behaviour. Shareholder value is a specifically Anglo-Saxon management concept, coined by Alfred Rappaport in his book *Creating Shareholder-Value: The New Standard for Business Performance* (1986). The concept arose from the need to protect one's company from hostile takeovers during the 'mergers and acquisitions' period of the 1980s in the United States by increasing its market value and subordinating management exclusively to the interests of the owners. It is a business management framework which is supposed to provide an above-average return on shareholders' investments. The management's sole obligation is to the owners, which means that the development of the company share price in comparison with that of competing firms in the sector acts as the measure of management success. In order to create an optimum incentive structure, the management is rewarded in part by share options and bonus payments based on profits. Shareholder-value capitalism enriched managers considerably, while at the same time putting them under constant pressure to increase the value of the company. Institutional investors, who were also under pressure to produce high returns, kept a close eye on managers and even penalized them, along with the growing number of financial market analysts and financial journalists.

There was a widespread belief in the objectivity and rationality with which the financial markets and their actors would value companies as realistically as possible and guarantee the 'fair value' of a company through market mechanisms. Criticisms of financial market mechanisms and their inherent tendency towards 'irrational exuberance' were dismissed as antiquated.[9]

Within the framework of shareholder value, the concentration on financial market numbers in the form of share prices and short-term yields, both for financial institutions and manufacturing companies, became more and more important. The burgeoning significance of financial markets and the dynamics of the financial system had structural effects on the corporate sector, especially with regard to company management. With the retreat of the banks from their traditional role of a 'house bank' and their turn towards investment banking, there was a convergence of the continental European financial system and the Anglo-Saxon model, in which the financial market has taken on a central function. Since companies must constantly worry about their valuation on the stock market, major industrial corporations have been forced to rethink their strategic orientation.

Contrary to the claim of efficiency theory that the shareholder-value strategy increases the pursuit of profit in companies, with positive welfare effects for society, the results of the past years reveal the fundamental failure of a one-sided concentration on financial market indicators. The development of the shareholder-value principle has had a dramatic effect on working conditions in the direction of more flexibility and the outsourcing to other or new companies of specific enterprise functions, ranging from accounting to cleaning. Many companies which took over functions traditionally performed within the company could remain competitive only on the basis of lower pay and precarious working conditions for employees.

A very interesting result of empirical corporate governance research is evidence that the focus on financial indicators in accordance with the shareholder-value model has a negative effect on innovation in an economy.[10] The shareholder-value model can be characterised as a model of 'profits without investment', since profits are sought by means of short-term strategies, including mergers and acquisitions. The shareholder-value model can therefore lead to low investment and low growth, which brings with it considerable systemic risks with regard to the financial structure of the economy. Even Alfred Rappaport (2005) has chastised the short-term orientation of modern management for its dire effects on the real economy. It is also doubtful whether the shareholder-value principle has really subjected management to the control of company owners. It seems rather that management has been able to enrich itself at the expense of the shareholders. The stakeholder system was clearly much better able to control management.

The orientation towards financial indicators leads to the sacrifice of investments in productive capital – such as employee training – which are essential for maintaining competitiveness even if they do not directly increase returns, in favour of a calculus of rationalisation oriented towards capital markets. Furthermore, there has as yet been no definite proof of a significant positive correlation between a shareholder-value orientation and an increase in the value of the company. The power of shareholder value has its primary source in propaganda for consulting concepts and a one-sided shift in power within large companies. Shareholder-value management concepts, accordingly, constitute a central component in the societal debate on the organisation of capitalist production and the distribution of socially produced wealth.

In the next and final section of this chapter, we jump from the level of shareholder value to the concept of rationality, which is the basis of the whole story of financial market efficiency. We have seen in practice that there is something wrong with the assumption of efficient and rational financial markets and their corresponding glorification of shareholder value. In the next section we therefore deconstruct the bigoted assumption of rationality.

THE ILLUSION OF RATIONALITY

Behind the conservative revolution lay powerful concealed interests, not least of the financial industry, which had lobbied for the unleashing of the whole financial system. However, the changes were also backed up and underpinned in theoretical terms. This calls for detailed examination since effective reform alternatives require a theoretical understanding of financial markets. The Keynesian compromise between neoclassical and Keynesian thought (the neoclassical synthesis), which had arisen from traditional neoclassical thought and the ideas of the economist John Maynard Keynes against the background of economic and political catastrophe in the 1930s, was largely superseded in economic debate from the 1970s by a revival of neoclassical thought. The macroeconomic approach, embracing the whole economy, came to be regarded as old hat, while a microeconomic approach focusing on individuals came to the fore. On the basis of these microfoundations, developments at the macroeconomic level – that is, the national economy – were inferred from the analysis of a single economic entity. Single enterprises or single households were implicitly equated with the business sector or the sum of all households – it was merely a matter of aggregating them. To many economists a separate macroeconomic model no longer seemed necessary. The microfoundations of the overall economy also shaped the analysis of financial markets: if all micro-entities act rationally and are considered stable, then the same applies to the financial system as a whole. Financial market regulation concentrated on the stability of micro-entities and therefore ignored macroeconomic systemic risks.

In the 1980s, economic debate came increasingly to be dominated by the approach of 'rational expectations', which can be traced back to Robert Lucas, Thomas Sargent and others.[11] The concept of rational expectations assumes that individuals in an economy – that is, employees, consumers, entrepreneurs and investors – are able to calculate the future development of all important economic indicators, such as share and commodity prices, interest rates, inflation, unemployment, wages or GDP, on the basis of objective probabilities and can base their economic actions, such as purchase, employment or investment decisions, on them. Among other things, it must be assumed for this purpose that individuals know all future events and can give all these events precise probabilities so that the sum of the probabilities adds up to one. Individuals must understand the causal mechanisms of the economy. Economic actors must therefore be able to infer how the variables just listed respond to unexpected events such as an increase in public spending, a war or new technological developments such as the internet. Rational expectations do not necessarily require that individuals be clairvoyant. It is assumed that they can use past data, for example past volatilities, past default rates and so on, to form objective probabilities. The past is seen as a perfect guide to what will happen in the future. Some individuals may make mistakes in their calculations, but it is assumed that, *on average*, they correctly predict the future. For economic models, rational expectations simplify matters radically as expectations become identical with the outcome of economic models and lose influence on economic development.

This approach neglects a whole series of problems. First of all, not even experts agree on how the causal connections of the economy really work. The open debate among economists about the depth of the recession after the outbreak of the subprime crisis, as well as the appropriate economic policy response, is sufficient to illustrate the multiplicity of interpretations to which an economic event can give rise. But if even experts are unable to estimate causalities with any precision, how are the broad mass of workers, investors and small-business owners supposed to do it? The second problem is that the concept of rational expectations assumes that individuals don't even need any time to make out the fundamental structures of the economy. Even structural changes are recognised immediately in this model and are immediately incorporated in individuals' calculations. Third, since future events are not known, one has to fall back on previous developments. The implicit assumption is that knowledge of the past enables us to know the future. But that is far from being the case.

In the area of financial market analysis, the assumption of efficient markets corresponds to rational expectations. Eugene Fama, an economist at the traditionally economically liberal University of Chicago, argued in 1970 that rational economic actors operate in asset markets and so asset prices reflect all the available information. Investors are rational if they analyse the value of assets on the basis of so-called fundamental data. If new information about the future cash flow, and so the value of the assets, emerges, the market immediately jumps to a new price which represents the new state of information. The logic underlying this assumption is rather simple: if an individual investor finds out that, for example, an enterprise has a promising new invention that is not yet reflected in the share price, he or she will buy shares in the enterprise until the share price once again corresponds to the price in accordance with those new 'fundamentals'. If on the contrary investors find out that an enterprise has got into difficulties and that this is not yet reflected in the share price, they will sell shares until the price has fallen so far that it reflects the new information. Since every rational investor who receives the new relevant information behaves in the same way, market prices always seem to reflect all information available to any investor.

This basic model is not substantially altered if individual economic actors do not behave rationally. Mistakes balance each other out if irrational economic actors are crowded out of the market as a result of their losses. In this model, continuous longer-term upward and downward movements in markets over weeks, months or years are ruled out. Yields above the market average can be earned on such markets only if an investor comes into possession of previously unknown information on the fundamental development of a company, branch or whole economy. But such a thing is excluded. Since all investors react immediately to new information, price bubbles on asset markets are as unlikely as speculative gains – a circumstance which, outside theoretical circles, would be regarded as somewhat preposterous.

The assumptions of efficient markets and rational expectations have little to do with reality. A fairly hefty dose of ignorance is required to make the assumption that *all* market actors evaluate the fundamental structures of the economy in the same way and predict the future on the basis of historical data in such a way that, on average, their predictions do not diverge systematically from reality. Equally out of touch with reality is the assumption that speculative bubbles would not develop in the financial markets. Nevertheless, many economists vehemently defended the hypothesis of rational expectations and efficient financial markets for a long time – and many continue to do so, even today.

The theoretical foundations for the critique of efficient capital markets and rational expectations were provided by John Maynard Keynes. For him, uncertainty was a decisive category for understanding capitalist economies. With uncertainty, every historical development is a one-off, so that statistically the future cannot be inferred from the past. Not all future events are known, and even known events cannot always be assigned much probability. Even if investors look for fundamentals they will not find them. Moreover the expectations of economic actors differ even if they look for fundamentals. In particular, the most important economic decisions, such as investment in a production plant or the purchase of a house, are one-off decisions, which must be taken in the shadow of uncertainty.[12] Consider the valuation of the shares of a steel company. It would be difficult to calculate the future cash flows of a steel company over the next 40 to 50 years and it would be absurd to suggest that all economic actors, even if they are looking for fundamentals, would make the same assessment. We simply do not know – that is how Keynes (1937: 214) characterised how things stand in many decision-making situations.

If one goes along with Keynes, asset markets are driven by expectations and it may not be assumed that these expectations are somehow anchored in fundamentals. First of all, such fundamentals are difficult or impossible to identify and, in any case, different economic actors evaluate them differently. Expectations, therefore, rest on very shaky foundations. Furthermore, expectations do not depend on economic factors alone; political and institutional factors also play a role in the formation of expectations. Many market actors also operate within a short time horizon, in which they do not bother to look for fundamentals but rather act mechanically on the basis of 'chart analyses'. Typically, a general sentiment forms which reflects developments in society and can be stable: for example, periods of optimism or pessimism. However, rapid and far-reaching changes in sentiment are possible. Asset markets are characterised by 'herd behaviour', in which everyone follows the leader of the pack, which tends to be a large investment fund or investor. Such behaviour leads to cumulative processes and irrational bubbles, which can subsequently burst in costly and catastrophic fashion. Economists such as Keynes (1937), Fisher (1933), Kindleberger (1996), Minsky (1975) and Stiglitz and Greenwald (2003) have clearly worked out the characteristics of asset markets as described here.

Unlimited supply? The credit cycle

There is another important aspect of financial markets, namely that the volume of credit in modern financial systems can, potentially, be expanded without limit. This is because money and credit can, as the Austrian-American economist Joseph Schumpeter (1926) put it, be conjured out of nothing and can be multiplied almost at will. Commercial banks give credit by recording a credit item on the borrower's account. If all banks issue more loans in step, then the balance of the banking system continues without financial bottlenecks emerging at individual banks. To be sure, an expansion of credit requires additional central bank funds, on the one hand because of the cash withdrawals of borrowers, and on the other hand because of the banks' minimum reserve obligations. The commercial banks can obtain the additional funds they need from the central bank, which cannot directly limit their refinancing, but can only influence their behaviour indirectly by changing interest rates on refinancing. Credit expansion in the financial system and so, indirectly, the development of the money supply, are every bit as dependent on expectations as price development on asset markets. In the case of positive expectations, credit expansion increases, while in the case of negative expectations it leads not only to higher interest rates for risky debtors, but typically also to a contraction of credit.

Asset-market inflation and credit are mutually reinforcing. The credit system expands like a concertina during a period of asset-market inflation, leading to a double feedback effect: on the one hand, the value of debtors' securities and creditors' equity capital rises and, with it, the willingness of creditors to provide credit, while on the other hand, the positive effect of asset-market inflation leads to increasing demand for credit on the part of debtors. The responsiveness of the price of assets is, in the short term, very low and sluggish even in the long term. For this reason, unbridled credit expansion can lead to an enormous increase in asset prices, because if the demand for stocks rises, new stocks are not issued automatically. A strong increase in real-estate prices will stimulate a construction boom, but it will be years before the real-estate supply increases significantly. If an asset bubble bursts, it gives rise to negative feedback effects. Conversely, falling asset-market prices depress the value of securities and also the equity capital of financial institutions. Both reduce the volume of credit in the economy. In the case of falling asset prices, financial institutions may fail and a systemic financial market crisis emerge, interrupting the allocation of credit which society needs.

The potentially unlimited possibilities for credit expansion in modern financial systems, the excessive bubbles which this makes possible, and the potentially catastrophic consequences of the probable subsequent implosion make strict regulation of credit issuing institutions absolutely necessary. This is the reason why, for example, credit expansion in the commercial banking sector is limited by means of capital requirements, minimum reserves and other provisions. If a financial system comes into being which can expand in an unregulated fashion and so create bubbles, cumulative processes on asset markets and the destructive implosion of such bubbles are virtually preordained.

The principles of efficient financial markets, with their super-structure of rational expectations, for years served to justify the actions of many actors on these markets. Take for example 'value at risk' (VaR), which became a favourite way of calculating risk in relation to portfolios. VaR is a measure of risk which indicates the possible losses of a portfolio within a certain timeframe with some degree of certainty. The calculation depends entirely on data related to the past. On the same level, methodologically, is the Black–Scholes model, well-known in the financial world, which is used in the assessment of financial options and in which the past market fluctuations play a decisive role.[13] Risk management in the financial system has indeed made great strides since the 1970s, but trust in the possibility of reducing systemic risks in the financial system has also grown. However since such models are based on past data, risks in phases of positive economic development were rated as very low, while in the case of negative developments risks are exaggerated. As a result, these risk models have a strong procyclical effect; in other words, they amplify the build up of asset-market bubbles and the costs when such bubbles burst.

The changes introduced into accounting provisions from the beginning of the 1990s were also based on the assumption of efficient markets. Emanating from the United States, rules based on historical costs were replaced by evaluation corresponding to prevailing market values ('fair-value accounting'). If an investment fund buys a share at a certain price, then the value of the share will be entered in the books of the investment fund at first at the purchase price. If the value of the share then rises, the new, higher price will be entered in the books, representing a profit for the investment fund. Under traditional accounting methods, even in the case of an increase in the share price, the value of the share in the books would have remained unchanged. Under the new accounting rules, during a period of asset-market inflation the asset in the company balance sheet and the profits rise accordingly, without being justified by an improvement in the company's income and expenditure. The consequences include high bonus payments to management, high dividends and the incentive for higher borrowing. In many countries, a lot of companies were observed to be buying their own shares in order to drive the share price upwards and so to increase bonus payments and dividends.

During periods when the value of these assets falls, fair-value accounting leads to an undue reduction in equity capital, even to the point of solvency and viability problems. Where there are particularly high dividends in the wake of asset-market inflation, under some circumstances the danger arises that companies will be bled dry and so be poorly prepared when a crisis emerges, due to their poor equity position. If asset values do not reflect fundamentals, fair-value accounting leads to procyclical tendencies: in other words, it excessively intensifies developments and thereby becomes a shock amplifier for the whole economy.

In the past few decades impetus has been given to the central problem not only because actors on asset markets were increasingly prepared to take risks and came to rely on company-specific risk models, but also because control agencies in the financial system, such as rating agencies and bank regulators, made false assumptions. They worked on the assumption of market efficiency and the belief that the systemic risks of the financial market could be checked with the help of ever more complex mathematical risk models. The development of a shadow banking system – an unregulated banking system which operated and conducted transactions beyond the regular banking system – was accepted, but the fundamental stability of financial markets was taken as given. The underlying error of the prevalent view of regulation in recent decades was the belief that such models of risk calculation could capture and avert systemic risks. The assumption that one could extrapolate from the analysis of microeconomic entities to the economy as a whole goes against the basic principles of economics. Microeconomic risk models are simply not capable of capturing systemic risks.

For this reason the equity capital agreement of the Basel accord of 1988 (labelled 'Basel I') was based on the so-called standardised approach, which envisages fixed percentages of capital requirements for certain risk classes, for example, loans to a state or company. Basel I was the first uniform international capital requirement principle which obliged banks to cover loans with equity capital. In 1993 the Basel Committee on Banking Supervision proposed a regulatory concept which followed this standardised approach and sought to develop it further. The banking sector protested violently and as a result of colossal lobbying by the financial industry the Committee recommended, within the framework of the Amendment to the Basel Accord in 1996, a model which was based to a considerable extent on the company-specific risk models of the banks, which could develop the models themselves and have the supervisory authorities sign off on them, and which envisaged capital requirement provisions corresponding to these risk models.

The proposals around Basel II followed this logic: practically speaking, all major banks use their own risk models which, in accordance with a risk assessment of a loan to a company, lead to a specific level of capital requirements. As an alternative, banks could use external ratings, thus further enhancing the role of the rating agencies (which use similar risk models). If a bank refuses to take either option, the capital-adequacy requirement becomes very high. What is decisive here is that the introduction of bank-specific risk models or external ratings led to a decrease in the legally prescribed capital requirements in the banking system, compared with the previous rules. This had been one of the goals of the financial industry lobby. In addition, the voluntary capital requirement beyond that, which would act as a buffer for financial market shocks, also decreased. For example, this ratio at Deutsche Bank or UBS has fallen from around 10 per cent of their balance sheets at the beginning of the 1990s to 2–3 per cent in the recent past.[14] People blindly trusted their own risk models, which helped to bring about very low equity ratios and, at the same time, undreamt-of returns on equity capital.

Without a fundamental change here, including the regulation of asset markets, a genuine restructuring of these markets and hence of the economy as a whole is inconceivable.

3

GLOBAL IMBALANCES FUEL
GLOBAL INSTABILITY

While the system of flexible exchange rates between the central
currencies arose at practically the same time as the end of the Bretton
Woods system in 1973, the transition to free capital movement was
more gradual. There had already been a phase of deregulation of
international capital movements in the years before the collapse of
the Bretton Woods system. After 1973 little changed with regard
to the regulation of international capital movements until well into
the 1980s. Among the developing countries, in fact, only some
Latin American countries opened their capital accounts. A second
wave of deregulation began to develop at the start of the 1990s. In
the course of the decade, not only the industrialised countries but
also most emerging and developing countries rapidly lifted their
restrictions on international capital movements.

Theoretically, the advocates of flexible exchange rates and free
movement of capital had predicted that in the world they were
propagating, on the one hand, individual countries would have
more economic policy autonomy, and on the other hand, world
saving would be allocated in the most efficient way and flow to
the places with the highest productivity. Furthermore, there was
also the hope that free capital flows could help undeveloped
countries to make investments more quickly and so to improve
development.

In fact, the opposite happened: exchange rates between the key
currencies in the world began to fluctuate erratically and violently.
Instead of serving as a means of stabilisation for the world economy,
exchange rates became a shock mechanism. Countries whose
industry at one moment was extremely competitive, and whose
exports were booming, often found themselves confronting major
foreign trade problems only a short time later because of a massive

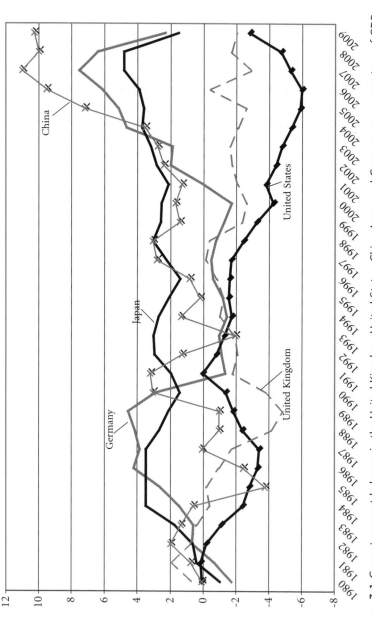

Figure 3.1 Current account balances in the United Kingdom, United States, China, Japan and Germany as a percentage of GDP, 1960–2009

Source: IMF International Financial Statistics 2010.

devaluation by trading partners. Countries whose currencies had devalued, in contrast, found themselves confronted by a violent bout of inflation and reduction in living standards. In many cases, particularly in smaller countries, national economic policy was suddenly compelled to subject itself to the caprices of the foreign exchange markets instead of to the needs of the domestic economy.

The second forecast – that long-term unsustainable trade and current account imbalances could be averted – did not come true, either. Figure 3.1 shows the development of current account balances for the United Kingdom, United States, China, Japan and Germany as a percentage of GDP. The figure shows that the differences between the current account balances in the 1970s were relatively low, only to skyrocket to unprecedented highs from the 1980s.

Calculating the average from 2007 to 2009 in billion US dollars, the five biggest current account deficit countries in the world were the United States (-468), Spain (-125), Australia (-48), Greece (-46) and the United Kingdom (-42); the five biggest current account surplus countries were China (436), Germany (185), Japan (148), Saudi Arabia (76) and Russia (61), which was closely followed by Norway (60). During the above period the EMU had a relatively small current account deficit of US$2.3 billion and a relatively balanced current account.

Immediately before the current financial and economic crisis the imbalances reached their apogee. The US current account deficit reached almost 6 per cent of GDP in 2006; Spain's deficit came to almost 10 per cent of GDP in 2008; and a few small Eastern European countries, such as Latvia, even produced deficits of up to 23 per cent. In direct contrast, some countries have run enormous surpluses. Among the large economies in 2007 in particular, Germany, with a current account surplus of 7.6 per cent of GDP, Japan, with a surplus of 4.8 per cent and China, with a surplus of 11.3 per cent, stand out.

The effects of the subprime crisis corrected the trade imbalances in some cases with brutal dispatch. For example, capital inflows to the Baltic countries were rapidly choked off. As a consequence, current account deficits fell from high levels before the subprime crisis to zero. This abrupt correction has been paid for by a two-digit drop in economic performance and a trebling in unemployment. What we are seeing in the Baltic countries is a classic boom-and-bust cycle, which has been observed in far too many countries since the deregulation of capital flows since the 1970s. However, the subprime crisis reduced imbalances of the key surplus and deficit countries only moderately and did not bring any solution to the unsustainable imbalances in the world economy.

The prospect of faster economic development held out to emerging and developing countries if they deregulated capital movements did not prove to be well founded. It is not only that the poorer countries were hit by a multitude of dramatic currency, financial and debt crises. As recent research, for example by Joseph Stiglitz, has shown, the countries that had liberalised their capital movements in no way developed better or faster than those countries that had been more cautious.

INTERNATIONAL CAPITAL FLOWS AS SOURCE OF INSTABILITY

The reason for the large fluctuations on foreign exchange markets, as well as for the massive global imbalances of recent years, is the market mechanism itself by which capital flows are determined. Traditional economics[1] describes how flexible exchange rates supposedly keep imbalances in international trade within sustainable limits based on fundamental factors, and insulate countries from potentially harmful effects caused by events in the rest of the world. In reality, however, this description does not apply to foreign exchange markets where there are free capital flows.

Instead, foreign exchange markets function like asset markets, which are fundamentally determined by expectations. German investors, for example, who buy US government bonds, do so not necessarily because of the difference in the two countries' interest rates (which in recent years has been quite low), but rather because they hope that the US dollar will increase in value. They buy dollars, therefore, when they believe that dollars will appreciate in value, and sell them when they fear that the rate will fall. Consequently, the price of currencies in a system of flexible exchange rates is as unstable as the price of shares or real estate in unregulated share or real-estate markets.

To be precise: in unregulated international capital markets, a currency's exchange rate depends on domestic interest rates, foreign interest rates and the *expected* exchange rate. If other things remain unchanged, an increase in US interest rates leads to a devaluation of the euro because capital will, consequently, flow into the United States. If Eurozone interest rates rise, the value of the euro will increase because capital will be invested in the Eurozone. When expectations about future exchange rates change, this also immediately influences current exchange rates in accordance with the logic of all asset markets. If a future appreciation of the exchange rate is expected, capital flows into the country in question, altering the exchange rate. If there are doubts about the future stability, funds flow out, weakening the currency today.

While it is difficult enough in the case of shares to make plausible assumptions about future profits of the company in order to establish at least a relatively accurate share price, for exchange rates it is much more difficult, because the judgement requires nothing less than an overall assessment of a country's economic and political situation and its development.

The neoclassical approach assumes that capital flows and exchange rates are driven by fundamentals because the latter determine expectations. The widely used concept of 'rational expectations' implies that expectations, on average, are identical with the prediction of the economic model (see Chapter 2). The most famous neoclassical model for explaining exchange rates is the purchasing power parity theory, which states that a certain basket of goods should have, expressed in a common currency, the same price in all countries. Otherwise, a country with lower prices would experience an export surplus, which in turn would increase demand for the national currency of the country and lead to an appreciation of the exchange rate, as a result of which prices would be brought into line again. According to this theory, exchange rates move according to relative inflation rates. If the prices of goods and services in the EMU rise by 5 per cent while remaining unchanged in the United States, the euro would be immediately devalued against the US dollar by 5 per cent. As soon as individuals get the information that prices in the EMU are rising they would expect a depreciation of the euro, and the consequent capital outflows from the EMU to the United States would immediately lead to a euro depreciation.[2]

Unfortunately, the purchasing power parity theory does not even come close to explaining the exchange rate between the dollar and the euro (or, before that, other European currencies). Medium-term exchange rate fluctuations between the euro and the dollar are in the double-digit range, while inflation rate differences between the currency areas are only a few percentage points.[3]

Among all the relevant factors, neither the different inflation rates, developments in current account balances, productivity, different GDP growth rates nor different national fiscal policies are sufficient to explain exchange rate fluctuations. Dornbusch and Frankel (1988: 67) got to the heart of the matter quite some time ago when, on the basis of econometric tests of exchange rate developments, they found out that most exchange rate movements cannot be explained by fundamentals like the ones mentioned above. The failure of its approach to exchange rate determination condemns neoclassical theory to its most profound defeat.

The Keynesian approach to exchange rate determination is a lot more plausible. John Maynard Keynes emphasised that the formation of expectations is a social process, interconnected with the historical situation, specific institutions and the particular country. However successful economic actors may be in their search for fundamentals, it will not be in their power to discern their future development. The first problem is that there is not even agreement on what the decisive fundamental data are. Sometimes, economic actors look for future changes in price levels, which is not particularly advisable, given empirical developments, and sometimes they compare the growth or productivity development of different countries. None of these factors or their combination can explain exchange rate developments among the world's leading currencies. It is crucial to understand that the factors which play a role in the formation of expectations with regard to exchange rates go far beyond economic developments in the narrow sense. Especially in the case of exchange rate developments, political, social and even military factors are relevant. Ultimately, economic actors seeking to ascertain fundamentals for exchange rate determination really need to undertake comprehensive country studies to enable them to form long-term expectations – a Herculean task, given the fact that, on this point, even experts rarely agree.

So far, the assumption has been that economic actors seek long-term factors in order to determine exchange rates. Trading on foreign exchange markets, however – as on all asset markets – is also subject to short-term expectations, which are independent of expected long-term developments and can lead to speculative extremes. Speculators can, for example, get out of the euro and buy dollars if they take the view that the value of the dollar will increase in the medium term, while believing at the same time that, over the long term, the dollar must experience a massive devaluation. In this case, it is rational for the sake of short-term speculative gains to buy, despite the assumption of long-term devaluation. As in all asset-market bubbles, this culminates in an accumulation of factors which positively reinforce one another: a short-term increasing dollar rate arouses expectations of a further increase in value and can trigger further capital flows into the United States, which bring in their train another dollar revaluation. A herd mentality can set in among investors, fuelling speculation, until some unforeseeable event bursts the exchange rate bubble, perhaps triggering speculation in the opposite direction.

Research shows that foreign exchange dealers do not form long-term expectations, but operate within the framework of an extremely short-term time horizon. They try to assess in a matter of seconds how other market actors will react to new information, and transact buys or sales accordingly. If exchange rate developments are going in a certain direction, so-called trend-following systems are initiated: on the basis of high-frequency data (for example, ten-second rates) computer trading systems trigger 'buy' signals, which drive an exchange rate further in one direction. More slowly reacting technical models give rise to further buys, which further reinforce the direction of exchange rate movement. These models are used to try to identify, by means of charts of past exchange rate trends, recurring formations and turning points. Economic theory tends to regard such technical analysis with some scepticism. However, it must be considered that, in an area of high uncertainty, such methods can give the appearance of at least a degree of certainty. It can be shown that foreign exchange dealers realise systematic speculative profits, which runs counter to the theory of rational expectations and efficient financial markets.[4]

To summarise, we can say that systems with flexible exchange rates produce a toxic brew, on the one hand because long-term expectations can scarcely be formed and are unstable, and on the other because many actors on the foreign exchange market base their trading not on long-term expectations, but rather on short-term speculation, computer trading systems or mystical technical analyses. The system of flexible exchange rates is a chaotic system dominated by unstable international capital flows and it is incapable of furnishing a rational framework for international trade and the global economy. The problem is, however, that exchange rate movements have consequences for the rest of the economy as they determine the relative price between domestically produced and foreign goods and services. Goods, labour and asset markets are disturbed. Flexible exchange rate transform international credits into a lottery, and sometimes even a form of Russian roulette.

Foreign exchange markets follow boom–bust cycles.[5] Over 90 per cent of cross-border lending takes place in US dollars, euros, sterling, yen and Swiss francs. This can be explained by the fact that creditors evidently have sufficient faith only in these curren-cies. A creditor is often unwilling, in particular, to grant developing countries foreign credit in their domestic currency. These countries suffer from 'original sin'.[6] The leading currencies of the world continue to enjoy the privilege of exemption from this 'original sin' and the relevant countries are able to obtain foreign credit in their own currency. The United States is the prime example and, as the world's largest net borrower, has been able to run up its foreign debt mostly in US dollars.

If a country's economic prospects are expected to be favourable, international investors pile in and its currency increases in value. If investors expect that a currency will rise even higher, they are more than willing to invest further or to grant credit to the relevant country's citizens and businesspeople because their dealings, profits or real estate suddenly appear much more valuable. In such a situation, a country can easily live beyond its means for an extended period and have access to ample credit from the rest of the world. However, such circumstances diminish a country's chances of developing positively over the long term. Currency appreciation triggered by capital inflows undermines the competitiveness of domestic industry. The latter is driven out of export markets, while domestic consumers buy more imports instead of more expensive domestic products. As a consequence, imports rise while exports decline.

This scenario corresponds to the situation in the United States in the first half of the 1980s, the second half of the 1990s and the 2000s: due to the strong dollar, American companies and the government received much more money than they actually earned. Nevertheless, international investors happily pumped their money into the United States, thereby creating an enormous current account deficit. The dollar's continuing strength, maintained by capital inflows, also led to US industry losing ground in world markets. Also in the 2000s, a number of Central and Eastern European countries suffered a similar fate. Because they expected a prosperous development in these countries international investors granted these countries practically unlimited credit before the subprime crisis. The building sector and domestic consumption boomed, while the external balance sheet slid ever deeper into the red and there was a continuous rise in credit demand, which foreign countries were happy to meet.

Such processes are always under threat of rapid reversal in the opposite direction. If investors come to their senses, the external value of the currencies of these countries collapses in expectation of devaluation while everyone tries to shift their monetary wealth into other, more stable currencies in an effort to safeguard their assets' value. With companies and households often indebted in foreign currency, the depreciation leads to an increase in the debt burden. As a consequence, companies are forced to curtail their investment plans, individuals have to reduce their consumption and the country slips into crisis. Because foreign exchange markets and international capital flows are driven by expectations, it can easily happen that countries get sucked into such a maelstrom even when their fundamentals are basically sound. During the Asian crisis in 1997–98, for example, even countries with robust fundamentals, such as South Korea, were caught up by the change in mood among investors.

For a country such as the United States, whose debts are almost entirely in its own currency, such events can pass off almost without serious consequences. For emerging and developing countries, however, the danger is that they can find themselves in deep crisis, with numerous insolvencies among banks, companies, private households and even state budgets, solely as a result of the whims of foreign exchange markets. The external debts of these entities have to be usually serviced in foreign currency, while company sales, workers' wages, tax revenues and so on are paid in the national currency. If the national currency now devalues, the burden of debt can rapidly become overwhelming and insolvency becomes inevitable. This process is also described as a 'twin crisis', in which devaluation destroys the domestic financial system, confidence in the economy declines further and capital flight leads to further devaluation.[7] Twin crises happened not only during the Asian crisis in 1997–78, they can be found during the 'lost decade' in Latin America in the 1990s, in Mexico in 1994, Russia 1998, Argentina 2001 and during many other occasions.

THE UNITED STATES AS THE BATTERED HEGEMONIC POWER

The special roles of the US economy and the US dollar in the world also play an important role in the development of large current account imbalances. From the 1950s until the end 1970s the US current account was relatively balanced. Then in the 1980s a first wave of deficit developed which became even bigger in the 1990s and 2000s (see Figure 3.1 above). It is a truism that current account deficits are only possible if there are corresponding (net) capital inflows. If (net) capital flows to the United States suddenly dropped to zero the US current account deficit would disappear. Since the Second World War the United States has always been a hub for international capital inflows and capital outflows. From the 1980s onwards, the United States was confronted with high net capital inflows and with correspondingly high current account deficits. The US net international investment position has deteriorated over the last decades. The net asset position of over 10 per cent at the 1970s became a net debtor position of over 20 per cent in 2008.[8]

One of the reasons for these large capital inflows is the fact that the US dollar has been the world's key currency since the end of the Second World War, when the Bretton Woods system gave it a special role. Inertia and the lack of a viable alternative explain why the dollar has remained the key international currency until today, with 60 per cent of all foreign reserves held by central banks being in US dollars.

Under a constellation of deregulated international capital flows, part of the world's wealth outside the countries producing it will be kept in the world currency. Thus, we can expect that individuals, firms or banks worldwide will prefer to keep some percentage of their wealth in US dollars as a safe haven. When international capital flows were deregulated, these types of capital flows increased. Increasing US current account deficits are clearly correlated with the deregulation of international capital flows. Especially in crisis situations the United States has been confronted with capital inflows, as its capital markets and its currency are seen as a safe haven. Paradoxically, this was the case even during the US subprime crisis when capital from countries such as Brazil or Korea was moved towards the United States even though the crisis had in effect originated there.

The actions of government institutions also contribute to US capital imports. After the Asian crisis in 1997 and its spread to many emerging countries, central banks in many developing countries (except Japan which at this point joined the developing world) started to intervene in the foreign exchange market to prevent currency appreciation and current account deficits. If we compare the sum of the US current account deficit in the years from 2004 to 2008 with the increase in official reserves held by central banks outside the United States during this time, and assume that around 60 per cent of the increase is held in US dollars, then over 70 per cent of the US current account deficit is financed by central bank interventions. During this period, the People's Bank of China, the Chinese central bank, financed over 40 per cent of the US current account deficit.[9] Without central bank interventions, the US current account deficit would have been substantially smaller.

The explosion of official international reserves after the Asian crisis, especially within the group of countries which peg their exchange rate to the US dollar, has led to speculation that the world economy has implicitly returned to a revived Bretton Woods system.[10] The idea is that countries from the periphery peg their currencies against the US dollar, or at least prevent large exchange rate changes of their currencies vis-à-vis the dollar, and at the same time push for current account surpluses. The United States is passively pushed into running high current account deficits and becomes a demand engine for the rest of the world. The new system, it is argued, is of mutual benefit and could last for decades, allowing the periphery to achieve export-led growth and the United States to realise high welfare gains due to its overvalued currency.

For the United States the system is a mixed blessing. Clearly it increases current real consumption in the United States, but it also reduces domestic growth and employment. Looking at the situation in the United States, from the 1980s onwards – and particularly in the 2000s – it was difficult to achieve a stable long-term growth in demand for US products because high current account deficits resulted in structurally low demand for domestically produced goods, and hence a permanent threat of rising unemployment.

The United States faced a dilemma. In responding to demand weakness, its policy-makers had two options: they could either accept increasing unemployment or try to balance the weakness of demand for US goods and services with an expansionary monetary or fiscal policy. Under its statutes, the Fed is tasked with ensuring not only price stability, but also as high a level of employment as possible and moderate long-term interest rates. And it does indeed pursue these objectives. Since, at the same time, both foreign trade and domestic income development gave rise to slow growth in the demand for domestically produced goods, the Fed was left with little choice but to keep interest rates very low for a long time. The fact that the Federal Reserve, under the chairmanship of Alan Greenspan, also accepted the subprime and securitisation booms can also be explained in terms of this logic. Since, without this boom, underemployment would have grown and probably triggered falling wages and deflationary tendencies in the medium term, the Fed was willing to tolerate the emergence of a real-estate bubble and the accompanying huge credit expansion.[11] The main blame for the subprime crisis must thus be seen in the general policy of deregulation, especially of the national and international financial systems, and their endogenously self-amplifying effects.[12]

The world current account imbalances, which are centred upon the US deficit, are dangerous in several ways. First, over recent decades the United States has taken on the function of a demand engine of the world and alleviated the harmful effects of mercantilist strategies of many countries in the world. If the United States is not able to fulfil this function in the future, which is likely, the mercantilist strategies of too many countries may come into conflict, leading to additional instability of the world economy. Second, a too rapid breakdown of the United States as the demand engine of the world economy would have a detrimental effect on the global economy. Third, the huge current account deficits and the already high foreign debt burden of the United States have implications for the US dollar. The US foreign debt is mainly denominated in domestic currency, so this will not lead to a debt crisis there as it would in emerging countries. However, the scale of debt poses a threat to the stability and international reputation of the US dollar because of the way that the negative US international investment position will burden the US current account with interest payments and/or profit transfers and trigger negative expectations about the future value of the US dollar.

The future of the US dollar is difficult to predict.[13] However, it seems to be clear that the US dollar will not be able to regain the absolute dominance it enjoyed in the 1950s and 1960s. The hypothesis of a revived Bretton Woods system is not very convincing as the constellation is not based on an international treaty; rather it is a kind of private cartel to stabilise the exchange rate of the US dollar. The euro does not take part in the revived Bretton Woods system. Should the external value of the US dollar collapse, only the first central bank switching from reserves held in US dollar to reserves held in euro or other currencies will avoid losses. As the number of countries in the revived system is large, the cartel may break down any time when the smaller central banks in particular, but also even the more important central banks, start to reduce their dollar holdings. There is a danger that the revived system could break down violently and add to worldwide exchange rate instability.

The most likely future of the international currency system is a further movement towards a leaderless currency system, as Benjamin Cohen (2009) predicts. In the near future the US dollar will of course play the most important role, followed by the euro. The yen has lost its international importance; Japan was pushed off its prosperous growth path after the end of its real-estate and stock-market bubble in 1990–91. The Chinese renminbi in the near future has not the capacity to take over international functions. The pound sterling is also unable to play an important international role, as is the Swiss currency; both countries are too small to take over more then a niche role. This means that during the next decade the competition between the US dollar and the euro will be at the centre of the world currency system. In the long run, depending on geopolitical shifts in the world power structure, more currencies will most probably take over international functions. Also fewer currencies are likely to peg their currencies to the US dollar in the near future, especially if economic integration in Asia deepens.

More intensive currency competition will most likely lead to more instability.[14] Governments and central banks may actively fight for a leading international position for their national currency. The decisive economic means to achieve this are policies designed in the interest of wealth owners and political and military dominance. But independent of such policies wealth owners, banks, investment and pension funds, or companies can create competition between currencies. If a country with an international reserve currency does not meet the expected standards of price level stability or follows economic policies which do not strongly promote currency stability and protect the interest of wealth owners, capital will be withdrawn and relocated to competing currencies.

Intensive currency competition creates a high level of uncertainty. Only the first ones to leave a currency in danger of depreciation will save their wealth. In this scenario wealth owners must be very alert so that they do not miss the crucial point of time for switching from one currency to another. Periodic shifts of potentially huge funds therefore characterise currency competition. Exchange rate movements between US dollar and euro (and earlier the deutschmark) very closely fit the scenario described. The special problematic of the present constellation consists of the fact that both the US dollar and the euro are unsatisfactory reserve currencies. The US dollar has lost its external stability; current account deficits as well as high external debt and a permanent decline of the United States' relative position in terms of GDP, international trade, technological leadership and political dominance (though not so much of military power) will weaken the role of the US dollar. The euro area has about the same economic size as the United States, but the euro suffers from deep and unresolved internal problems (see below). What we have is competition between two crippled giants, which makes unstable international capital flows even more likely.

CHINESE MERCANTILISM

Another important factor contributing to global imbalances has been the rise of China. Between 1978 and 2010, real GDP in China increased by a spectacular average annual rate of (nearly) 10 per cent and GDP per capita by over 8 per cent. Taking US$1 a day as a threshold, over the past decades China has been the country with the largest absolute reduction in poverty in the world despite its alarming and increasingly unequal income distribution. An overall gradual strategy was chosen with far-reaching government interventions. China did not follow recommendations in the tradition of the Washington Consensus pushed by IMF and other Washington institutions, but probably because of this fact was economically overall successful.[15]

China has implemented a comprehensive system of capital controls which has been only slightly relaxed in the past few years. The logic of the capital control system is simple: all types of capital flows are controlled with the exception of foreign direct investment (FDI) inflows. However, capital inflows have been dominated by FDI and capital outflows by central bank interventions in the foreign exchange market. To a large extent, China has been able to structure capital flows in its own interest and in addition to follow a domestically oriented monetary policy with generally low real interest rates.

Chinese development has been driven by two growth engines. First, investment has been exuberant and, in spite of high FDI inflows, mainly driven by a highly regulated financial system. Second, China has never accepted lasting current account deficits. From the late 1990s, current account surpluses in China started to explode and quickly became among the biggest of the world. The greatest trade imbalance exists between China and the United States. These surpluses clearly are politically motivated and enforced, and reveal that China, starting in the 2000s, followed an aggressive mercantilist strategy intended to accumulate current account surpluses.

In 1994, following a major depreciation, China pegged its exchange rate to the US dollar at a level which made Chinese products internationally competitive. This peg was successfully defended until 2005 when China started to peg the renminbi to a currency basket and a crawling peg regime that led to very moderate appreciations vis-à-vis the US dollar. The People's Bank of China (PBoC) has been steadily intervening in the foreign exchange market to prevent or slow down the appreciation of the Chinese renminbi.

Interventions in the 2000s were so strong that China became the country with the biggest international reserves of the world, around US$2.4 trillion at the end of 2009.[16] Since the end of the 1990s China has amassed a huge double surplus, one in its current account and an even greater one in its capital account, stemming from FDI inflows and partly also from other legal or illegal inflows. Without the PBoC's interventions in the foreign exchange market and without changes in capital flows China would be pushed into a huge current account deficit.

In order to understand Chinese policy, however, it is important to recall that, in other countries, development strategies based on broad liberalisation of financial markets and flexible exchange rates have often foundered. Furthermore, during the Asian crisis of 1997–98, the Chinese government had to stand by and watch while other countries in the region, sometimes with fairly low current account deficits, were dragged into the crisis by global financial markets. The logical consequence of this experience was for a country to attempt to shield itself as much as possible from the swings of global capital flows. By accumulating current account surpluses, China avoided having to borrow abroad and so was able to go its own way, independent of the caprices of foreign exchange dealers and international investors. For the purpose of this strategy, it was also important to keep the renminbi at a low level so that exports exceeded imports. China's export surplus can therefore be interpreted as self-defence against a global currency system which is dysfunctional for developing countries. Another, more stable world financial system would have moderated this strategy.

However, there is no doubt that China's current account surpluses are harmful to economic growth in other countries, as are the high surpluses of Germany and Japan. As argued above, they lead to problems of aggregate demand management in other countries as well as a growing instability of the world economy. There is also some irrationality in the Chinese strategy, as it is clear that the accumulated monetary wealth denominated in US dollars and held by the PBoC must lose its value when the US dollar depreciates. We support the use by developing and emerging countries of a strategy to avoid current account deficits, and the use of capital controls and central bank interventions to implement such a strategy. It is also a wise strategy for countries like China to peg the exchange rate to one of the world currencies or a basket of currencies. However, the current account surpluses in China simply are too big. Also the high proportion of exports as a percentage of GDP makes Chinese growth very dependent on world market development, especially development in the United States, as the main channel for Chinese exports.

The combination of a moderate depreciation of the renminbi and a more balanced domestic demand structure to increase the share of consumption on GDP are the policies we would recommend. An exchange rate adjustment needs to take place in a coordinated way in Asia, as China is not the only country following a mercantilist strategy. Domestic demand stimulation in China could be combined with a policy to reduce income inequalities.

DESTABILISING IMBALANCES IN THE EUROPEAN MONETARY UNION

While Europe as a whole has not contributed much to global imbalances, the global problems have their mirror image at the European level, the development of which can only be understood after taking a look at the history of European integration. European economic policymakers, as long ago as the collapse of the Bretton Woods system, were not prepared to allow extreme appreciations and devaluations among their own currencies in accordance with the whims of the market. From 1973 onwards, six European countries (Belgium, Denmark, France, Germany, Luxembourg and the Netherlands) therefore tried to keep their exchange rates in narrow bands, at first within the framework of the 'currency snake', with the German mark as anchor currency. In 1979 the Europeans introduced the European Currency System, in substance a small Bretton Woods system, but without an institutionally determined leading currency, and even went so far as to replace their own national currencies with the euro in 1999.

The release from exchange rate risk within the EMU has been obtained at the expense of the accumulation of enormous current account surpluses and deficits between individual participating states. Since the EMU came into being, from a current account deficit, Germany has built up a record current account surplus, as have Luxembourg, Austria, Finland and the Netherlands. Germany's high surpluses represent a particular problem since it is the largest economy in Europe. The current account deficits of all other EMU countries have deteriorated since the advent of euro. The deficits in Greece, Portugal and Spain are particularly high, with double-digit current account deficits, as a percentage of GDP. As in the case of global imbalances, surpluses and deficits emerged primarily in the years directly preceding the crisis. These imbalances, too, can partly be explained in terms of excesses in the real-estate markets in countries such as Spain, Greece and Ireland. In contrast to the global imbalances, these imbalances have more to do with economic policy problems within the Eurozone than with the caprices of global financial markets. To be sure, the EMU is, in the first instance, a political project and not an optimal currency area, but it can also be understood as a reaction to instabilities in the global economy, with its erratic exchange rate fluctuations.

National deficits and surpluses conceal strongly diverging developments in demand *and* cost trends within the EMU: while in countries such as Ireland or Spain in recent years demand was driven primarily by domestic consumption and a construction boom, economic growth in Germany was based almost exclusively on strong export growth and corporate investments in the export sector. Wage cost trends, determined by changes in nominal wages and productivity, also diverged. Wage costs rose only minimally between 1999 and 2010 in Germany; indeed, between 2004 and 2006, they even fell. In Italy and Spain, by contrast, costs rose rapidly, while France was slightly above the EMU average.

Overall, the differences in the development of wage costs are enormous. In Spain, Portugal, Greece and Italy, since the EMU came into existence, they have risen by over 20 per cent, while in France they have increased by a good 15 per cent in comparison with Germany.[17] If wages increase in one country more strongly than in the rest of the EMU, it means two things: on the one hand, that country will lose competitiveness and on the other, the domestic inflation rate will rise because production costs will increase for non-tradable goods and services and producers will pass on these higher costs to consumers. The uniform nominal interest rate fixed by the European Central Bank for the whole EMU represents a lower real interest rate in a country with a higher national inflation rate. Lower real interest rates tend to make investment more attractive. Since this effect in the foreign-trade-oriented sector of the economy is offset by the loss of price competitiveness, the lower real interest rate works primarily to stimulate the real-estate market and the construction sector. A real-estate boom kick-started in this way is further reinforced if price increases exceed mortgage interest rates. At this point, the attractiveness of real-estate transactions increases to such an extent that speculative buyers enter the market. During such a boom, moreover, consumption accelerates more quickly than in the rest of the Eurozone, on the one hand because disposable income is increased by strong wage growth, and on the other because property owners feel richer on account of rising property prices.

Supported by the lack of an exchange rate risk, current account deficits within the EMU were easily financed via the European banking system and the capital market. Little account is taken in this respect of the macroeconomic indebtedness trends of the deficit countries. Instead, at least for the time being, there is implicit faith in their creditworthiness. Since, during a real-estate boom, the value of securities in these countries increases, banks in the rest of the EMU are also willing to help finance the boom for an extended period, even when the debt-ridden countries are living beyond their means.

The real-estate boom described came to an end with the outbreak of the subprime crisis. As the countries with the boom had lost much of their competitiveness, the weakness of the export sector added to the economic problems and pushed these countries in a deep and most likely long crisis. The building sector will have to shrink back to normal size, leading to job losses. The country affected will also be compelled to try to regain lost competitiveness through an extended period of wage agreements below the Eurozone average. During this period the national inflation rate now lies below the EMU rate and the national real interest rate is therefore higher than in the EMU average. These factors only intensify the crash of the real-estate market, while slower wage growth or even falling wages imply deflationary dangers in these countries with additional problems for the financial system and low domestic demand. In other words, falling wages and prices would very negatively affect some services, handicrafts and other forms of local production.

De facto, Germany sets the wage standard for the EMU. It is not only the largest economy within the Eurozone, but also the country with the lowest increase in wage costs, which is due not to very high productivity increases but primarily to its very low money wage increases. If wages in Germany continue to develop as they have hitherto, the countries that have had higher wage cost increases in the past will be forced to swallow significant wage cuts in order to regain competitiveness. It would be an illusion to hope that significantly higher productivity growth in these countries could restore competitiveness. It is doubtful whether large nominal wage cuts are even possible in those parts of the EMU which have lost their competitiveness, because workers and trade unions normally oppose such cuts. After the outbreak of the subprime crisis, countries such as Greece, Italy, Portugal and Spain face a stark dilemma at least as long as wages in Germany and other EMU surplus countries do not rise sharply: they have a choice between, on the one hand, stagnation due to a lack of competitiveness within the EMU and an exhausted real-estate bubble or, on the other, deflationary wage cuts which would raise the real debt burden of some companies and part of the population and depress domestic demand. At first, the southern EMU member countries tried to stabilise their economies via expansionary fiscal policies when the subprime crisis spread. Yet these attempts quickly had to be stopped as markets started to turn against these countries and investors demand rising risk premiums, putting these countries into the danger of default. In 2010 Greece became the first country to fall into an outright sovereign debt crisis and had to call in the International Monetary Fund. At the time of writing, market pressure is still high for Ireland and Spain. The cases of Ireland and Spain are especially instructive as these countries had a seemingly robust budget position prior to the crisis. Until 2007, they were even running surpluses. Only with the implosion of tax revenue, the increase in recession-related spending such as unemployment benefits, and the bank bail-out packages necessary in the crisis did these countries get into the downward spiral of high deficits, rising risk premiums and a strongly rising public debt level.

To be sure, wage increases in the southern EMU member states have sometimes been much too high. But it would be misguided to blame these countries for the current distortions within the EMU which, if there is no fundamental policy change, will only increase in the future. Wage and price increases in Germany have been too low, compared with what would be reasonable wage growth in macroeconomic terms and for the EMU, leading on the one hand to above average high real interest rates in Germany and, on the other hand, to strongly increasing current account surpluses in relation to almost all the other EMU countries. Wage development in Germany has been at least as problematic for EMU cohesion as that of Spain, Portugal or other countries which had to record well above average wage increases. The excessively low increases which brought Germany almost to the brink of deflation are due on the one hand to its mercantilist tradition, which favours export-oriented development with high current account surpluses and was backed by important interest groups, including some trade unions. On the other hand, the high levels of unemployment in Germany and the erosion of labour market institutions have also contributed to low wage increases (see Chapter 4). Whether or not as a deliberate strategy, Germany, and to a lesser extent the smaller surplus countries, have de facto instigated wage dumping within the EMU and so have exported unemployment through their export success. That is the case despite the fact that for Germany this development has not paid dividends with regard to growth and employment, due to the low domestic demand which corresponded with wage dumping.

Reform options are as clear as they are politically difficult. Necessary measures are wage coordination on an EMU level, including institutions which allow this, and a centralisation of fiscal policy in the EMU. Without such reforms the EMU will be troubled with deep distortions. In particular, wage increases in Germany need to be higher and Germany, as the biggest EMU country, has to abandon its aggressive mercantilist strategy.

4

LABOUR IN THE WAKE OF MARKETS

The aim of this chapter is to take a closer look at the role of wages in order to work out their crucial role not only in our everyday life, of course, but also on the broad economic level of states and even on a global level. Trends in wages are fundamental for understanding what went wrong in the past 20 to 30 years and why our economies crash so predictably today. In order to get the full picture of the role of wages we have to proceed in several steps. First, we will put wages into the context of the academic debate, while trying not to be overly academic in our language ourselves. For that we need to dig a bit deeper into the role of wages in different economic paradigms, which are constantly competing to be the one that will explain the world to us. Then we get a lot more practical by turning to the erosion of labour market institutions during the market-liberal revolution. Key to understanding the increasing proneness to crisis of our economies is a sober account of changes in income distribution over the past few decades – developments in this sphere are closely connected to the excesses on the financial markets. At the end of this chapter we demonstrate the concrete effects of labour in the wake of markets by elaborating on some short case studies.

LABOUR IN THE FACE OF PARADIGMS

In parallel with the deregulation of financial markets, from the 1980s the market-liberal revolution also pressed ahead with deregulation of labour markets. The neoclassical model, which developed in its macroeconomic variant at the end of the nineteenth century, from the beginning regarded overly high wages and rigid labour market regulation as the main causes of unemployment. After the Second

World War, a specific version of Keynesian thought became popular which, on the one hand, emphasised the connection between wages and employment. On the other hand, this school traced economic disruptions back to inadequate demand for goods, which had to be combated by means of monetary and, above all, fiscal policy. The basic idea of this so called neoclassical synthesis was that – in the longer run – the neoclassical model is in fact valid and so also is the need for flexible labour markets, but that in the short term 'Keynesian' disruptions can arise in the form of a lack of demand for goods. The core of neoclassical thought was preserved in this 'bastard Keynesianism'.

We have to dig a bit deeper into labour market theories in order to be able to understand the labour market's role in the recent crisis and in capitalism more generally. In the 1970s, the neoclassical synthesis was plunged into deep crisis. A central difficulty of this model lay in its inability to really come to grips with the problem of inflation. Rising inflation rates, the view was, should lead to rising employment. In the 1970s, however, this was far from being the case, when inflation rates and unemployment rates went up simultaneously. That, in turn, ushered in the era of monetarism, whose most famous representative, Milton Friedman, had always been a sworn enemy of the neoclassical synthesis. Since the end of the 1960s, his influence over economic policy had been increasing. Friedman's views were based on the unadulterated neoclassical model, according to which monetary policy was duty bound to maintain price stability, while the task of the labour market was to ensure a high level of employment. Disturbances of the labour market in the form of a wage-formation mechanism dominated by trade unions and employers' associations and not by the play of the free market, including regional and professional imbalances with regard to labour supply and demand, were identified as the cause of a 'natural' unemployment rate. Labour market deregulation, according to this approach to economic policy, is the most effective way of combating unemployment. Monetary and fiscal policy are unsuited for this purpose because they could only have a short-term effect which, besides, would be difficult to evaluate. State budgets should always strive to remain balanced, while the central bank should increase the money supply at a constant rate.[1]

Friedman's victory in the academic realm was short-lived in comparison with his political influence. In the 1970s, a more radical variant of neoclassical thought began to develop and dominated the academic debate. Robert Lucas, a pupil of Friedman at the University of Chicago, was one of the most important co-founders of the New Classical School. This school also stressed that the labour market is of central importance for economic performance and employment, as well as the reasons for unemployment. According to Friedman and Lucas, each household offers the number of working hours at which the utility of the additional income offsets the disutility of labour from the additional working hours. Households will usually increase the labour supply when real wages, the basket of goods which can be earned in one hour work, go up. Companies' demand for labour continues as long as the physical output produced by a worker corresponds to the real wage. Let us assume a worker earns 5 kg of corn per hour. Then a capitalist will only employ that worker when his or her output is at least 5 kg of corn, otherwise it is unprofitable. In addition it is assumed that each additional employed worker will produce less output. The outcome of this line of analysis is that only falling real wages can increase the demand for labour. Flexible wages will find their level when the labour supply matches labour demand. In this model, unemployment is always voluntary and could be eradicated. The New Classical School even argues that markets adjust very quickly and labour markets always are in equilibrium.[2]

Methodologically, this approach followed a microfoundation of macroeconomics. That might sound rather complicated, but it is quite simple in fact. Microfoundation means examining a rational acting individual household or an individual company and directly extrapolating the results to the macroeconomic level. Any notion that the rational behaviour of individuals can lead to unintended consequences at the macro-level ceased to play a role in economic thought. But, to take a simple example, it is obvious that the individual rationality of standing up in a theatre in order to get a better view of what is happening on the stage will not lead to everyone getting a better view if the whole audience follows suit. In this instance, a rational micro-decision results in something worse for everyone. Unfortunately, this line of analysis of the labour market is politically very powerful as it seems to be quite plausible. Telling a different story is a bit more complex. For a single firm, lower wages indeed increase its competitiveness and can lead to higher employment. If wages for all firms decrease, the outcome will be different.

In response to the New Classical School, the New Keynesian School developed in the 1990s. The latter accepted the notion of microfoundation from the New Classical School, but deduced that there are rational grounds at the microeconomic level which lead to wage rigidities, drawing unemployment in their wake.[3] This once more made room for an effective monetary and fiscal policy, although the New Keynesians considered that the basic problem of unemployment lay in labour market mechanisms. For example, so-called efficiency-wage models were developed, according to which workers idle away their time and do not do their best. If a company increases its wages, however, workers risk being caught out and fired, thereby forgoing the higher wage available in that firm. If all companies operate in accordance with this logic, wages will rise too high and unemployment will ensue. Another example is the so-called insider–outsider problem. The trade unions, which organise the workers, are the insiders who obtain high wages for their members, although wages then rise too high and create outsiders in the labour market. Wages are fixed on the basis of wage negotiation systems and outsiders cannot force them down.

As far as both traditional neoclassical ideas and their modern incarnations are concerned, trade unions, minimum wages and a burgeoning welfare state are very much a bad thing, since in the face of unemployment they make it difficult to bring down wages or can encourage households to prefer claiming social benefits to working. Supposedly stable market mechanisms, regarded as a marvellous machine for generating social welfare and harmony, should be helped to prevail. In the market-liberal view, deregulation leads to the revitalisation of economic development and to positive employment effects. It is therefore not surprising that the majority of economists and economic advisers who believe in the traditional neoclassical model or even in the New Keynesian approach recommend labour market deregulation and wage cuts to fight unemployment. Even governments that are in principle labour-friendly, like the Social Democrat–Green government in Germany of Gerhard Schröder (1998–2005), based their policies on these ideas.

Whatever school you refer to, Keynes himself saw things totally differently. In his magnum opus, *The General Theory of Employment, Interest and Money* of 1936, written in the shadow of the global economic crisis of the 1930s, Keynes interprets the labour market in the context of aggregate demand in goods markets. Goods demand is the main feature which determines production volumes, employment and unemployment in the economy overall. In Keynes's view, labour markets take the lowest place in the market hierarchy and are dominated by asset markets and goods markets. Investment demand is determined in asset markets by the level of interest rates together with companies' expectations, although consumer demand also depends on asset-market developments, for example in the availability and cost of borrowing and the development of share and real-estate prices. If the economy is not working at full capacity and unemployment arises, investment and consumer demand, together with state and foreign demand, determine production volumes and, therefore, employment. Only very rarely does the physical availability of means of production limit the volume of production, employment and incomes.

Generally speaking, the capitalist dynamic depends on the level of money advances (the sums entrepreneurs use to carry out production processes, to buy investment goods, intermediate goods, labour, etc). This can be explained by the general formula of capital which, alongside Karl Marx (1867), Keynes also posited, although he disagreed with Marx on many other points. Money is advanced for means of production and labour in order to produce goods, which are then sold. The return obtained through sale must be higher than the money advanced because the whole business only makes sense if a profit remains. Production processes are not only financed by own means, credit plays a vital role in the determination how much money is invested for productive purposes.

Crucial to this viewpoint are expectations. Keynes (1936) spoke of 'enterprises' and 'animal spirits', and Joseph Schumpeter (1926) of 'entrepreneurship', the gist of which is that companies' investment decisions cannot be explained strictly in economic terms but also depend on a range of expectations with regard to the future. Needless to say, the expected demand for their products plays a crucial role for entrepreneurs. But this cannot be predicted with any certainty and so the general investment climate is also important. The problem of insufficient investment might have another cause, namely when companies are unable to obtain financial resources. As a result, the availability of loans and financing costs also play a key part in the growth process. Financial institutions and wealthy households also base their decision on expectations which do not have firm grounds. When, for example, the financial system is disrupted and companies cannot obtain enough money, growth and employment will be low. Typically, this happens precisely when companies, on the basis of negative expectations, do not really seek loans for investment purposes anyway. So, investment moves in waves. Empirically, this manifests itself in the constant rise and fall in investment activity, growth and employment which have characterised economic dynamics since the emergence of capitalism. Ultimately, the central bank also can reduce the amount of money

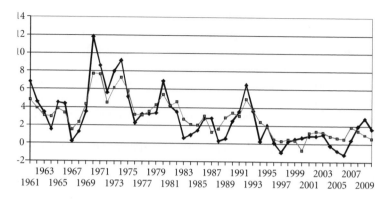

Germany

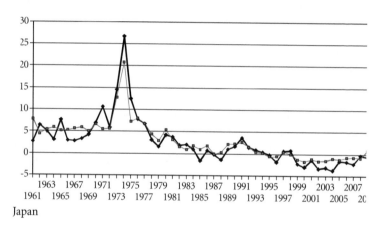

Japan

Figure 4.1 Unit wage costs and inflation rates (percentage change over the previous year) Germany, the United States, Japan and the United Kingdom
Source: Ameco (2010).

invested in productive and income-creating activities in the economy by means of a restrictive monetary policy. In many cases, it is the central bank which raises interest rates in order to combat inflation and so reduces investment activity. It is one of the above-listed factors which limits production and income generation – and not the physical availability of labour and means of production.

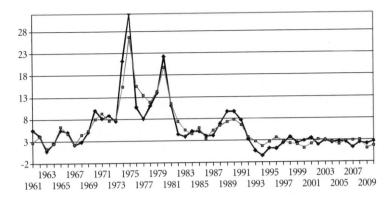

United Kingdom

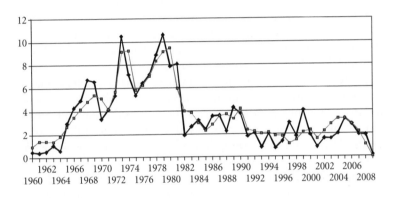

United States

- ◆ Nominal unit labour costs
- ▣ GDP deflator

In capitalist economies, productivity rises along a relatively stable path and reflects technological and organisational improvements. Evidently, it is the pursuit of extra profits which promotes permanent innovation of all kinds in market economies, and companies that cannot participate in this process risk going under. Many economists have emphasised this power of capitalist economies, including Karl Marx and Joseph Schumpeter, as well as John Maynard Keynes.

Demand for labour basically depends on production, with the development of productivity coming into consideration as an additional factor. Employment in the medium term increases whenever the volume of production grows more strongly than the development of productivity. When the volume of production in the economy grows by 5 per cent and productivity by 2 per cent, for example, employment rises by 3 per cent. Unemployment exists when more persons want to work than labour is demanded by economic growth and productivity. Thus, labour demand does not depend in any direct way on wages – as the neoclassical model wants to make us believe in all its versions. Labour supply depends on population growth and participation in the labour market. Wages only play a subordinate role in explaining the supply of labour. Difficulties in the labour market usually arise when, over the long term, the increase in the volume of production lags behind productivity increases.

The implication of the above analysis is that wages do not directly determine employment. However, they are of key importance for the price level in an economy. John Maynard Keynes pointed out that wages are negotiated in national currencies, which means wages in dollars in the United States, wages in pounds in the United Kingdom and so on. They are not negotiated within an overall basket of goods. At least on the assumption of a closed economy, wage costs expressed in a national currency have the function to determine the national price level. Keynes developed this approach in his *Treatise on Money*, which was published in 1930 and is just as important for Keynesianism as the *General Theory*, which contains nothing on inflationary and deflationary processes.

The development of the price level is determined, first and foremost, by production costs. In a closed economy, unit wage costs represent the most important cost component and become the nominal anchor of the price level.[4] If they increase, the price level rises; when they fall, deflationary developments ensue. Unit wage costs are made up of two factors: on the one hand, money wages, an increase in which also increases unit wage costs, and on the other hand, labour productivity, an increase in which will reduce wage costs. Figure 4.1 illustrates the development of unit wage costs in a number of countries. Germany after 1995 is characterised by very low increases in unit wage costs and price levels. In the United States and the United Kingdom unit wage costs also increased substantially in the 1970s, but became relatively stable in the 1990s and 2000s.

The situation in Japan shows that unit wage costs can also fall. Empirically, the connection between unit wage costs and the development of the price level is astonishingly close and stable.

However, in spite of the paramount role of wages in determining the price level, other factors also play a role. For example, the price level rises as a result of higher commodity prices or a rise in VAT. Changes in the exchange rate alter the price for imports and raise or lower costs in a country and so affect the price level. Especially in small countries with a high import quota, the exchange rate can become the second anchor for the price level in addition to wage costs. Common to the cost components of the price level determination is that they function by a way of a 'price–price effect'. Thus, even without excess goods, market demand that increases costs will increase the price level. Finally, imbalances between supply and demand in goods markets can also play a role in determining the price level and lead to demand inflation or demand deflation.

This brief account of the role of labour in the face of paradigms has shown that it makes a great difference how one looks at labour. Labour is crucial in all economic paradigms, but is certainly more crucial in some such models, such as the one developed by Keynes himself.

EROSION OF LABOUR MARKET INSTITUTIONS

The rising unemployment figures in almost all OECD countries in the 1970s, together with high and increasing inflation rates, were among the main reasons the neoclassical analysis was able to win out. The neoclassical synthesis which dominated economic thinking in the 1950s and 1960s was not able to explain a combination of increasing inflation *and* rising unemployment. Keynes could easily explain such stagflation. Money advances in production processes and thus GDP growth rates were too low to provide employment for all, while at the same time increasing costs (in the 1970s particularly wages and oil prices) led to a cost-push inflation. In that decade, however, the neoclassical paradigm started to dominate economic thinking and its proponents began to push for labour market deregulation in the fight against unemployment. The campaigns for making labour markets more flexible were undoubtedly decisive and most economists never got tired of extolling the virtues of flexibilisation.

Conservative political interests played a major role in pushing through this paradigm; the power of trade unions and the protection of workers had always been a thorn in their side. Power relations

in enterprises were to be rearranged so that employees would have
to passively accept management decisions. Politically, the decisive
break in labour market policy took place after the election victories
of Margaret Thatcher and Ronald Reagan. In the 1980s, in both
countries there was an overt policy against the trade unions and in
favour of dismantling labour market regulation. By way of illustra-
tion, in the United Kingdom, there was a miners' strike in 1984–85,
which lasted a year. The miners were defeated, paving the way
for the reform of trade union legislation. Most Western countries
followed the lead of the United States and the United Kingdom
after some delay, even those with social democratic governments.
Ultimately, only a few Scandinavian countries continued to hope
that the problems on the labour market which had accumulated in
the 1970s could be solved without resorting to deregulation.

Economic developments stepped up the pressure on employees
and increasingly weakened the trade unions. Unemployment figures
rose in most OECD countries. Germany provides a particularly
graphic example here, since between 2000 and 2008 the unemployment rate climbed from below 1 per cent in the 1960s to almost
9 per cent. It is important to note that the proportion of employed
persons who were temporarily affected by unemployment is higher
than may be apparent from the unemployment rate.

The globalisation model which arose from the conservative revolution was one which tended to produce constant economic shocks.
Exchange rate shifts altered the competitiveness of entire economies
overnight. Furthermore, new and important countries pushed their
way into the international division of labour and demanded their
share. These included not only China, but also the countries of the
former Soviet bloc and countries such as India and Vietnam. Whole
industries in a large number of countries were deprived of their
competitiveness, in the course of shock-like developments, through
no fault of their own. Restructuring in the corporate sector as a
result of mergers and acquisitions, as well as shifts in the supply
chains of multinational companies around the globe, had become
much more important. Increasingly, skilled industrial jobs were
lost in developed countries. In addition the change in technologies over the last decades reduced the scope for unskilled jobs in
manufacturing. Outsourcing often followed the 'logic' of regulation
arbitrage from firms with good salaries and/or strong unions to
sectors or regions with low wages, precarious jobs and no unions.
As a consequence of market-liberal globalisation, pressure increased
on the workers to accept wage cuts and flexibilisation to improve

the survival chances of companies whose outlook was sometimes desperate. The relocation of production – or often just the threat of it – did the rest, weakening the workers and forcing them to make concessions.

The process of labour market deregulation was intensified in many countries by the dismantling of social security systems. High unemployment rates, the creation of employment relationships with no liability for social security contributions, and demographic developments in most countries increasingly put social security systems under pressure.

Another important development since the 1970s has been the shift of wage negotiations from central to enterprise level in many countries. Enterprise-level wage negotiations weaken trade unions, which have to agree to all kinds of special provisions at that level. Negotiators in enterprises are the management and the employees, who are dependent on the management. Enterprise-specific trade unions also have a tendency to pursue strategies together with the management, who seek to furnish their own enterprise with competitive advantages by means of wage restraint and flexibilisation at enterprise level.[5] A microeconomically rational policy of falling wages can lead to deflation at the macroeconomic level, however, thereby making things worse for all enterprises in the economy.

Of course, there are exceptions which stand out against the general trend. For example, in Portugal and Spain wage negotiations were shifted from company to industry level. It is important to note that this shift does not automatically entail a stronger coordination of wage formation or the inclusion of macroeconomic needs. Wage developments in individual industries can also exclusively reflect the specific conditions of those industries and lead to harmful wage developments in a country.

Industrial production, with its traditionally high level of trade union organisation, was increasingly relocated from industrialised countries to the rest of the world, while industries with a traditionally low level of trade union organisation, such as services, gained in significance in the industrialised countries. In many countries, the trade unions are suffering from a severe image problem. Even within the left-wing movements they are in many cases seen as dinosaurs from a bygone age. These developments are reflected in falling trade union membership, especially in the United States, the United Kingdom, Japan, France, the Netherlands and Germany. However, this is by no means an inevitable tendency. A number of countries, for example Belgium, Denmark and Finland, can point to a stable or rising level of organisation.[6] Employers' organisations have also seen their position undermined in many countries.

In most industrialised countries, there has been an increase in precarious employment characterised, for example, by fixed-term contracts, temporary agency work, part-time working, low employment protection or work without payment of social security contributions. Although this trend has been seen in higher-wage segments such as higher education and research, precarious employment is by and large concentrated in the low-wage sector. Overall one can say that living and working conditions have become much more insecure for a considerable portion of the population due to misguided responses to rising unemployment and the deregulation of labour markets.

INCREASING INEQUALITY

A key characteristic of the market-liberal globalisation model of the past few decades has been a significant change in income distribution. In view of the increasingly unequal distribution of income and assets, and so also of opportunities, capitalism has been moving from a more decent to a more brutal form, as is clear even if it is viewed through ideologically tinted spectacles. In what follows, the various dimensions of change are presented and explained.

Let us begin with the so-called functional income distribution. In almost all countries, *wage shares* have fallen significantly from their highest levels in the 1970s; the term 'wage shares' describes the ratio of wages to total income. In comparison to the 1970s, wage shares have fallen most sharply in Austria, Finland, France, Germany, the United Kingdom, Greece, Ireland, Italy, Japan and Spain.[7]

This development can be explained primarily by the increase in the power of the financial sector, which has been able to achieve a higher profit mark-up. In this connection, the interest rate should be seen as the lowest rate of profit, since over the long term no company would accept a profit rate which was below the interest rate. But falling wage shares cannot be explained primarily in terms of high interest rates. A different mechanism is at work: institutional investors, such as investment banks, pension funds, hedge funds and private equity funds, have intensified the pressure on enterprises to generate higher returns. The proportion of financial institutions that are willing to take risks has also grown and the demand for returns has increased in the financial industry and the whole economy. The triumph of the shareholder-value principle, which is linked to the changes in the financial system and pushes management to follow only the interests of owners and generate returns that are as high as possible in the shortest possible time, added to these tendencies.

The level of monopolisation in goods markets is also crucial, since it is possible to achieve a higher profit rate in oligopolistic and monopolistic markets than in markets with many suppliers.[8] So, for example, the significance of multinationals has undoubtedly grown over the past few decades, although globalisation has increased competitive pressure on goods markets, slowing this process down somewhat. Compared with the changes in the financial sector, we believe that this factor is of secondary importance.[9]

Let us come to changes in wage dispersion. Many countries relied on a low-wage sector to combat unemployment, or passively allowed the development of such a sector. Thus, statutory minimum wages were not used to prevent the development of a low-wage sector. Strong trade unions almost always prevent the development of a big low-wage sector. However, as already mentioned, unions in many countries lost much of their power.

The strongest *wage dispersion* is to be found in the United States, followed by Canada, the United Kingdom and Ireland. By far the lowest wage dispersion is to be found in the Scandinavian countries. Austria, France, Germany, Spain and also Japan lie somewhere in the middle.

Inequality in the wage structure has increased markedly in most OECD countries. Comparing developments from the mid-1990s onwards, three scenarios emerge: in the case of a 'collapsing floor', lower wages break away and an expanding low-wage sector forms; Germany is the most extreme case of the exceedingly rapid development of a low-wage sector. In the case of a 'rising ceiling', the wages of high earners escalate; Canada, Germany, the United Kingdom, Ireland and the United States fit this scenario from the 1990s. It must also be emphasised, however, that in the Anglo-Saxon countries the low-wage sector grew strongly in the 1980s and that this development was at least partially blocked in the 1990s by a policy of increasing state minimum wages. In contrast, there were countries which were able to reduce wage dispersion; the most successful was Spain, but such reductions were also found in France.[10]

The *state* also clearly intervenes in personal income distribution, through social security systems, tax and contribution systems and state expenditure. Over the last decades in many countries, governments have followed tax and other policies which privileged high-income groups. In 2005 the Scandinavian countries, Austria,

Belgium, the Netherlands and France showed a comparatively equal income distribution. In the group of industrial countries, the United States has the most unequal distribution as far as disposable household income is concerned, but countries such as Canada, the United Kingdom, Greece, Ireland, Italy, Portugal and Spain are also characterised by relatively sharp inequality. Germany lies in the middle, near the OECD average. Comparing 1985 with 2005, distribution became less equal in many countries, especially the economically dominating ones, but a number of countries reduced inequalities with regard to disposable household income; the latter included Belgium, France, Greece, Ireland and Spain (the latter three countries have traditionally been characterised by very high inequalities with regard to personal income distribution).[11]

A simple comparison of distribution with GDP growth rates shows that the countries which have the most egalitarian income distribution have not done badly economically; quite the reverse, they register comparatively high growth rates and low unemployment figures. This applies particularly to the Scandinavian countries. A policy of increasing income inequality cannot, therefore, be justified on the grounds of possible higher growth and employment. Between 2000 and 2008, however, countries with sharp income inequality also grew strongly: for example, the United Kingdom, Spain and the United States. In these three countries, however, growth was driven by strong credit expansion, particularly in the housing sector, which proved unsustainable with the outbreak of the subprime crisis.

THE SITUATION IN THE UNITED STATES, GERMANY AND CHINA

No fundamental legal changes were needed to deregulate the *US labour markets* as they were never regulated as tightly as, for example, in continental Europe. In the United States, protection for workers in the 1950s and 1960s came from relatively strong unions which established benchmarks for wage developments in key industries which in turn spread to the whole economy, and in addition an active policy to adjust a minimum wage policy. The 1980s brought big changes. The poorest 10 per cent of employees had to accept harsh real wage reductions in the early 1980s. Only the boom in the 1990s allowed them to regain their former real hourly wages by the early 2000s. but in that decade wages stagnated at the level of the late 1970s. Fifty per cent of all employees had to accept stagnating real wages from the late 1970s until the mid-1990s. Then, real hourly wages of this group increased by around 10 per cent and stagnated again until today. The top 1 per cent of national income receivers took about 10 per cent of the national income between the late 1930s and the late 1970s. Their share increased to around 18 per cent by 2005 without allowing for capital gains, and to 23 per cent including capital gains.[12]

One of the key factors that explains increasing wage inequality in the United States is the weakening of unions. Union membership decreased from 22.3 per cent of the workforce in 1980 to 11.6 per cent in 2007, and the fall in the private sector was much bigger.[13] As an important element of the conservative revolution, President Ronald Reagan followed a fundamental ideological policy against unions. The Professional Air Traffic Controllers Organisation went on strike in August 1981 for better working conditions and higher wages. After an ultimatum, all the striking air traffic controllers lost their jobs, trade union leaders ended up in jail and the trade union was decertified. Disputes with similar outcomes in other industries characterised the 1980s in the United States. At the same time the so-called Treaty of Detroit broke down. The 'Treaty' dated back to negotiations between the United Auto Workers and the big-three car producers in the United States shortly after the Second World War. It conferred stable medium-term wage increases, extensive health, unemployment and pension benefits, and expanded vacation time. This arrangement served as a model for other industries. Wage and other negotiations in the car industry served as benchmarks for almost all other industries and guaranteed a relatively equal wage development in all regions and professions in the United States.[14]

After the conservative revolution, minimum wage policies ceased to be used to prevent an expansion of the low-wage sector. Expressed in 2006 US dollars, statutory federal minimum wages decreased from around US$7.50 in 1979 to slightly above US$5 in 2006. The absolute level of federal minimum wages in the 1990s and 2000s in real terms fell to at most about two-thirds of the level in the 1960s. In 2007, however, federal minimum wages were lifted to US$7.25.[15]

No wonder Alan Blinder and Janet Yellen in the United States speak of traumatised workers who see their jobs as constantly under threat and their life situations as unstable.[16] Living standards in many cases could only be maintained by increases in households' indebtedness.

Turning to Germany, we have to distinguish between the old model of wage setting which was established after the Second World War and was in place until the early 1990s and the new model which developed afterwards. In the old model wage negotiations took into account the macroeconomic effects of wage development and were highly coordinated. Traditionally, the annual wage round started in Baden-Würtemberg in the metal industry, of which it is a stronghold. As early as the 1950s, productivity-oriented wage increases had become a guideline for stable macroeconomic wage development. The need to maintain the international competitiveness of German companies played a role in the negotiations as well. The outcomes of the negotiations in Baden-Würtemberg were adopted more or less automatically by the entire German metal industry and by all other industries with only minor modifications. As in the Scandinavian countries, Germany had no statutory minimum wage but the wage bargaining mechanism prevented the development of a low-wage sector.

It was only in the course of the 1990s that the traditional system of wage bargaining eroded and a dual wage bargaining system in Germany developed. One of the key elements of the new system is that the benchmarking effect from the metal industry to all industries in all regions broke down. The erosion of the old system came in two waves. The first related to reunification in 1990, when it was found that the West German wage-setting mechanisms could not be established in East Germany. After reunification, even negotiated wage rises in some industries, especially service industries, became very low in both the West and the East. Second, labour market reforms under the Social Democrat–Green government in Germany under Gerhard Schröder failed to fill the institutional gap by introducing statutory minimum wages or policies to strengthen unions and the wage bargaining process; labour markets were reformed in a market-liberal way. Among other things, in the early 2000s entitlements to unemployment benefits were cut; long-term unemployment benefits and social assistance were amalgamated into a single flat rate, while benefits became means-tested; requirements for the unemployed to accept job offers were tightened.[17]

In the metal industry, the chemical industry and the public sector, the old wage-bargaining system still exists. However, companies have been granted more flexibility to alter agreements reached in industry-wide negotiations. In addition, independent unions of small groups and professions like airline pilots, hospital doctors or engine drivers have gained strength and have been able to achieve above-average wage increases. Wage increases in the modified traditional wage sector have remained low but positive. But, as mentioned, the benchmarking effect to all sectors has broken down.

In 1998, 76 per cent of all employees in West Germany were covered by collective agreements; by 2007 this percentage had declined to 63 per cent.[18] As statutory minimum wages do not exist, wages started to fall to the very low social assistance level. Between 1995 and 2006 the real hourly wages of the lowest paid quarter of workers decreased by 13.7 per cent, the next quarter had to accept a cut in real wages of 3.2 per cent. Overall, the real hourly wages of all workers increased by 0.2 per cent.[19] There should be no surprise that consumption demand stagnated in Germany.

Low German wage increases have been a disaster for the EMU as they gave Germany a huge competitive advantage over other countries in the monetary union. The latter had realised wage increases which were much more in line with macroeconomic needs than the German wage development, but faced great stress from Germany's competition and its wage cost advantage.

In the Chinese labour market, it was only after the reforms started in the late 1970s that market mechanisms came into effect.[20] Since then a largely deregulated and opaque labour market has been developing. Trade unions do exist, but they are largely controlled by the Chinese Communist Party and are not allowed to negotiate wages. The Chinese economy is divided into a formal and an informal sector. In the former, there are state employees, employees of state-owned enterprises, enterprises with (partly) foreign ownership and large and medium-sized private enterprises. The latter comprises mostly small private companies which usually do not have unions or even written individual working contracts. This sector has a labour market of a 'Manchester' type, with very bad working conditions and often very low wages. In the formal sector too, enterprises pay very low wages for unskilled work and do not always provide written working contracts. Migrant workers from rural areas can be found in both sectors of the labour market. Statutory minimum wages exist, but are very low. Their development gives a certain benchmark for wages in the lower-wage segments, including the informal sector, but is not a sufficient instrument to coordinate wage developments in the whole economy. As collecting bargaining seldom exists even on a firm level, individual working contracts dominate the scene. This creates high transaction costs. For example, skilled workers will leave their employers as soon as competing companies pay higher wages. Thus, rather than retaining and developing qualified personnel, firms have to keep looking over their shoulders at changes in an unpredictable labour market and not to lose qualified personnel. Recently the Chinese government has given unions a new role: to control labour laws in companies and to experiment with wage bargaining at the firm level. But as long as unions are not politically independent they will not be seriously regarded by workers as legitimate representation of their interest. The frequent and increasing outbreaks of industrial unrest are in almost all cases not organised by official unions.

Labour market institutions in China are problematic for several reasons. First, wage development has no stable anchor and is very much driven by microeconomic logic. Where there is a shortage of skilled labour, wages quickly increase and lead to inflation, whereas in a recession wages quickly fall and lead to deflation. In the early 1990s, for example, China experienced over 20 per cent inflation; then, after the slowdown of GDP growth after the Asian crisis in 1997, it suffered several years of deflation. Second, the absence of real unions has led to a dangerously high level of wage dispersion which, together with a lack of a comprehensive social security system, is one of the key factors for the relatively low increase of domestic consumption demand; this in turn has forced the Chinese to attempt to keep GDP growth high by pushing for high current account surpluses. Third, as employers' associations are weak or non-existent, and there is no institution which could express the common interests of the company sector, there is – much as in the United States – no incentive for vocational training or other measures to improve qualifications at the firm level.

5

THE NEXT STAGE OF THE CRISIS

FROM PRIVATE DEBT TO SOVEREIGN DEBT

As this book goes to press, the overall economic situation worldwide has significantly improved compared with the depths of the financial and economic crisis. In the months after the Lehman Brothers' insolvency, when inter-bank money markets had frozen shut and the volume of global trade was in free fall, a number of observers warned that the US subprime crisis might turn into something similar to the Great Depression of the late 1920s and early 1930s. In early 2010, when leading indicators globally had turned, employment in the United States was growing again, and China and other Asian countries were actually debating new fears of overheating, the panic of the winter of 2008–09 seemed like a nightmare slowly fading from memory. While there was still some dispute about how quickly the world economy and especially the economies of the OECD countries would recover, there was for a while very little fear of a prolonged period of stagnation or a double-dip and a return into recession.

Yet, in May 2010, there was a stark reminder that everything was not necessarily well in the world economy. In July that year, testifying before the Senate, Federal Reserve Chairman Ben Bernanke warned of an 'unusually uncertain' outlook for the US economy.[1] By the end of the year there were fears in a number of countries of very low growth rates in 2011. It all started with the Greek government admitting that it had cheated with its latest budget data. According to the updated figures, the Greek public sector debt was higher than previously thought. While the correction was far from dramatic, it was enough to attract investors' attention to the Greek budget situation. With a budget deficit of more than 13 per cent of GDP in 2009, a public debt-to-GDP-ratio of about 120 per cent and the economy significantly contracting, investors panicked and started to sell Greek government bonds. Yields on Greek bonds on the secondary market skyrocketed and the government in Athens became increasingly anxious about how long it would be able to continue borrowing and paying its bills. With the still fresh memory of the Lehman Brothers' bankruptcy shocking world financial markets into a state of panic, policy-makers in the other European capitals were reluctant to just leave Greece to default. In particular, the fact that German and French banks with their already diminished equity capital had large exposures to the Greek government as well as to Greek corporations led to hectic attempts to construct a rescue package for the country.

The situation was complicated by both the legal provisions of the EU treaty and the diverging interests in the EU member states. As the EU treaty contains a no-bail-out clause stating that 'a Member State shall not be liable for or assume the commitments of central governments, regional, local or other public authorities, other bodies governed by public law, or public undertakings of another Member State' (article 125 of the Lisbon Treaty on the Function of the European Union), a number of politicians and economists rejected the idea of a rescue package by the EU or EU member states. They argued that the right institution to turn to would be the IMF, which, however, could not provide the huge amount Greece would need to repay government bonds that would become due over the coming months. In some countries, notably Germany, there was strong public resistance to rescue packages for Greece or other southern European countries. The feeling here was that Greece should do its own homework and that German taxpayers' money should not be used to bail out the profligate southern partners. Discussions in Europe about how to help Greece therefore dragged on for weeks.

This delay proved to be toxic for financial markets. While the European Union was finalising the Greece rescue package and collecting the necessary votes from national parliaments, the market for government bonds of other EU countries started to dry up. As Bundesbank President Axel Weber later explained in a parliamentary hearing, at one point only German government bonds could find a liquid market, while investors shunned even bonds from core European countries such as France.

At the same time, the possibility was on the table that not only the Greek government but also other EU countries such as Spain, Portugal, Ireland or even Italy might default on their debt. While some economists had claimed that the global banking system as well as the world economy could easily withstand a bankruptcy of small Greece, it certainly would not be able to sustain the much larger blow from the simultaneous default of a number of OECD countries.

Within a very short time, the European Union leaders stitched together a much bigger rescue package from which all Eurozone countries could draw in times of crisis. Using IMF money as well as a newly created special investment vehicle to be founded in Luxemburg, the rescue package had a volume of €750 billion, enough to impress the financial markets and calm them down.

Yet the Greek incident did not remain an isolated event. The crisis made it clear that government finances in the Western world have deteriorated sharply over the past couple of years. In the United Kingdom after the May 2010 general elections, the need for severe budget cuts was underlined by politicians referring to the fate of the Greek government. In the United States too, the events on the other side of the Atlantic focused attention on the fact that the government debt burden had grown sharply since the onset of the crisis.

The questions is, how had we come that far? How could we suddenly find ourselves at a point where the government of the world's ninth largest economy, Spain, which for years had been praised for its sound public finances, had come close to government default? In order to understand the sad state of the Western countries' government finances, we need to go back and look at the way the world economy was pulled back from the brink in early 2009.

HOW WE MOVED AWAY FROM THE ABYSS

When the initial crisis signals hit in autumn 2008, it seemed at first that no adequate economic policy reaction to the collapse in economic output would materialise. Economic theory was very clear on what to do in such a situation. With private investment contracting at a record speed, people becoming unemployed by the millions and global trade almost coming to a standstill, even economists who usually follow the neoclassical paradigm were willing to turn to Keynesian solutions. While Keynes had always insisted that his 'General Theory' was not just a theory for special occasions, many economists had held that Keynes had written a 'crisis theory'. If ever, this was the crisis in which to enact deficit-financed tax cuts, spending programmes and to slash interest rates.

With a very active public debate and a long tradition of using fiscal stimulus, the United States acted quite quickly. As the US economy had already entered recession in late 2007, US policy-makers got their first economic stimulus package off the ground as early as the end of 2007. When the situation deteriorated further in 2008, US politicians were busy discussing more stimulus measures during the election campaign.

However, given the momentum of the downturn, US policies would probably not have been enough to stabilise the world economy. Unfortunately, the second other big economic player of the Western world, Europe, was at first deeply divided on the subject of joint action for most of 2008. At that time it was Germany above all which, thanks to its low public deficits, moderate public debt levels and high current account surplus, had some scope for economic stimulus packages. Yet it was the Germans who dug their heels in when the European partners presented proposals for economic stabilisation. For example, in late summer 2008 the then finance minister Peer Steinbrück expressed the view that the crisis was a US problem and therefore Germany did not need a stimulus package. Requests from French President Nicolas Sarkozy and British Prime Minister Gordon Brown for European spending programmes or tax reductions were rejected at that time not only by Steinbrück, but also by Chancellor Angela Merkel. In response, Sarkozy and Brown pointedly met in London without Merkel in order to discuss further action with regard to the crisis. Only a few days after US investment bank Lehman Brothers went bust in September 2008, Steinbrück declared, in the budget debate in the Bundestag, that Germany was not at risk of recession and the German economy would grow by more than 1 per cent in the following year.

As we now know, this assessment was wrong (and would have been wrong even if Lehman Brothers had not gone bankrupt). German GDP had begun to decline, measured in quarter-on-quarter terms, as early as spring 2008; according to the standard definition, the economy had already been in recession for six months when Steinbrück made his speech. The background to the German position, which almost wrecked a European response, comprised, on the one hand, an intellectual aversion on the part of many German politicians and economists to Keynesian economic policy and, on the other hand, Steinbrück's personal goal of achieving a balanced budget (a goal which was completely shattered by the crisis). Obviously it was hoped that Germany could overcome the crisis by stimulating exports and taking a free-rider position.

Given the, at first, far from constructive position of the German government, there was general surprise when, only a few weeks later, it did an about-turn and cobbled together its own, larger, economic stimulus package in the first days of January 2009. Those involved in the negotiations report that, with the worsening of the situation after the bankruptcy of Lehman Brothers, representatives of both large industrial companies and trade unions decided to seek talks with the governing parties and to alert them to the seriousness of the collapse in orders and production. Both the Social Democrats and the Christian Democrats (CDU/CSU) partners of Chancellor Angela Merkel in the then 'grand coalition' decided to boost the economy with fiscal policy measures.

With the German package passed, all the major industrialised countries adopted enormous stimulus packages of their own by spring 2009. According to OECD estimates, on average these packages totalled more than 3 per cent of GDP (OECD 2009). Although the individual packages differed in details, there were a number of similarities: practically all the packages contained elements for expanding infrastructure, though these did not take sufficient account of urgent ecological needs. Many countries subsidised the scrappage of old cars and the purchase of new ones, and there were also widespread tax cuts. Although in some countries some of the measures had already taken effect in 2008, the bulk of the programmes came into force in 2009. Only in a few exceptional cases, such as Germany, were the main effects of the stimulus schemes discernible only in 2010. It is also important to mention that in some smaller crisis countries, such as Hungary, Iceland and Ireland, governments found themselves compelled to raise taxes or cut spending, which no doubt worsened the problems there.

The large emerging economies also joined the rush for stabilisation policies in an unprecedented way. As countries such as China, India and Brazil had entered the crisis with robust fiscal balances and current account positions, they were able to use expansionary fiscal and monetary policies to counteract the downturn. Even countries with a less stable economic situation, like for example Vietnam, engaged in large stimulus packages. China announced a stimulus package amounting to a staggering US$585 billion in late 2008. This was close to the amount committed by the US government up to this point, yet it came from an economy only about a third of the size of the US economy. Of course, the money allocated was not all new spending. Some money was just moved from other budget lines. However, even after taking these facts into account, the stimulus package still remained quite large both in relation to the Chinese economy and in absolute terms compared with that of other countries. Brazil and India also increased spending to counteract the downturn.

All in all, the fiscal policy reaction of the major industrialised countries, most EU member states and also the largest emerging markets was pretty much what was required in a crisis – even if the details of the packages, such as the relative weight of spending increases and tax reductions, can be argued about. In particular because of the lack of formal institutions for the effective coordination of economic policy in the Eurozone as well as at the G20 level, this was a positive surprise.

The governments of Europe and of other OECD countries also merit praise with regard to labour market policies. In contrast with other crises in recent decades, such as the long period of low growth in Germany from 2001, these governments have refrained from any measures which might weaken the wage anchor. On the contrary: in the crisis, many governments even extended social protection beyond unemployment insurance.[2] In Finland and France, for example, the period during which an employee must have worked before becoming entitled to support was shortened. In the United States, the period of entitlement for unemployment benefits was extended.

In a number of countries – including Germany – financial incentives were also offered to enterprises to retain staff despite shrinking order books. For example, in Austria, the Czech Republic, Germany and Italy the rules on short-time working were liberalised for a period. Some smaller countries even introduced such rules for the first time.

As a result of all this, in a number of countries – including France, Italy and Germany – unemployment increased much more slowly than might have been expected, judging by the experience of previous crises. Furthermore, demand was propped up through unemployment benefits. Overall, in this way the pressure on trade unions to consent to nominal wage cuts was alleviated. However, these policies could not prevent unemployment rates jumping to record levels in some countries, for example in the United States or in Sweden.

The central banks also deserve some praise for their response. Although the European Central Bank can be reproached for raising interest rates as late as July 2008, thereby intensifying the downturn once more (Dullien 2008), it subsequently took the right approach:

not only did it significantly lower interest rates by mid-2009, but it also introduced new instruments and credit lines for banks, which provided them with liquidity. The actions of the US Federal Reserve, which at times even bought commercial paper directly from enterprises, circumventing the banking sector, must be regarded as a positive step towards stabilising the economic situation. Central banks in emerging markets also slashed interest rates sharply, helping to provide a large global stimulus.

In addition to the fiscal and monetary stimulus, governments across the world saw themselves forced to help the banking sector through the crisis. In developed countries such as Germany, France, Switzerland and the United Kingdom, large financial institutions found themselves heavily exposed to the US subprime market. Some of the banks had directly invested in collateralised debt obligations (CDOs) backed by US mortgages. Others had even formed their own special investment vehicles to take part in the 'originate and distribute' business, buying mortgages from US banks and mortgage associations and trying to divide them into CDOs and sell them to other investors. When the crisis hit and these assets became illiquid or even worthless almost overnight, governments were forced either to buy problematic assets from banks in their countries, to provide guarantees, or to give loans or even inject capital into the ailing banking sector. Of course, the measures taken differed in detail. In countries such as the United States and Germany, governments were initially very reluctant for ideological reasons to inject equity capital into banks or nationalise banks, as they saw this as an abandonment of free-market principles. In the end, however, most governments introduced these heavy-handed options for at least some selected banks.

In the emerging markets, banks were not exposed directly to US subprime mortgages to the same extent as banks from rich countries, as financial institutions had seldom entered upon a foreign investment spree. However, the problems in the banking sectors of the OECD countries also had impacts on developing countries and emerging markets. With large financial institutions suddenly experiencing heavy losses, they cut back their exposure to investments perceived as risky. Capital was pulled out of countries such as Brazil and Korea and the exchange rates depreciated strongly. Hence, banks in developing countries and emerging markets suddenly saw themselves cut off from credit lines from the rich world. While, thanks to strong fundamental conditions in many emerging markets, the exchange rate volatility did not create an outright crisis in most cases, the governments there nevertheless felt compelled to act, and extended loans from the government or the central bank to domestic financial institutions to keep credit flows going. The lesser the degree of integration of national financial systems into the world financial system was, the better a country's situation was at that particular moment. Due to capital controls and regulations, the financial systems in India and China were not substantially destabilised by the meltdown of the financial system in the developed world and were able to continue to finance real economic activities. In addition, in countries like China, India and Vietnam the banking system is largely state-owned and could be used by governments as a second channel to stabilise demand.

WHO RESCUES THE RESCUERS?

All these measures were the right things to do at the time. Even if not all politicians have understood all of the underlying logic, these policy steps corrected at least temporarily the problems created by the US subprime mortgage crisis and its spread across the world.

Injecting capital into banks or buying 'toxic assets' from the banking sector meant taking over liabilities from the private sector and thus helped to solve the problem of overly indebted households and firms in countries such as the United States, the United Kingdom and Spain. The private sector's liabilities towards the banking sector were written down in the process of credit defaults and foreclosures. In order to save the banking sector, the government then increased its own debt and used the proceeds to fill the gap in the banks' balance sheets. De facto, this process led to a shift of the debt burden from the private sector to the public sector in a number of countries, and to an international shift of the debt burden from the private sector in countries which had previously experienced a mortgage boom, such as the United States, to the public sector in countries such as Germany or the Netherlands which had previously lent their money abroad.

Governments also helped to solve the problem of inadequate demand which was created when the private sector suddenly could not count on further credit expansion to keep increasing its demand. Just when private households in the United States, the United Kingdom and Spain cut back on consumption and housing construction – and in particular when US households stopped behaving as the 'consumer of last resort' for the world economy – governments jumped in with public infrastructure projects and subsidies for new cars, and so prevented the economy from moving into a downward spiral where new job losses cause new spending cuts which then lead to more job losses.

All of these measures together have thus without any doubt helped the world economy to pull back from the brink. However, they all had one drawback: governments needed to borrow money first in order to then spend it on stimulus packages or hand it over to the banks in order to stabilise the financial system. In addition, the violent drop in economic activity across the world also hit government revenue hard, leading to additional holes in government budgets. While the costs of a world economy falling into a depression comparable with the one in the 1930s would have been catastrophically large, the cost of averting this also proved to be high: in 2009, budget deficits in the industrialised world had thus reached heights unknown for decades. Spain was borrowing 11.2 per cent of its GDP, UK government revenue fell short of expenditure by 11.3 per cent of GDP, and the US government had to plug a budget hole of 11 per cent of GDP. In all major OECD countries, public debt levels rose significantly from the onset of the crisis in 2008 through to 2010 and are set to continue increasing as the budget deficits cannot be corrected overnight. For the OECD as a whole, the debt-to-GDP ratio is set to increase from 73 per cent prior to the crisis (2007) to roughly 100 per cent at the end of 2011. In absolute terms, this means an increase of government debt in this rich-country group of about $10 trillion, or about 80 per cent of the annual output of the United States, in a matter of not even half a decade.

THE DANGER OF A LONG PERIOD OF LOW GROWTH

It is far from clear how the issues of large deficits and large government debts are to be resolved. While government actions have clearly stabilised the world economy in the short run, they have not solved the basic structural problems of the world economy. As has been described in the earlier chapters, the debt trend which led to the crisis has to be seen as part of a broader scheme of deregulation of financial markets as well as a fundamental change of income distribution between capital and labour and within the working class.

Governments have assumed the role of economic actors, increasing their own debt as a way to keep the economy growing. For a long time, investors did not mind much. Indeed, demand for government bonds as a safe investment remained very high into 2010, which can be seen at the low level of return on a 10-year US or German

government bond. However, at some point, financial market participants became nervous at least about some countries such as Greece,
Spain, Ireland and Portugal. While countries with a national central
bank and government debt in their own currency such as the United
Kingdom or the United States have been spared from market panic
so far, the Greek crisis has increased politicians' awareness of the
problem of high public debt. While of course a government has more
options to increase its revenue than private households – namely by
increasing taxes – there is also a limit to how much debt a government can shoulder. At some point, interest payments will make up
an unacceptably large part of tax revenue, especially if interest rates
increase again. Thus, governments cannot go on forever borrowing
at the same level as in 2009.

Pulling back from the recent expansionary fiscal policy, on the
other hand, might not turn out to be easy either. The economy
will only continue its recovery in the wake of rapid government
retrenchment if the private sector increases its demand again. The
problem is that income trends in the private sector at the moment
do not provide the fundamentals for a rapid recovery of consumer
spending: in a number of large economies, unemployment has risen
sharply and now exerts a downward pressure on wages. Even in
countries where unemployment remained relatively stable such
as Germany, the heavy drop in corporate profitability during the
crisis will prevent meaningful wage growth. Only in some emerging
markets, including China and Brazil, does the situation seem to be
different: Here, private demand growth has actually accelerated.
However, even though China's and Brazil's importance for the world
economy has grown over the years, their consumer spending still
is not sufficient to pull the world economy out of the doldrums.[3]
Also, developments in some of the high-growth countries hide some
ominous trends. China and other developing countries suffer from
dangerous real-estate bubbles and may also need to be forced to
refrain from aggressive mercantilist policies.

It is very likely that during the next decade or so households and
corporations will refrain from expanding their spending. Private
households' debts as well as corporations' debts in almost all OECD
countries are at record levels. In such a situation, creditors and
debtors are reluctant to borrow. Real-estate prices in countries like
the United States are likely to fall still further; overcapacities in the
real-estate sector in many OECD countries are very likely to depress
the construction sector for a long time. The stock-market boom that
started in 2010 seems to have feet of clay. Moreover, international

imbalances and indebtedness have not been structurally corrected. Sudden exchange rate adjustments with ensuing destabilising effects cannot be ruled out. It is a realistic scenario that growth in most OECD countries will be low and unstable, which also means that there will not be much relief in labour markets. A widespread Japanese-style stagnation scenario, which has been predominant since the real-estate and stock-market bubble in Japan in the 1980s, is far from being unrealistic.[4] In almost all OECD countries the next cyclical downturn, including a new major financial crisis, may easily lead to a systemically critical economic situation. Labour markets are deregulated, and both trade unions and social democratic parties are rather weak in most OECD countries. In a situation of high unemployment and falling wages, a serious deflationary development cannot be excluded. In this sense one cannot at the point of writing (winter 2010) rule out the scenario of a depression comparable with the one in the 1930s.

Given these dangers, it is high time for a fundamental turn-around of the world economy. The following chapters will outline what a world economy which prevents the errors of the past decades could look like.

PART II
THE PATH TO DECENT CAPITALISM

6

MAIN FEATURES OF A NEW ECONOMIC MODEL

A sustainable economic model, a decent capitalism, should include three interrelated dimensions. First, the model should be ecologically sustainable: preventing global warming, changing to a renewable energy basis and preventing other problematic developments such as a reduction in biodiversity. Second, it should be formed in such a way that the targeted growth process is not jeopardised by either asset-market inflation or ensuing deflation (so-called boom-and-bust cycles), and does not result in the excessive indebtedness of individual sectors or even whole economies, thereby leading inevitably to the next crisis. At the same time, such a model should promote innovation and, therefore, technological development necessary both for solving ecological problems and, in the medium and long term, increasing labour productivity and so holding out the possibility of growing prosperity for all. Third, in our view, it is critical that all population groups have a share in social progress. Inequality of income and wealth distribution must be at politically and socially acceptable limits. Everybody should have a decent living.

In the following sections we present some basic reflections on the formation of a decent economic model.

FOCUS ON DEMAND AND GREEN GROWTH

Let us first take a look at the drivers of growth. A society's volume of production is ultimately determined by its level of demand; the latter is made up of investment demand, consumption demand, government demand and exports minus imports. If demand and production volume increase more slowly than productivity, the employment of labour falls. If working time and labour participation remain unchanged in such circumstances, unemployment rises. If development is to be lasting, the volume of demand must grow at a stable and adequate rate. That requires a certain proportion between the different components of demand. For example, it makes no sense to build up economic capacities through high investment if consumption and the other components of demand are too weak to make full use of these capacities. As consumption demand is the biggest demand element (usually between 60 and 70 per cent of GDP) it is important to have a regular expansion of consumption demand based on the incomes of households.

Of paramount importance is, of course, investment demand, which comes from private sources and also from 'public households' (that is, the institutions of central and local government, and indeed of government at all levels). Investment does not only create demand; investment goods embody new technology and are vital for economically sustainable growth in the future.

In order to allow sufficient demand growth on the part of private households, it must first and foremost be ensured that the wage bill – at least over the economic cycle – increases at the same rate as GDP. It is true that, ultimately, profit income also flows to private households. For most households, however, wage income represents the bulk of their earnings and so defines their consumption possibilities. Furthermore, experience shows that the consumption rate is much lower in the case of profit income than in that of wage income. An increase in profits and thereby of household incomes with a high savings rate, without a corresponding increase in incomes in general, therefore does not suffice as a driver of demand. In such a scenario, households dependent on wage income could increase their consumption sufficiently only by increasing their debt. Primarily credit-driven consumption demand is not sustainable and extremely dangerous, as the subprime crisis has clearly demonstrated.

Government demand is also important. Governments deliver many important public goods like education or health care and in this way structure consumption in a society in a positive way. Governments are also of key importance in delivering infrastructure, as well as for ecologically sustainable growth. Many of the most successful countries in the world have a high proportion of public expenditures to GDP, as for example in the Scandinavian countries. If governments have to deliver important public goods and also want to modify unacceptable market-given income distribution, public households cannot be made 'lean and mean'.

A country can stimulate its demand by focusing on exports and pushing for trade and current account surpluses. Such export-driven growth is, however, naturally a zero-sum game, as the export surpluses of one country lead to import surpluses in others. Excessive and enduring export-driven growth strategies of single countries are therefore generally harmful for the rest of the world and would have to be limited by global regulations.

We see a fundamental conflict between the present method of production and consumption on the one hand, and ecological needs on the other. If we do not quickly begin to tackle ecological problems, the survival of large parts of the world population will be endangered, creating extreme conflicts about areas in the world in which to live and work, about water and food, and last but not least about natural resources like oil. What we see today is an enormous and lethal failure of the market mechanism to combine economic growth and ecological needs. This does not only involve present methods of production and consumption; it also involves the type of technological development which has been taking place over the last two centuries. That development is not the fault of individual firms and consumers. It is the failure of the price system which for centuries sent out wrong signals about technological development, production and consumption. In spite of this fact, we do not see a fundamental conflict between growth as such and ecological needs like the prevention of global warming or finding methods of production and consumption without depleting non-renewable resources. With radical changes in the structure of production and consumption and technological developments, which will of course deeply affect our way of living, green growth without negative ecological effects is possible. We do not assume that growth is needed forever. Whether growing prosperity based on technological development takes the form of higher consumption or more leisure time is a question that a society must ask itself once a certain stage of development and level of living standards have been reached.

The market-liberal globalisation project has been combined with the unsustainable accumulation of debt in many sectors. For example, even if the private household sector as a whole has a creditor position, it is detrimental to the stability of an economy if a substantial proportion of private households have extremely high debts. Governments too have become highly indebted (measured in per cent of GDP), as have whole states. It also makes a difference which sector is in question. The enterprise sector, for example, can be indebted to a much greater extent than private households, because the latter cannot engage in production and value creation on the market. However, enterprises and financial institutions in the market-liberal era have also neglected to increase their equity sufficiently.

The fact is that growth in demand cannot be generated on a lasting basis if one individual economic sector builds up excessive debts, while other sectors accumulate surpluses. The same applies, in global terms, to individual economies. It is not necessary for the balance sheets of individual economic actors, sectors and economies to be identical. In fact, that would be extremely harmful. But indebtedness (always measured as a percentage of GDP) should keep within certain limits to avoid the over-indebtedness of sectors or of entities within sectors.[1]

Consumption demand and investment demand under a *laissez-faire* regime do not automatically develop in ways that allow stable and sustainable development. John Maynard Keynes made this clear many years ago: 'This disturbing conclusion depends, of course, on the assumption that the propensity to consume and the rate of investment are not deliberately controlled in the social interest but are mainly left to the influences of *laissez-faire*' (Keynes 1936: 219). What is needed is a coordinated grip on consumption and investment demand in the interest of the economy and society as a whole. Achieving steady and satisfactory demand growth without dangerous tendencies towards indebtedness requires the imposition of a certain framework and economic intervention by the state. The institutional framework must be worked out in a way that leads to a relative equality of income, and that reverses the redistribution that has worked to the heavy detriment of lower-income groups. At the same time investment has to be stabilised by government interventions. A public enterprise sector can play an important role here, as well as infrastructure investment and cooperation between the private and the public sector.

To change production and consumption in an ecologically sustainable way will require a major change in the way energy is produced, mobility is organised, and houses are built. Such a fundamental change will inevitably have to be combined with a massive wave of new investment. The next decades, if fundamental ecological change happens, will lead to new private and public investment and GDP growth, as we will show in Chapter 10.

A FINANCIAL SYSTEM FOR GROWTH AND INNOVATION

Financial systems represent something like the brain of the economic system. They are of crucial importance for dynamic development, although they can also drive economies to ruin. In fact, a well-functioning financial system has at least four tasks in a modern economy which are indispensable for sustainable growth.[2]

First, by means of creating credit it enables enterprises – and, in particular, innovative enterprises – both to invest and to produce. The credit system can create money and credit, so to speak, *ex nihilo*, without the need for previous savings. These funds can be made available to entrepreneurs, who can use them to purchase materials or machines for production. The circuit closes when the investments of an individual enterprise increase the capital stock and so the production potential of the economy, as well as incomes and savings, thereby ensuring, almost retrospectively, the financing of investment. Since this process often goes hand in hand with innovation, the financial system supports the development of productivity in an economy at a crucial point.

The second central task of the financial system is the redistribution of risk. Although this function has fallen into disrepute somewhat in the wake of the subprime crisis, the redistribution of risk between different economic entities remains an important function of the financial system. Investments in individual projects often bear an enormous risk, up to the point of total failure. Individuals would therefore be reluctant to bear such risks alone, or would do so only with the promise of substantial returns. However, since the financial system makes it possible to spread the risk among many investors, and moreover individuals are not compelled to commit their entire assets, the aggregate willingness to invest in such projects increases.

Banks' credit allocation is an important part of the liquidity and risk transformation of the financial system. The banking system amasses the short-term deposits of the general public while at the same time granting long-term loans to investing enterprises. Stock markets can take on this function, because shareholders buy a long-term investment in the form of a share which they can sell at any time on the secondary market. Non-bank financial institutions such as investment banks, which are usually more risk-prone, also finance risky activities and can (provided they are properly regulated) support growth. A society in which the financial sector provides more liquidity and risk transformation will have a higher capital stock, and thus higher labour productivity and also higher material prosperity, than a society which lacks such a financial sector.

The third task of the financial sector is to make capital and credit available to the sectors and enterprises which offer the most promising investment projects. By exploiting economies of scale in the procurement of information, the financial system tends to judge better than individual investors which projects are likely to bear fruit. The allocation mechanism for the distribution of financial resources to their most efficient application is compatible with low general returns. Thus the general rate of return could fall to almost zero, and income from technology for innovative companies could become the sole substantial source of higher returns.[3]

The fourth function of a financial system consists of accumulating the assets of small investors and using them to enable much bigger investments.

Against this background there can be no question of striving for an economic order that tries to manage without a financial system or without the indebtedness of individual sectors. The problem is that, over the past few decades, a financial system came into being which either does not carry out the above-mentioned functions or does so only in a form which leads to instability. In our view, there are five basic dimensions with regard to the necessary regulation and reform of the financial system. We present them at this point without going too much into details, as we will dig deeper into that sector in Chapter 9.

First, risk-taking non-bank financial institutions like investment funds and hedge funds should be separated from commercial banks. The latter should not be allowed to give loans to non-bank financial institutions and there should be no proprietary trading by commercial banks – an idea, which was put forward by former Fed Chairman Paul Volcker. Such a framework would still provide sufficient capital for riskier ventures.

Second, it is not acceptable to allow the development of a shadow banking system which, by exploiting regulatory loopholes and shifting activities to less regulated areas of the financial system or even to states with wholly unsatisfactory regulation, systematically withdraws transactions from the regulated financial system. All financial institutions have to be regulated. Financial institutions have operated not only with ever-greater leverage, but also in a riskier, more short-term, more speculative and more return-demanding manner, with yield expectations climbing to irrational heights. It is equally unacceptable that financial institutions have been able to constantly reduce their equity capital ratios, ending up with little in the way of an equity capital buffer when crisis hit.

The third dimension consists of the creation of anti-cyclical instruments for macroeconomic governance in general and of the financial system in particular. In financial markets in particular – even with the best regulation – excesses regularly arise which have the potential to destabilise the rest of the economy, unless the state intervenes. This tendency of financial markets has been intensified by misguided supervisory regulations (the so-called framework of Basel II) and accounting reforms. The rules of the game in the financial market, therefore, must be substantially rewritten in order to make the financial system once again capable of performing its important functions in the economy.

Within the framework of anti-cyclical policies, the central bank as well as the finance ministry attains a key position in the financial system. As soon as matters appear to be going off course, as in the case of a real-estate bubble, it must be possible to counter it by administrative means. Interest rate increases to stop bubbles are not sufficient, and are potentially harmful for the whole economy. Other policies should also be deployed more robustly in order to correct certain macroeconomic mistakes. For example, tax policy can combat excesses in real-estate and stock markets by taxing speculative profits.

Fourth, all financial products (especially all types of derivates) need to be approved by a supervisory agency before they are allowed onto the market. Trading has to take place in organised exchanges only. These rules would allow sufficient opportunities to hedge risks and do not increase costs for firms in any relevant way. Rating agencies also should be supervised by public authorities as well as institutions defining international accounting standards.

Fifth, international capital movements pose another problem. Individual central banks are barely able to influence them by means of interest rate policy, but they can lead to huge current account imbalances and destabilising exchange rate turbulence. Here, too, central banks are in need of additional instruments to enable them to intervene in international capital movements. On the whole, the developments of recent decades appear to us to be misguided, since the instruments at central banks' disposal dwindled progressively, until finally they were left with nothing more than interest rate policy. Central banks should once again be furnished with instruments with which they can actively combat domestic asset-market bubbles and unstable international capital flows. Such instruments should be part of the normal toolbox of central banks.

MORE EQUITABLE INCOME DISTRIBUTION

In recent decades, a marked inequality has increasingly arisen with regard to income distribution. This jeopardises the social and political cohesion of societies. Apart from that, income distribution which is too unbalanced is macroeconomically destabilising. If households consume primarily from their income, an increasing inequality in income distribution comes to have a detrimental effect on consumer demand, because those with high incomes have a higher savings rate. Germany and Japan are typical examples of substantial changes in distribution, with the growth in precarious living conditions further choking off consumer demand. In other countries – for example, the United States and the United Kingdom – household consumption has been maintained, despite increasing inequality of incomes, by the increasing indebtedness of private households. These countries experienced higher growth from the 1990s until the outbreak of the subprime crisis, but this was accompanied by the build-up of financial instability. Such a model cannot be sustained in the long term, since it leads to the excessive indebtedness of sections of the population.

A decent capitalist model must reverse the negative changes in income distribution and grant all population groups an adequate share in the wealth created in society. One secret of the success of regulated capitalism after the Second World War was the increasing mass purchasing power of workers, based on growing incomes and relatively equal income distribution. It is now becoming clear that the old model has to be regenerated.

Income distribution has three important components: functional distribution of income in wages and profits, distribution within the national wage sum and the national profit sum, and state redistribution policy. A fall in the wage share is the result of a higher profit mark-up. The latter was possible, according to our analysis, on the basis of deregulation, in particular due to the increasing power of the financial sector and its willingness to take risks in pursuit of higher returns. The shareholder-value approach and the increasing role of institutional investors drove enterprises to pursue higher profit mark-ups. Correspondingly, the structures and rules of the game in the financial sector must be changed in such a way that the profit mark-up falls again.

The profit mark-up also depends on the level of monopolisation and power structures in goods markets. The task of competition law is to prevent the monopolisation of individual markets, because growing market power tends to go hand in hand with increasing monopolistic or oligopolistic profits, which in turn lead to more marked income inequalities and so to problems with steady demand growth in the economy as a whole. On the one hand, market-liberal globalisation intensified competition on goods markets, and on the other hand, multinational companies are becoming bigger all the time, due to growth, mergers or takeovers, so that the level of competition is decreasing. In many cases, natural monopolies – such as energy and water supply or the railways – were privatised without creating sufficient competition, as a result of which high profits have been made in these sectors. We see no need for privatisation in these fields. If state organisations were to take over production and service provision in sectors characterised by a natural monopoly, this could also reduce the profit share.

Recent decades have been characterised by significant wage dispersion. In almost all countries in the world the low-wage sector, as well as that of precarious employment and informality, has increased, especially in the sector of goods and services that are not internationally tradable. Globalisation trends, therefore, cannot directly explain the emergence of these sectors. They are the result of labour market deregulation. These unjustified income inequalities among wage earners must be dismantled by means of labour market reforms. The collective bargaining system must be strengthened, backed up by other labour market institutions to achieve the decent work conditions stressed by the International Labour Organization. Minimum wages and social security guaranteed by the state also play a crucial role in this.

Even with strict regulation, markets do not lead to a politically acceptable income distribution. In addition to that, not everyone has equal chances in the market. The disadvantaged – whether on the basis of gender, childcare responsibilities, handicap, age, race and so on – can drop out of the market and be deprived of an income, or at best obtain only an inadequate one. Ultimately, by no means all incomes are obtained on the basis of personal achievements; consider, for example, large inheritances, which are an intrinsically alien element with regard to capitalism. Tax law and social systems must be deployed in order to organise income distribution in a socially acceptable manner. Tax law should therefore include a clear redistributive component, and this need becomes more pronounced the more evident it is that market outcomes alone will lead to growing inequality. Against this background, not only is a markedly progressive tax system important, but above all regulations which ensure that incomes from capital are adequately taxed. Tax evasion, for example, should be combated by the 'draining' of offshore centres and other measures. Public spending can also be used to reduce income inequalities, for example by providing public goods, such as education, health care and public transport. This also applies to state transfer payments and social security systems, which can contain markedly redistributive components.

ROBUST FINANCING OF STATE BUDGETS

We have already mentioned that economic sectors should not constantly register increasing debt ratios. This also applies to state budgets. A very high public debt stock, measured as a percentage of GDP, has a number of negative effects. First, a high level of public debt can lead to negative redistribution effects, for example if state interest income flows into higher income brackets and taxes are paid by medium or lower earners. Second, a period of high interest rates, coupled with a high public debt, can cause the budget deficit to escalate to such an extent that budgets face refinancing difficulties. Third, state budgets can also become excessively indebted and cut off from the credit market. This typically occurs when the debt is in foreign currency, and has afflicted numerous less developed countries that have experienced currency crises in recent decades. But it can also happen when the debt is in the domestic currency. An example is the debt crisis of Greece and other counties in the EMU. A very high level of public debt ultimately limits governments' room to manoeuvre. In turn, it can cause legitimate demands for currency reform or other ways of alleviating public debt which are hotly contested politically and can be destabilising.

We are not calling here for the fixing of a particular debt ratio for public budgets, and certainly not for the fixing of a ratio for new borrowings. During sharp economic crises, such ratios cannot be maintained in the short term. Moreover, they could be harmful in the current economic circumstances, for example if the fiscal policy required by the economic situation is hindered by regulations on indebtedness, of whatever kind. Our argument is that the public budget should be divided into a consumption budget and a capital budget, with the latter financing public investment. The consumption budget should be balanced in the medium term and ordinarily financed by taxes and contributions. For public investment, public debt is justified, especially if measurable returns in the form of revenues from investments can be expected. However, in the long term a stable percentage of public debt to GDP should be achieved. In the short term, an active fiscal policy with sharply fluctuating budget balances is compatible with these norms.

At this point, the distinction between a capital budget and

a current budget is helpful. The current budget includes state consumption expenditure and should be balanced in the medium term, while public investments are entered in the capital budget, which can be financed by long-term credit. In order to stabilise demand across the economy, first and foremost the capital budget should be deployed, bringing forward or putting off public investments in accordance with the economic situation. In the current budget however, the automatic stabilisers which result from changes in tax revenues and public spending due to the economic cycle should be accepted, as only a medium-term balancing of the current budget is needed.

LEVELS OF REGULATION

The fundamental problem of the globalisation model of the past few decades lies in the asymmetry between economic globalisation and the largely still national regulation. Existing structures for the regulation and governance of the world economy are too weak or have too little reach, although economic processes have long had a global dimension. This is not confined to the economy in the narrow sense, but also encompasses many other areas, such as environmental problems. The lack of global governance also manifests itself in the fact that the production of international public goods, such as the prevention of further global warming, coordination of global economic policies or the provision of a stable international reserve medium, is inadequate.[4] One function of global governance is to establish a more stable international exchange rate regime and a mechanism which prevents excessive current account imbalances. Without a certain degree of control of international capital flows, such a system is difficult to establish. Despite the claims of the protagonists of the Washington Consensus, it is clear that free capital flows are not in themselves a value. In many cases they increased volatility, created shocks and currency crises and were definitely not growth and efficiency promoting.[5]

Not everything can or should be regulated and governed at supranational level. A great deal can remain at the national level. Which measures should be regulated at which political level should be decided on a case-by-case basis. In summary, what is needed is to furnish economic policy institutions with macroeconomic governance mechanisms – either by introducing new ones or by restoring some which have been lost over the past few decades – in order to be better able to control and correct market developments which jeopardise the stability of the national and global economy or even the future of humanity.

MARKETS AS PART AND PARCEL OF FREEDOM

In order to avoid misunderstanding, our proposals do not provide carte blanche for regulation and state intervention of all kinds. Not all forms of intervention by the state are capable of or suited to promoting stable economic growth or the steady development of incomes and demand. A number of forms of intervention are even harmful over the medium and long term. Within a state-given framework that takes account of ecological needs, the liberalisation of markets for products and services is the driver of innovations which increase productivity and living standards. The enormous impetus given to innovation by telecommunications in recent decades would not have been possible in a more heavily regulated market with higher entry barriers.

The costs of state intervention must, therefore, always be weighed against their benefits. It must above all be ensured that intervention does not nullify elements of the market economy which ensure that product and process innovations occur of the kind which brings about higher productivity or simply higher living standards. As Joseph Schumpeter and Karl Marx showed, competition between enterprises and the possibility of achieving above-average returns by means of innovation are drivers of the development of the economy's productive forces. The possibility of achieving success in the market, as well as of failing in the market, is a central element in economic dynamics. This is the mechanism which underlies the market economy's superiority over attempts at central economic planning.

Furthermore, despite their many negative elements, markets must be regarded as an emancipatory achievement which increases the space for individuals to decide how they prefer to work and consume. For example, from research into happiness it is known that the self-employed tend to be more satisfied with their lives due to their largely self-determined daily work routine. As long as a move to self-employment is not the result of the economic pressure imposed by unemployment and does not lead to constantly deteriorating working conditions, the opportunity to start up a business must be considered a positive instance of freedom. Markets which are as open as possible without unnecessary red tape are important here because they tend to allow more people to choose how they want to live.

There is also no question of transplanting the economic system back to the regulatory situation characteristic of, for example, the 1960s or 1970s. Instead, the general principle underlying the new framework and state intervention must be to retain the emancipatory elements of liberalisation that have appeared over recent decades, while bringing the destabilising elements of deregulation back under control.

We – once again – agree with Keynes:

> For my part I believe that capitalism, wisely managed, can probably be made more efficient for attaining economic ends than any other alternative system yet in sight, but that in itself it is in many ways extremely objectable. Our problem is to work out an organisation which shall be as efficient as possible without offending our notions of a satisfactory way of life.[6]

Whether capitalism as we know it today will survive the next few centuries is highly improbable. In any case, the question has little relevance in view of current problems and the foreseeable future. The existing economic and societal formation provides the necessary and binding point of departure for reforms and modifications.

7

RESURRECTING THE PUBLIC SECTOR

In our economic world, the structure of government revenues and expenditures inevitably constitutes a decisive element. Governments have to become a lot stronger and more active again compared with what they used to be under the logic of market-liberal globalisation. The public sectors' activities are an area in which policy has one of the most pervasive and sustained influence on the economy. Beyond regulation, taxes and expenditures are also central to the distribution of income and wealth. Governments should deliver public goods by investing in education or in research and development. Furthermore, bans and rules, taxes and expenditures are important to radically change technologies and the way we produce and consume with regard to ecological needs. These elements are important within the framework of the economic model presented here in order to ensure that economic output is stable and ecologically and socially sustainable, and comes as close as possible to full capacity and high employment. Over the medium to long term, the most important task of expenditure and tax policy is, on the one hand, to provide the framework for continuing eco-friendly productivity growth by means of adequate investment in education and infrastructure, and on the other hand, to prevent the divergence of incomes between various groups by means of tax and spending policy.

We want to approach this issue in three broad steps: first we ask, what would be the strategic fields of activity for the public sector today. Then, in a second step we take a closer look at where the money for an increased role of the public sector should come from in a way that is economically effective and at the same time makes for fair taxation, which also steers technological, green development. Finally, we take up the role of public households as so-called 'automatic stabilisers' in times of crises, and consider also the other means available to governments to steer and influence our economies through sometimes only cyclical and sometimes very stormy times.

GOVERNMENTS' STRATEGIC SPENDING

In this first step towards explaining the role of the public sector in the economy, we consider what public spending is for, how funds are acquired and how large the public sector's participation in the economy should be. This question is independent of fiscal policy in the narrow sense: that is, from the question of how the government can influence economic fluctuations by varying its spending and revenues. But even with regard to fiscal policy, the structural effects and the repercussions for income distribution should be taken into account.

Leaving things to the market results in inadequate provision of public goods (or often none) and for this reason alone cannot be relied on as the sole mechanism for generating green development and social welfare. Public goods are goods which can be used by different persons or enterprises with no disadvantage to any of the users. Often, the consumption of a public good simply cannot be prevented. There is another theoretical concept which, for our purposes, focuses on market failure in relation to the production and use of goods. In the presence of so-called 'externalities', market prices fail to function as signals of shortages or surpluses. We want to pick out two examples which are crucial to the role of the public sector in our model: education and infrastructure.

Investment in education and infrastructure

Technological progress and productivity growth in a socio-ecological economy are the most important determinants of medium and long-term increases in living standards in an economy and should therefore be promoted and supported. Public spending on education, but also on infrastructure and research and development, as well as support for investment by enterprises in promising areas, are central to boosting productivity growth and, thereby, living standards. Education and research and development are public goods which are not adequately provided for in the private sector. They also generate 'positive externalities', since enterprises benefit from a high level of education and good infrastructure and unleash positive synergies.

Education has yet another important function: its dissemination in society helps to avoid unequal income distributions in the medium and long term. In a society in which the lowest qualified are only in a position to perform the simplest assembly-line work, but in which the best qualified rapidly develop highly complex machines which replace assembly lines, an uncontrolled market creates enormous income differentials. Income policy instruments, such as minimum wages or industry-wide wage bargaining can slow this development, but it is difficult to entirely prevent it.

Education is therefore a crucial starting point. By raising the level of education of even the low qualified, it is possible to increase opportunities in society and, thereby, income mobility over a person's working life, which in turn curbs income differentials. In addition, a society's level of productivity is raised. Unacceptable wage differences that persist despite a rising level of education can be reined in by means of labour market regulations, for example, a statutory minimum wage.

Public education can also play a key role in combating poverty and bringing about more equality of income. If, in particular, crèches, nursery schools and schools are free of cost, besides producing the public good of education, this means that the poorer social strata

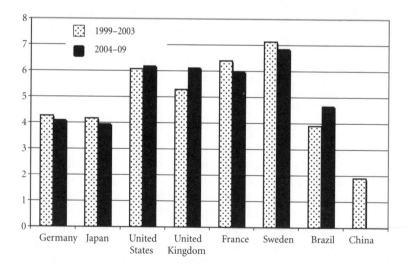

Figure 7.1 Government expenditure on education as a percentage of GDP in selected countries, 1999–2003 and 2004–09
Source: OECD Stat 2010 http://stats.oecd.org/index.aspx; UNESCO Data Centre 2010 http://stats.uis.unesco.org/unesco/TableViewer/tableView.aspx; own calculations.

will have easier access to basic education. Public education, as a rule, tends to have a more positive effect than the transfer of benefits to the poor.

There are significant differences among countries with regard to public spending on education, from crèches to universities (see Figure 7.1). Public investment in education, measured as a percentage of GDP, is around 6 per cent in Sweden and France, as it is in the United States and the United Kingdom which are considered more market-oriented countries. Governments in Germany and Japan spend only 4 per cent of GDP on education. Brazil also spends about 4 per cent of GDP, while China spends less. However, the last two countries have lower government expenditures as a percentage of GDP than most OECD countries. China in particular makes substantial efforts to steer government expenditures towards education, in pursuit of its policy to support human resource development.

Government investment in infrastructure is also central for sustainable economic development. If a country's motorways and rail network are in such a shoddy state that, for example, highly qualified mechanical engineers spend all their time stuck in motorway tailbacks while on the way to their clients, productivity cannot achieve its full potential. Again, there are considerable differences among different countries with regard to public spending on investment. As far as gross fixed capital investment is concerned, measured as a percentage of GDP, China leads the group of countries covered in Figure 7.2, followed by Brazil. This shows the efforts these countries are making to stimulate economic growth and to develop their infrastructure. Japan, followed by France and Sweden, also spend high percentages of GDP on public investment. The United States and the United Kingdom are rather 'underperforming' with regard to this indicator, reflecting the relatively poor public infrastructure in these two countries. Gross government investment in Germany is surprisingly low. If one turns to public net fixed capital investment the differences are even more marked. If one includes wear and tear and the dilapidation of public roads and buildings, for example, it emerges that in Germany investment, less depreciation, in the period in question was negative.

It is often argued that it is not necessarily the public which should spend more on education and infrastructure, but also the private sector. This is highly questionable. Education and infrastructure have a whole range of characteristics which make it probable that private solutions would result in the inadequate provision of these goods. First, investments in these two areas usually have positive

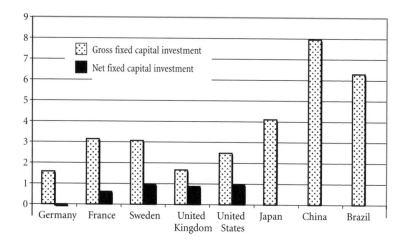

Figure 7.2 Government fixed capital investment as a percentage of GDP in selected countries, 1999–2008
Source: Ameco 2010; IMF *World Economic Outlook* April 2010; own calculations.

effects for the rest of the economy – externalities which cannot be precisely assigned. The same goes for infrastructure. If, thanks to good transport and good telecommunications links, the productivity of the economy increases, everyone benefits – assuming that income distribution mechanisms allow all to participate in national development.

Another problem with regard to investment in education and infrastructure is the long planning horizons: both education and investment in railway networks or motorways can deliver benefits for a good 40 years, and so the benefit increase of such investments in the distant future is very difficult to quantify. While private investors tend to shy away from such investments and could obtain funding only on adverse terms, the public sector can allow itself such an extended planning horizon. On the one hand, governments are in a position to fund themselves on favourable terms over the long term. On the other hand, they pursue a multitude of education and infrastructure projects. Even if some of them provide no benefit this is likely to be compensated by the success of other projects.

Areas of public goods and infrastructure are in many cases also areas of natural monopolies. Before the start of the market-liberal globalisation in the 1980s it was self-evident that the government should take responsibility for such productions and services. Starting in the United Kingdom and driven by ideology, it came to be thought that these areas had to be privatised. In almost all cases the outcome was poor. The cost advantages of privatisation were mainly based on wage cuts and an increase in precarious jobs, real efficiency improvements did not take place, long-term investment was insufficient, prices for consumers usually went up, and governments had to maintain or build up extended administrative capacities to control private companies in these areas. Charges for public services should be set at a level which enables incomes and working conditions in service companies to correspond to general social standards. Governments frequently had to reverse privatisations as the outcomes were disastrous in all respects. Well-known cases include the privatising of electricity in the United Kingdom, New Zealand and California which led to soaring prices and erratic supply, and the failure of the rail privatisation in the United Kingdom.[1]

In the areas of basic infrastructure where public goods, external effects and natural monopolies all play a role – as is the case in electricity supply, water supply and disposal, roads, railroads and local public transport – state-owned companies owned by different levels of government are the best legal form (though the organisations that run them can legally be stock companies). Equally critical are public–private partnership models, at least in those cases where private partners get a guaranteed profit and the public sector carries the risk. A large public enterprise sector can play an important role in changing the infrastructure in a way that favours green development, because it is capable of enforcing key technological decisions.

SOURCES OF SOLID GOVERNMENT REVENUES

In order to avoid increasing inequality in societies, it is essential to have a progressive income tax system, under which higher earners pay a higher tax rate on additional income. Generally speaking, progression of this kind is already a feature of most tax systems in the world. If incomes are not to diverge more and more, it is crucial that all forms of income are included and taxed in the same way. Furthermore, decisive action should be taken against tax flight and tax evasion. It cannot be disputed that, with the growing political pressure to return top income tax rates to the levels which existed before beginning of market-liberal globalisation, that means top rates of well above 50 per cent. Figure 7.3 shows clearly that top individual income tax rates were reduced after the start of market-liberal globalisation in the 1980s. To cut taxes and then use the

pressure of high budget deficits to cut expenditures is a strategy
which conservative governments frequently used. Tax policy under
Ronald Reagan in the United States in the 1980s perfectly fits to
this. Also global tax competition triggered cuts in top income tax
rates. In general, from the 1980s on tax revenues over the cycle were

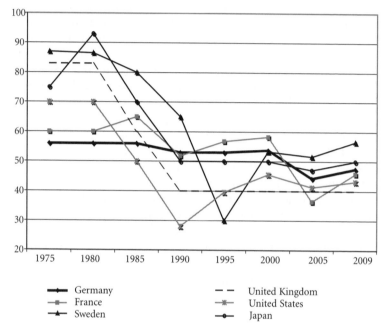

Figure 7.3 Top individual income tax rates in selected countries, 1975–2009

Notes

France: 1979–87: This is the top tax bracket for a married couple; 1984–91: The top
marginal tax rate was imputed from a table that outlined tax liabilities at different levels of
income.

Germany: 1981–96: This is the top tax bracket for a married couple.

Japan: Rate includes only the national tax, except from 1979–82 when is includes both the
national and local tax. Maximum tax payable (national + local) limit as percent of taxable
income: 1975: 80%; 1979–82: 80%; 1984: 80%; 1985–87: 78%.

Sweden: 1976, 1979: This rate includes both state and local income taxes. Average rate
for local income tax:1976: 26%; 1979: 28.5%; 1984 -1990: This rate includes the basic
state tax and the supplemental state tax rate; 1991-1996: This rate only includes the
national tax on employment income.

United Kingdom: 1981–87: This is the top tax bracket for a married couple.

United States: The top marginal tax rate shown here applies to married couples filing
jointly. The top tax rate does not include the effects of phasing out personal exemptions
or itemised deductions.

Source: OECD in figures, Statistics on the member countries URL: http://www.taxpolicyc-
enter.org/taxfacts/Content/Excel/oecd_historical_toprate.xls (28 September 2010).

in most OECD countries not sufficient to prevent and increase of public debt in per cent of GDP.

We favour the US tax law, under which US citizens are liable to tax even if they live abroad. Under such a rule all citizens, whether they live in the home country or not, would have to pay taxes there on all their income worldwide. If the person concerned has already paid taxes abroad, these can be deducted from the tax liability at home.

Besides a progressive income tax, the regular taxation of inheritances is also necessary in order to limit increasing inequality. No society with pretensions to being achievement oriented or a meritocracy can allow people to inherit enormous assets through no effort of their own and so acquire much better opportunities in life than people who inherit nothing. An increase in inheritance tax in most countries is needed.

It is claimed that a high inheritance tax would ruin medium-sized businesses because on the death of the owner the heirs would have to use the business's liquid funds to settle the tax debt. One possibility would be for the government to become a sleeping partner in those companies in which the heirs are unable to pay the inheritance tax right away. The government would then retain a certain share of company profits from the time of inheritance, but the heirs would have the right to buy the share back if they acquire money themselves. The normal business operations of a company would not be disturbed in this way. Furthermore, generous tax allowances might be applied in this area.

If a progressive income tax which takes in all forms of income equally and a regular inheritance tax are marshalled against rising income and asset inequality, the taxation of enterprise profits becomes less significant. In principle, these profits are either taxed when they are distributed to the owners or when the owners sell or bequeath their shares. In such a system, corporate taxes could be low without this resulting in funding imbalances for the public sector or dangerously increasing income and asset imbalances. Low corporate taxes would also contribute to strengthening the capital base of the corporate sector, making companies less reliant on debt.

With regard to corporate taxation, the primary aim should be to organise the system so that investment is encouraged. This is particularly important in light of the fact that innovations generally find their way into the economy and society in the form of new capital goods. Investment would receive a considerable boost if companies were offered generous tax write-off opportunities. This instrument could be used to stimulate green technologies and growth in areas which allow sustainable growth.

It is also important with regard to taxation that enterprises are prevented from reducing their domestic taxable profits by creative transfer pricing with regard to their foreign parent and affiliate companies. The OECD has made a number of recommendations which would help to prevent the abuse of so-called transfer pricing.[2] Other models, such as the US tax authorities, should also be looked at as they have to some extent managed to preserve their tax base, despite high tax rates, by limiting the transfer of profits.

One important instrument against tax flight is to prohibit the deductibility of borrowing costs, as well as royalty payments for using the company name or other rights.[3] Such an approach would make it more difficult to implement tax avoidance strategies and private equity strategies which replace the equity capital of domestic companies with borrowed capital for tax reasons. In order to make sure that small businesses and founders are not inordinately disadvantaged, special rules could be put in place to allow companies to set aside a small sum in terms of borrowing costs as long as the loans are used for new investment.

The economic model presented in this book relies heavily on balanced income growth among different population groups. Whenever markets deviate too far from this ideal state, the government has to step in to implement redistribution by means of taxation. An important factor in this is the government's ability to tax all incomes effectively – capital and rental income, as well as the incomes of freelancers and normal wages and salaries. In recent decades, nation-states' ability to do this has been increasingly undermined.

Tax policy became a key factor that persuaded companies to transfer their head offices or invest in low-tax countries. In this respect, tax competition pursues the logic of the lowest possible cost burden for companies. Countries are afraid that they can stay in the race for direct investment and production locations only if they adjust their national corporate taxation to the falling trend. Empirical research indeed confirms a connection between corporate taxes and location decisions.[4] A major part of international tax competition takes place in the financial sphere and tax administration of companies.

This is a separate matter from the way accounting is organised to ensure that in due course the profits are taxed as lightly as possible. By adjusting the structure of the enterprise in the most tax-friendly way and by taking advantage of legal loopholes in drawing up contracts and balance sheets, multinational companies and financial institutions such as private equity companies can minimise their tax liability. Taxes can also be avoided by taking a credit or granting a loan within multinational companies.[5] Profits can be shifted to holding and finance companies in tax havens.

The primary effect of these tax avoidance strategies is the draining away of the tax base from countries with a highly developed (social) infrastructure and therefore a justifiably higher tax burden. The developed industrialised countries in particular are affected by these methods of tax avoidance and lose revenues as a result. Tax competition changes the structure of taxes. It leads to lower tax burden on profit and interest earners and a heavier burden for workers, and a restructuring in the direction of indirect taxes such as VAT. In practice, this means a lightening of the burden on large multinational companies at the expense of small and medium-sized enterprises and, what is more, employees. Overall, tax competition has a subversive effect on the financing structure of welfare states and therefore on models of decent capitalism.[6]

The problem of competition between locations, which ultimately harms all countries, can be solved in everyone's interest by coordination. But agreement on common corporate taxation is extremely improbable due to the divergent interests of countries.

One possible compromise would be to impose a minimum tax rate on companies and capital, at least in the important industrial countries. Such a minimum tax would to some extent deprive tax dumping of its raison d'être. Assistance for countries not joining such agreements as well as other privileges should be made dependent on their cooperation with regard to tax issues. Naturally, a minimum corporate tax rate would make sense only if the relevant bases of assessment were harmonised. Otherwise, there is a danger that competition would shift from tax rates to exemptions and possible tax write-offs.

Offshore financial centres and jurisdictions with a high level of bank secrecy offer services as tax havens, and for money laundering and all types of criminal activities. Such centres are to be found in the Virgin Islands, Bahamas, Monaco, Jersey and many other places. They impose enormous revenue losses on the countries affected. In these areas tax policy should ideally be handled at the European level because the problem of tax flight affects all EU member states, not just individual ones. The big industrial countries, for example the G-20 with its considerable collective political and economic weight, could exert pressure on other countries with regard to global standards for transparency and tax fairness.[7] It would also be feasible for individual countries, for example, to restrict or even ban financial transactions with uncooperative offshore centres. The US government demonstrated in 2008, in an action against Swiss bank UBS, how pressure can be exerted on such countries and financial institutions. After the action brought against it for aiding and abetting tax evasion by creating phantom accounts in the amount of US$20 billion, the bank agreed to pay a fine of US$780 million and to provide confidential information on US clients.

Taxes to change the structure of prices

Whenever external effects come into effect, prices fail to give the correct signal to consumers and producers. Internalisation of external effects is one of the policies needed to change the structure of production, consumption and technological development. Internalisation means that all activities that pollute the environment or use up non-renewable resources are heavily taxed. For example, taxes on petrol, kerosene and electricity from non-renewable resources need to rise substantially in order to give incentives to change behaviour. As there is no objective way to measure external effects, the structure and scale of such taxes must be decided politically.

Environmental taxes have the advantage that they can be relatively easily handled. A disadvantage is that it is difficult to judge their environmental effect. For example, how much will the use of private cars decline if petrol becomes more costly? Trading of pollution rights or of the right to use certain resources has the advantage that the maximum consumption or pollution can be fixed. In carbon trading, for example, the government sets the maximum permitted emission of carbon dioxide (CO_2) and other greenhouse gases, and everybody emitting these gases must buy a certificate in an auction which allows a quantitatively fixed emission. Pollution rights can be traded in secondary markets like shares. One problem is that the price of such pollution rights can become very volatile and disturbing for the economy. But there are other problems with trading carbon that make such an approach incompatible with the concept of a decent capitalism. Carbon markets are purely quantitative mechanisms, which do not lead to qualitative changes of old-fashioned production facilities, and furthermore tend to play the North off against the South (and vice versa) and workers against workers under conditions of increased cost competition in that field.

An attempt to correct a market failure by means of a failing market is surely doomed to failure. We are convinced that a combination of requirements, bans and rules and environmental taxes, together with public infrastructure investment and key decisions about technological developments, is the bundle needed to bring about fundamental, qualitative changes. Revenues from both environmental taxes and pollution rights could be used by governments to invest in 'green' infrastructure or support sustainable technologies.

Taxes can also be used in other areas to change behaviour. A relatively high stock-market-turnover tax will make short-run speculation in the stock market more difficult and should be introduced. We also support a comprehensive financial transaction tax which taxes all financial transactions. As we show in the chapter on the financial markets, financial transaction taxes have important functions in raising revenues, but they are not in themselves sufficient to stabilise financial markets.

How big should the government be?

There is a great deal of discussion about just how large the public sector should be. Within the framework of the market-liberal globalisation project, it was fashionable to call for a reduction in the government spending ratio (measured as public spending as a proportion of GDP) and thus the tax burden to, for example, 'below 40 per cent'. Even a cursory examination shows that such a demand is arbitrary and unjustified. International comparison show that there are very successful countries, such as those in Scandinavia, with government spending ratios over 50 per cent, and countries with permanently crisis-ridden economies with a government spending ratio of below 40 per cent. It is noteworthy that countries with a relatively market-oriented approach such as the United States and the United Kingdom have a relatively high government spending ratio. Among developing countries, Brazil, for example, has a relatively high proportion of public expenditures to GDP (see Figure 7.4). This proportion in China is substantially lower. However, we should remember that China has a much lower GDP per capita than all the other countries shown in Figure 7.4, and that poor developing countries suffer from a lack of public resources.

In fact, the correct government spending ratio should be determined by the tasks the public sector is called on to perform and what it needs to fund them. Decisive in this is the question of what tasks the public sector performs better than the private sector. As already described, there are many activities in a society which have

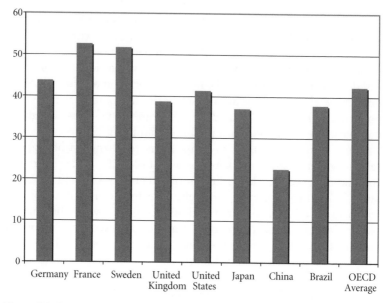

Figure 7.4 Government expenditure as a percentage of GDP in selected countries in 2008*

* The year 2008 before the deep recession in 2009 was taken. Data from 2009 would have shown much higher values as the result of fiscal stimulation and shrinking GDP; OECD average without Israel and Mexico.
Sources: *World Factbook* (2010); *OECD Factbook* (2010); AMECO (2010).

the character of public goods. Many of these tasks can be carried out better by the public sector that the private one. Also, in relation to network industries, such as electricity and water supply, or the railways, it is not obvious whether it makes more sense to run them as a private enterprise than under state ownership. Many past privatisations were ideologically, not economically, motivated. Furthermore, privatisation is of dubious social value if a private company can operate more cost-effectively only by reducing wages and working conditions.

In particular, if one takes the view – as we do – that the public sector should provide for medium and long-term stable and ecologically sustainable growth by supplying public goods, set technological guidelines by infrastructure investment, intervene in the economy to bring about tangible redistribution and perform an important stabilising function in the economic cycle by means of its revenues and expenditure, at the end of the day a government spending ratio of above 40 per cent seems more likely than one below that figure. In mature industrial countries which follow an ecological and socially sustainable development in the interest of the majority of their citizens, there is a tendency for government spending and also tax revenues as a percentage of GDP to be high and even to increase. But as we have already argued, a particular government spending ratio cannot be an end in itself, but emerges as a consequence of the set of tasks which the public sector must fulfil.

MORE THAN JUST 'AUTOMATIC STABILISERS'

A well-functioning social security system is also essential for stable growth. If people no longer have to fear the major economic risks of life this will lead, on the one hand, to more robust consumption growth. It can also be expected that people will accept financial risk, for example by setting up a company or moving jobs, if they do not have to worry too much about their livelihoods. Both these effects are conducive to a dynamic economy and economic development. The 'production' of security via a well-functioning social security system must be regarded as a public good, and it is unlikely to be adequately provided for by the private sector. The basic risks which should therefore be covered by the state include sickness, unemployment and poverty in old age.

Even if there were a more stable financial system, social security systems based on financial markets should be approached with considerable caution. Particularly important in this respect is pension insurance which, on account of its enormous volume alone, is eagerly competed for by the financial industry. Capital funding of pension insurance means that the young generation accumulates assets either collectively or individually, which are then consumed in old age. Pension funds led to an immense increase in the importance of banks and institutional investors in their role as fund administrators. One look at the United States, where capital funding of pension provisions has always existed, is enough to show the trend: there, institutional investors are the main actors in the financial sector and have a major influence on the economy as a whole, and on corporate governance in particular.

Germany played a pioneering role in social insurance in the nineteenth century through Bismarck's reforms. The German model is built on the understanding that the risks associated with old age, health and the workplace must be cushioned by statutory social insurance. Funding is provided exclusively on a pay-as-you-go basis: in other words, a system in which the young fund the old via current contributions. The contract between the generations, then, envisages that successive generations of young people will continue to fund successive older generations. The system in Germany has survived wars, the hyperinflation of 1923 after the First World War and the monetary reforms of 1948 after the Second World War. In Germany, for example, the contract specifically entails that only employees are subject to the system, and contributions are linked to wages. It is clear, however, that the German variant of the contract between the generations can get into trouble if, due to unemployment and increasingly precarious employment, the standard employment relationship is eroded and a diminishing proportion of the population pays into the social security system. As in, for example, Switzerland or the Scandinavian countries, the circle of contributors to mandatory pension insurance should be expanded.

With regard to pension systems, we propose the compulsory membership of all income earners in a country, in respect of which all forms of income shall count as a basis for contributions. An income ceiling for contribution payments would be sensible. In old age, all those who have paid in will receive a pension from the statutory pension insurance system. The system could include redistributive elements. The lowest pensions should be sufficient to prevent poverty in old-age, after a full working life. As the proportion of pensioners in a population increases, a compromise can clearly be worked out between contributions and the pension level. The funding problems of the pension system arising from demographic change could thereby be solved rationally.

Pension insurance should ultimately seek to approximate the living standards of working life. That does not necessarily entail pensions being as high as previous income from employment. Pensioners have lower expenses than employees, for example because they no longer have to travel to or dress for work. Furthermore, by the time they reach old age, people's children have generally grown up, which means that their education no longer has to be paid for. Pensions, therefore, should prevent poverty and maintain living standards, on the one hand, but be commensurate with contributions, on the other. We are not in favour of a model which aims at maintaining living standards solely by means of additional private insurance. These principles for a social system should not apply only to employees with a standard employment career, but also to those who, due to self-employment, child rearing or unemployment, have not had such a career.

The attraction of a capital-funded system from the market-liberal standpoint is that asset markets can profit from it and, at the same time, increase the interest of those in lower-income brackets in financial markets. A further attraction of a capital-funded pension system is that everyone forges their own destiny. Anyone who fails to put anything aside during their working life can expect only income support in old age. If a person's assets are destroyed due to a crisis, then tough luck – they should have selected their portfolio more wisely. One effect of the capital-funded system is that it removes the debate about how resources should be distributed between old and young from the political process and leaves the distribution to market forces. We consider such an anonymous and market-driven solution to an issue of such fundamental importance to every society as pension insurance to be deeply anti-social and inappropriate. Distribution between young and old must be the subject of political debate and decision-making. The pay-as-you-go approach is most suitable for this purpose, and to be preferred to a capital-funded system.

In a closed economy, the younger generation must always take full responsibility for the older generation. In any period of time, a society gives rise to a certain social product which must be distributed between the young and the old. This applies to both a pay-as-you-go funded system and a capital-funded system. A capital-funded system cannot overcome this simple fact. However, the hope is, with regard to the capital-funded approach, that the mature societies of the West, with their low birth rates, can invest their assets in the poor, high-birthrate societies of the developing countries. The argument goes that the developing countries would fund the old in the developed countries, thereby relieving the young in rich societies of their burden. First of all, it is questionable how robust such an effect is likely to be, above all because the more successful developing countries, such as China, have at least as serious a demographic problem as Germany. More important, however, is the fact that there is no guarantee that, in 30 or 40 years' time, the developing countries will be able or willing to pay. Argentina, for example, declared its foreign debts void in 2001.

We consider a capital-based system to be not only anti-social but is also dangerous. Pensions depend on the vagaries of financial markets. Furthermore, it is optimistic to say the least to assume that massive economic and political upheavals will not occur in the future. What is there to rule out hyperinflation or monetary reforms at some point? A capital-funded pension system, given future uncertainty, is quite simply too fraught with risk to serve as stable old age insurance.

Besides the certainty of crisis, a pay-as-you-go system – at least when one allows for temporary deficits and surpluses – has a stabilising effect in times of crisis. Such a system comes in the category of automatic fiscal stabilisers, in that, in crisis periods, people are cushioned and their purchasing power maintained. The liberal model, with its focus on private provision, suffers from procyclical effects. If asset prices and asset revenues fall, pensioners who obtain their pensions via the asset market must reduce their demand for goods.

For continental Europe with mostly pay-as-you-go systems it is highly advisable to stick with their systems and broaden them towards the Scandinavian version. The United States and other countries with capital-based systems will have difficulties in quickly switching to pay-as-you-go systems. In those cases, pension funds should be strictly regulated and limited in their investment decisions. For developing countries like China, capital-based systems are extremely dangerous as these countries are even more than developed countries likely to be affected by economic shocks of all types. The introduction of simple and transparent pay-as-you-go systems is their best option.

Health insurance should cover all necessary costs in the event of sickness, and some sort of individual contribution is entirely conceivable. As in the case of pension insurance, here too we are calling for obligatory membership of statutory health insurance. Health insurance should insure everyone in a country, which implies that all those in receipt of an income should pay into a statutory health insurance fund. In this way, all forms of income would be brought in to fund health insurance. An element of redistribution can be built into health insurance, although there should be an income ceiling on contributions. A model based on obligatory membership leaves room for additional private insurance in certain areas. There can also be various statutory health insurance funds which could compete in accordance with established rules. However, one should be aware that there are limits to the benefit of competition in the health insurance sector. If competition is done by varying the extent of coverage, the theory of adverse selection predicts that competition will lead to the coverage of the treatment of certain conditions increasingly being dropped from contracts, until only those definitely needing these treatments buy insurance for them, which in turn makes the insurance extremely expensive. Moreover, there is always the danger that insurers will try to maximise profits by competing for the healthiest 'customers' instead of bringing down treatment costs, cutting their own administrative costs or offering better services. Thus, a publicly run health insurance system with a limited number of large players seems to provide the more efficient provision of universal health care than competition among a large number of private insurers.

Most industrialised countries in the world already provide health insurance along these lines. For a long time, a notable exception was the United States, with roughly 20 per cent of its population being uninsured prior to the passing of the 'Patient Protection and Affordable Care Act' in 2010. This Act, which will be phased in up to 2014, will extend coverage to roughly 30 million US citizens who were until now not covered.

While the US health care reform passed in 2010 makes progress, especially in increasing the number of individuals covered, it has some shortcomings. It still leaves about 20 million people without cover. It produces an overly complicated system of health care regulation, and protects a fragmented market with a large number of insurance companies. It does not do anything to prevent the insurers from competing in a way that increases marketing costs or aiming to lure in the healthy while trying to keep the sick out of insurance contracts, and it does nothing to limit the attempts of insurance companies to circumvent well-meant regulation and increase their profits at the expense of the insured. It would have been better to include a 'public option', a health insurance plan offered by the government which could also work as a default option, and to finance the coverage of the chronically ill and poor in this system by a levy on privately sold health insurance.

Unemployment insurance – to mention another important 'stabiliser' – should alleviate people's fear of temporary job loss. We do not consider it wise for unemployment insurance to sustain a standard of living above that of those who obtain it through working. This would rapidly call the legitimacy of the system into question, which over the long term might have political repercussions, undermining robust social security. The living standard guarantee provided by unemployment insurance can be generous, but within reason. What should certainly be avoided is that, during prolonged periods of economic weakness, broad masses of the population are forced out of normal unemployment insurance and become threatened by poverty and insecurity. This sort of danger can be counteracted by the sustained payment of unemployment benefit.

The problem can also be avoided by extending the entitlement period for unemployment benefit in a recession, as is customary in the United States. Although the United States is not noted for particularly generous social security provisions, unemployment insurance there has a couple of very sensible features. On the one hand, this prolongation of unemployment benefit in a recession is implemented by means of automatic rules, and on the other hand, Congress has increased the benefit duration of unemployment aid by law in every recession since the 1970s. In China, as in almost all developing countries, unemployment insurance is only at an embryonic stage. It is difficult to measure unemployment in China because of the size of the informal sector and the huge underemployed labour force in the countryside. For China, basic unemployment insurance for all employees in the formal sector of the economy and a strategy to reduce the informal sector is the best strategy. In the European Union, the introduction of European unemployment insurance is advisable.[8] Under such a system, all European workers would pay into a basic insurance scheme. Individuals who become unemployed would receive unemployment assistance from Brussels based on their former income. On top of this basic insurance, each country could offer additional insurance. This system would help to curb the divergence of economic cycles: if the economy of one country is booming, more money will flow to Brussels and thence to countries that are not doing so well. This would also ensure that, during periods of weak growth when budgets are under financial pressure, individual countries do not cut their unemployment insurance. Finally, such a basic European insurance would provide a minimum insurance against unemployment and so prevent a 'race to the bottom' with regard to social protection. European unemployment assistance, which might be introduced initially only for EMU countries, would also contribute to European integration.

TARGETED MEASURES BEYOND 'AUTOMATIC STABILISATION'

In the short term, governments can deploy active fiscal policy to support macroeconomic demand during the usual economic downturns and, even more, in response to unforeseen events such as natural disasters. In a downturn expenditure is increased and taxes may be reduced. Of course, the ensuing deficits should be reduced again in the upswing because, essentially, the public budget should be balanced in the medium term; a permanently increasing level of public debt to GDP as a result of government consumption is unsustainable and unwanted. There is no argument, however, against governments using credit for investment purposes when a direct cash flow is created; the classic example would be public investment in a bridge where the government can charge a toll for crossing it. In general public investment is difficult to measure, and/or has no clear return, and/or the returns are very long-term, for example in the case of government-run public schools. As these types of investment are difficult to evaluate, they too should be financed from taxes.[9]

Overall government debt in many countries has increased substantially. In the United States, gross public debt increased from an average of around 45 per cent in the early 1970s to over 90 per cent (net debt over 65 per cent) in 2010; during the same period, public debt increased in Germany from around 20 per cent to over 80 per cent (net debt over 70 per cent), in Japan from around 40 per cent to nearly 230 per cent (net debt over 120 per cent), and in the United Kingdom from nearly 70 per cent to nearly 80 per cent (net debt slightly above 70 per cent). Gross public debt in the EMU in 2010 was nearly 85 per cent (net debt nearly 75 per cent).[10] These figures show that during the market-liberal era, in spite of the ideological orientation towards a balanced budget, public households were not financed in a sound way. This has to do with the economic instabilities experienced since the 1970s and the political reluctance to raise taxes to levels which cover expenditure over the business cycle.

Public gross debt in China is below 20 per cent. However, in the Chinese case we have to take into account that the state-owned banking system is used to finance fiscal stimuli and also undertakes tasks which in developed countries have been taken over by the government. For example, the banking system for a long time financed the social security system in China, which used to be based at the company level. The accumulated non-performing loans can be considered as quasi-fiscal deficits.

During the subprime crisis especially in 2009 and 2010, the United States, Japan and also China increased budget deficits much more (by 8 to over 10 per cent of GDP) to stabilise their economies than Germany did (with budget deficits below 4 per cent of GDP).[11] Germany, as a country with a big current account surplus, would have had the internal and external ability to give a bigger fiscal stimulus and also stabilise economic development in Europe and help to adjust current account imbalances in the EMU. It seems that in 2011 and the following years, many industrial countries and not only Germany will try to reduce budget deficits. This seems to be too early to support a sustainable recovery from the subprime crisis. To compensate for mistakes in fiscal policies in the past decades and try to reduce public debt as a percentage of GDP now seems to be a misguided policy.

There is no clear limit as to when the ratio of public debt to GDP becomes too high. Nonetheless, high public debt has several negative effects. First, it can lead to a more unequal income distribution. If the tax system does not interfere substantially in market-based income distribution, high public debt can lead to redistribution from the poor to the rich. Second, public interest payments and budget deficits can explode in a cumulative way when interest rates increase sharply and public debt to GDP is high. Governments' room for manoeuvre definitely shrinks when the ratio of public debt to GDP permanently increases. Third, high public debt to GDP ratios can erode confidence in whether a government can sustain payments on interest and principal. This can lead to an explosion of risk premiums or even a refusal to give new credit to the government. In 2010, Greece and other EMU countries suffered from the scenario mentioned here. Fourth, if private investment is stagnating, fiscal policy in the end will not be able to stimulate the economy in the long run. Keynes argued that it is not fiscal policy that is of key importance to overcome a long-run stagnation, but rather the control of public and private investment, which goes far beyond traditional fiscal policy.[12]

Finally, we turn to the more political problems of high public debt. A refusal to give credit to the government is hardly acceptable for national leaders as it would entail the collapse of vital government functions. It is very likely that in such a situation governments will – and indeed must – force central banks to give direct credits to governments (or force commercial banks that are financed by the central bank to do this). Printing money and pumping it into the economy can easily erode the stability of the national currency. Other political ways to get rid of bone-crushing public debt include currency reform and very high taxes on monetary wealth. We do not argue that such developments are unavoidable; the argument is that we cannot exclude such developments for political reasons if public debt is exploding.

There were several institutional attempts to prevent budget deficits or increases in public debt ratios. The most ambitious and far-reaching regulations are the Maastricht Treaty of 1992, and even more the Stability and Growth Pact, which was adopted in 1997 to prevent high budget deficits. The Stability and Growth

Pact in particular became the cornerstone of fiscal policy regulation for the member-countries of the EMU. The essence of the Pact is that countries, except in exceptional cases such as deep recessions or natural disasters, were not allowed to have a budget deficit exceeding 3 per cent of GDP. At the same time, gross public debt in relation to GDP was not to be greater than 60 per cent of GDP. Should a country not abide by the pact's rules, sanctions in the form of fines would be imposed to force them to obey. In 2005 the rules were relaxed without changing the substance of the pact.

In a similar spirit, as a result of exploding budget deficits under the rule of Ronald Reagan in the 1980s, in the United States the Gramm–Rudman–Hollings Emergency Deficit Control Act (1985) and the Budget and Emergency Deficit Control Reaffirmation Act (1987) were passed with the aim of achieving a balanced budget. They provided for automatic spending cuts if the deficit exceeded deficit targets. However, in 1986 such cuts were judged unconstitutional and the acts were accordingly revised in 1987.

In both Europe and the United States, these laws were violated as budget deficits were not reduced sufficiently to fulfil the regulations. One of the problems with these acts is that during economic booms governments are not forced to bring down budget deficits, for example in the case of the Stability and Growth Pact to levels sufficiently below 3 per cent. In periods of low growth, budget deficits then become greater than 3 per cent. The pacts also have the shortcoming that governments have to meet a target they cannot easily control. To a large extent budget deficits are determined by economic development. During economic slowdowns tax revenues decrease as the tax base shrinks and at the same time expenditures for unemployment benefits and other measure rise. Endogenous budget surpluses decline and, in typical cases, budget deficits increase. Theoretically, in such situations the budget deficit can be reduced by changing tax laws to increase government revenues and/ or by changing government expenditures. However, such a policy is extremely costly and undesirable because policies to reduce the budget deficit reduce aggregate demand, make economic development even worse, reduce tax revenues and lead to new holes in the budget. Thus, consolidating balanced public budgets in a context of economic crisis is not a very wise policy.

In spite of negative experiences with budget-deficit acts, Germany undertook a new attempt in this direction. In 2009 a balanced-budget law was added to the German constitution. Under this law, in 2016 and thereafter it will be illegal for the federal government to run budget deficits over the business cycle of more than 0.35 per cent of GDP and, beginning in 2020, the 'Länder' budgets (the German States) will have to be completely balanced over the business cycle, i.e. with no deficit. This law is much stricter than the Stability and Growth Pact and seems to be closer to the US Gramm–Rudman–Hollings Act, which also aimed at reducing budget deficits to zero in the medium-term. One does not need much imagination to predict that the German version of the balanced-budget law is also likely to fail.

The US Budget Enforcement Act (which was passed in 1990 and expired in 2002) replaced the failed fiscal acts of the 1980s. The act was no longer aimed at limiting the budget deficit but at controlling public expenditure. Here, a distinction was made between legally binding and discretionary expenditures. According to the Act, an increase in discretionary expenditures was only possible according to strict rules. Every increase in discretionary expenditure or reduction of taxes had to be counter-financed.[13] The stabilisation of discretionary expenditures in the Budget Enforcement Act produced an anti-cyclical fiscal policy. Expenditures do not have to be cut during recessions to fulfil a budget target, as there is no limit set on the deficit. Thus, the government can incur high deficits in a recession whereas in economic growth phases increased revenues do not lead to greater expenditure since there is a cap that has to be complied with. However, the expenditure rules allow exceptions in deep recessions, when additional expenditure is needed to stabilise aggregate demand, as well as for cases such as natural disasters.

Fiscal policy as well as monetary policy has to react in a discretionary way to stabilise aggregate demand and economic development. In particular, rules to control budget deficits must be judged as being too rigid to react to historical developments, and can therefore lead to policies which are not optimal. If a country wants to impose a fiscal rule, it would be best to set a target of discretionary expenditures in such a way that these expenditures are allowed to increase by a certain percentage every year independent of the business cycle, so allowing the budget deficit to fluctuate endogenously. While expenditure rules may seem desirable at lower government levels, for central governments such measures can lead to unacceptable restrictions on fiscal policy and are not advisable.

Fiscal policy in Europe is especially inappropriate. There are a number of different approaches to this problem. One option would be to furnish the European level with a much bigger budget, its own tax revenues, and substantially more functions and competences, so that the EU-level institutions or, for a smaller-scale solution, those at the EMU level can significantly influence demand in individual regions through public spending or tax revenues from the central budget. Regional fiscal redistribution, like that within a nation-state, would de facto be established. The hope would be that the central budget would curb national economic ups and downs. In this way, the working of the Eurozone would more closely approximate that of traditional federal states, such as the United States.

Over the long term, such an evolution is essential. However, finding solutions in the existing structure of European economic policy is very difficult, if not impossible. As the subprime crisis has shown once again, in the absence of a European state it is enormously important that the individual nation-states are able to deploy their financial policies to counteract dramatic economic downturns. At the same time, it has become clear that the finances of individual states are a matter of keen interest to their partner countries. The bankruptcy of an individual euro-state would send shockwaves through the banking system of the whole Monetary Union. The so-called 'no-bail-out clause' in the Maastricht Treaty, under which the other euro-states will not assume the debts of an individual member, will, in case of emergency, founder on the economic realities of Europe's closely interwoven economies. This has been made abundantly clear by the rescue efforts European policy-makers made for Greece in the spring of 2010 and the liquidity facility that the European System of Financial Supervisors (ESFS) has designed for other euro-zone countries under pressure. The existing Stability and Growth Pact (SGP), which supposedly limits budget deficits to 3 per cent of GDP, provides no solution to this dilemma, as it has not and could not have prevented the fiscal problems of countries such as Ireland and Spain. Both these countries had robust public finances in the years before the crisis, with surpluses in their government budgets. Only the outbreak of the crisis with the consequent drop in government revenue and the requirements of rescuing the banking sector have sent these countries on a path of dramatically increasing debt-to-GDP ratios. The problem was that the existing Stability and Growth Pact completely neglected private sector debt, which in the crisis had to be taken over by the public sector.

The EMU will only be able to prosper, or even survive, if there is a further and substantial integration towards a real federal system with a strong central government and with the nation-states turning into federal states. As Nouriel Roubini and Stephen Mihm (2010: 282) put it: 'No currency union has ever survived without fiscal and political union.' Integration is needed in almost all fields – fiscal policy, tax and infrastructure policy, wage bargaining institutions, minimum wages and other fields. A concentration of political competencies at the EU or EMU level is inconceivable without the reform of democratic institutions. Such a project would require that the European Parliament elect a proper European government. Since some EU countries are at present still reluctant to go further with integration, and even at the EMU level there remains strong resistance, such a project will require several decades for fulfilment. The only realistic solution for a quick further integration in Europe is to allow different countries to integrate at different speeds, for example through an earlier economic and political integration of the core countries of the EMU.

In sum, one can say that the reduced role of the government in most of the industrialised world in the past 20 years has led to a substantial destabilisation of individual economies, but also the world economy as such. A government's appropriate role is not limited to setting rules and regulations. Public economic activity definitely should go further. In a number of markets, without public involvement crucial goods and services would be undersupplied. Often, this is less a question of rule-making or setting boundaries, but more of direct government involvement in the markets and of active redistributive policies. As governments also cannot embark on a path of ever-increasing public debt levels, these activities need to be soundly financed through taxes and other stable government revenue. Without a move away from the Pavlovian reflex against tax increases nurtured in many Western democracies over the past decades, this will not be possible. A strong, stabilising government needs sound revenue, and this revenue can only be guaranteed by a broad range of taxes and a progressive income tax system with top marginal tax rates close to or even exceeding 50 per cent. The idea of some economists that such a tax system would stifle growth can nowhere be supported by empirical data. If the government uses its weight in the economy to encourage investment in education and research and development as well as to prevent self-amplifying downturns and economic crises, the result will be more, not less, growth and welfare in the long run.

Beyond the direct economic impact of government activity on the economy, however, one must also not underestimate the influence of regulations on single key markets of the economy such as the labour market or financial markets. The next two chapters turn to those specific markets and explain how market forces there have to be reined in so as to achieve a decent capitalism which brings improvements in well-being to a broad number of people.

8

REVALUING LABOUR AND WAGES

In the wake of the market-liberal revolution, over the past few decades labour markets in many countries have been drastically deregulated. In most industrialised countries this has led to increasing wage dispersion, increasing inequality of income distribution, an increase in precarious employment and the danger that the nominal wage anchor will drag. In our view, the analysis that high unemployment is due primarily to labour market rigidities is wrong. We regard the cause of high unemployment and the failure to deal with it adequately as, first and foremost, a demand problem in goods market. As an outcome of market-liberal globalisation there is the danger of a long-term strain on labour markets.

Four factors are of importance and interact. First is the impact of the high indebtedness of private and public households and enterprises in many developed countries, combined with the more cautious investment behaviour of entrepreneurs and a more risk-oriented behaviour of financial institutions in many cases. These factors disrupted a financial system that was suffering from old and new non-performing loans, and are likely in future to keep investment in productive capital low. Second, unequal income distribution and the uncertainty of living conditions in most developed countries will restrict consumption that is paid for out of income. At the same time, credit-driven consumption will be more difficult to achieve in the future than it was in the past. Third, there is no tendency for markets solve international imbalances in current accounts by themselves. This can lead to new deep crises. Last not least, if there is no quick progress towards a global Green New Deal, global warming and shortages of resources may place heavy burdens on GDP growth.

We first focus on macroeconomic needs for wage development. Then we discuss how labour market institutions can be strengthened. Finally, we outline reform steps in the labour markets in the United States, Europe and China.

MACROECONOMIC NEEDS FOR WAGE DEVELOPMENT

Even though the labour market cannot spontaneously create employment, it has an important role with regard to economic stability, growth and employment. On the one hand, income distribution and thus consumer demand are affected by the developments of the wage structure. On the other hand, neither inflationary nor deflationary stimuli can be allowed to arise from the labour market because this destabilises the economy and would prevent monetary and financial policy from acting in the interest of stable economic growth.

We start with the second point. In Chapter 4 it was shown that developments in wage costs are of paramount importance in establishing price levels. To make wages a nominal anchor for the price level, the *wage level* should increase according to medium-term productivity plus the central bank's inflation target. If this is the case, wage costs increase at the same rate as the target inflation rate of the central bank. The medium-term productivity development should be taken as the measure of this, because statistically productivity is influenced by the business cycle. During a recession, productivity decreases as firms cannot and/or do not want to reduce employment as quickly as GDP; when, after a recession, GDP increases firms can increase output for a while without increasing labour input. No central bank in the world wants to have a deflation; all try to realise a low inflation rate. Monetary policy is asymmetric. Central banks can and did fight against excessive wage increases by restrictive monetary policy and by creating unemployment. In the end this will reduce wage increases. However, if wage costs decrease it is difficult for central banks to prevent deflation. Japan in the 1990s and 2000s is an excellent example of this.

It is also economically inadvisable, as well as unacceptable in terms of fairness, if wage dispersion becomes too great. In such a case, a disproportionately large share of wage increases goes to those on higher incomes, who spend a smaller proportion of it on consumption. Growth requires fairer distribution, which would raise the consumption of those on low incomes through higher wages. Otherwise, adequate growth in consumer demand is possible only if some wage earners go increasingly into debt – a development which, after the subprime experience in the United States and some other countries, should clearly be prevented. Another consideration seems relevant here. The more uncertain people's jobs and incomes, the lower consumer demand will be, since households will make provisions for the future. The high unemployment and the reorganisation of the welfare state in many countries over the past few decades have led to muted demand on goods markets for this reason.

Income distribution also depends on the wage share, which in recent decades has fallen in almost every country of the world, a fact which first and foremost reflects the increasing power of the financial system which was able to impose a higher profit mark-up. If stable growth is to be achieved, the wage share must be raised again, and this must be brought about above all through financial market reform. Government policies with regard to the tax system and public spending should also be employed to create a more equitable income distribution.

STRENGTHENING OF WAGE BARGAINING AND MINIMUM WAGES

In labour markets the pure market mechanism fails. If demand and supply alone determined the price in the labour market, unemployment would lead to a falling wage level and deflation. A flexible wage level leads to waves of inflation and deflation, and in addition to extreme wage dispersion. This is why in no country in the world is the labour market completely left to market forces.

Labour market institutions have to guarantee that the wage level increases at around the rate of medium-term productivity plus the target rate of inflation. Strong collective bargaining partners, who include the macroeconomic prerequisites of wage development in their calculations, offer the best chance of attaining a functional wage policy in accordance with the guidelines described above. It is often argued that strong trade unions primarily extract wage increases at the expense of non-members, and in the case of trade unions with a high membership ratio, at the expense of the unemployed. This argument is both empirically and theoretically wrong. In fact, strong trade unions conducting wage negotiations on a national level have a strong interest in negotiating wage agreements geared to stability. Since the trade unions know that, in the event of inflationary wage agreements, the central bank will raise interest rates – ultimately at the expense of employment, growth and their members' income – they have no incentive to make excessive demands. It would be equally unpalatable to conclude wage agreements which would lead to deflationary developments. If strong trade unions negotiate on wages with strong employers' organisations, this also ensures that the interests of the corporate sector are taken into consideration.

Under certain conditions, wage negotiations at industry level can also lead to a stabilising macroeconomic wage development. This is the case if, for example, one industry takes the lead as a representative of all trade unions and employers' organisations and concludes a pilot agreement which takes into account macroeconomic needs and then is informally taken up by all other industries. Even if there is no industry-wide agreement, the outcome of collective bargaining in key firms can have a benchmarking affect for the whole economy and lead to a stability-oriented wage development if the negotiations take into account macroeconomic conditions.[1]

Governments should support all institutions which lead to wage coordination. The ILO as part of its Decent Work Agenda recommends tripartite consultations at a national level between trade unions, employers' organisations and the government to negotiate wage guidelines and other matters important to trade unions and employers.

There is a whole series of institutional reforms and policies which could help to support collective bargaining. Not all reform options are suitable for all countries, but countries can certainly learn from one another.

One robust instrument worth considering as a way to reinforce industry-wide collective agreements is obligatory enterprise membership of an employers' organisation. The establishment of a level playing field in the labour market through uniform wages in each sector is a public good. It is not very constructive if managers put most of their effort into trying to lower their employees' wages. If all companies in a sector had the same wage level, managers could instead focus their effort on devising new products, improving customer care or introducing improvements into the production process. If voluntary membership of employers' organisations no longer guarantees a uniform sector-wide wage level, however, obligatory membership is a legitimate way of ensuring coherent approaches on the employers' side. In addition, employers' organisations have other important functions, for example the provision of training, which also have the nature of public goods. Obligatory membership would ensure that wage agreements apply automatically to all enterprises. Austria has not done badly with this model, in the form of economic chambers, and has almost 100 per cent collective bargaining coverage.

Another approach is to make collective agreements generally binding. In a number of European countries, collective agreement coverage – that is, the number of employees covered by collective agreements as a percentage of all employees – has been expanded by frequently declaring them generally binding.

Another instrument to bolster collective bargaining consists in allocating public contracts only to companies covered by collective agreements. This instrument could also incorporate other criteria, such as whether the company offers traineeships.

The trend towards deregulating labour markets, and thereby dismantling regular full and part-time employment, continues unabated in many countries. Such employment relations undermine statutory social security systems, since not all employees now pay into social insurance funds. Furthermore, the dismantling of regular full and part-time employment leads to the danger of poverty in old age further down the line. All policies that make it possible only in exceptional circumstances to treat full and part-time employment as other than the norm should be supported.

In our view, it makes no economic sense for different firms within the same sector and region to pay different wages for the same work. This distorts competition between companies and is economically unjustified. It is true that employment can be increased to a limited extent by reducing productivity in a particular sector by means of paying below-average wages in some companies. However, the negative effects of wage differentiation within a sector outweigh any benefits from this kind of lowering of aggregate productivity. If there really are good reasons for supporting individual firms, this is the task of the state.

An important labour market instrument is the use of minimum wages. First, they can operate as a dam against deflationary dangers. In the medium term and even long term there is the danger that unemployment will remain high. Given the weakness of trade unions and wage bargaining mechanisms in many countries that make it difficult to prevent falling wage levels and deflation, a minimum wage policy must play an important role in the fight against defla-tionary tendencies. Second, statutory minimum wages can change wage structures and, therefore, income distribution. Minimum wages should be adjusted on an annual basis in accordance with trend productivity developments in the country in question, plus the target inflation rate. In this way, they would contribute to the nominal wage anchor in a deflationary situation. If average wages in a country increase more quickly than the wage norm, minimum wages should be adjusted to the increase in average wages. The reason for this is that equitable distribution should not be sacrificed to a putative fight against inflation. If the wage structure in a country is to be changed, minimum wages should develop more quickly or more slowly than average wages. That is a political decision. In the United States, there is a Living Wage Campaign to decide minimum wages, and this has led to statutory minimum wages in a number of regional and local authorities being set significantly above the national level of statutory minimum wages.[2] Finally, there should be a sufficient difference between statutory minimum wages and income support. In our view, besides being unfair, it would establish adverse incentives if living on benefit provided the same or even higher disposable income than full-time work.

The United Kingdom, which very successfully introduced statutory minimum wages under Tony Blair's Labour government in 1999, provides a model for their annual adjustment. Adjustment recommendations are assigned to the independent Low Pay Commission. The Commission comprises representatives of the trade unions and employers, together with independent experts who, on the one hand, lend their expertise to the discussion and, on the other, exert a moderating influence within the Commission. Recommendations are then in practice accepted by the government, although it has the last word.

The conventional argument against statutory minimum wages is that their introduction or increase results in massive job losses in the low-wage sector. Empirically this argument is not justified.[3] Since an increase in statutory minimum wages raises the incomes of low earners at the expense of higher-income groups, an increase in aggregate demand for goods can be assumed. The fact is that low-income households generally have a greater propensity to consume than those with higher incomes. An employment increase is to be expected for precisely this reason.

CASE STUDIES: THE UNITED STATES, EUROPE AND CHINA

The United States

Let us start once again with the United States. From the 1980s on the development of the wage *level* more or less followed the increase in trend-productivity plus an inflation rate of around 3 per cent. This was very helpful for monetary policy and explains partly the relatively good growth performance of the US economy from the early 1990s until the subprime crisis. However, the development of the wage level was not the outcome of a coordinated wage bargaining mechanism; it was luck. What is needed in the United

States is the rebuilding of institutions which allow a coordinated wage bargaining mechanism. It is not possible simply go back to the Treaty of Detroit; however, an attempt in this direction that was also supported by the government would be a first step.

The development of wage dispersion after the start of the market-liberal revolution was a disaster. What is urgently needed in the United States is a policy to reduce the low-wage sector. Substantial wages increases for this group of workers would be an important element in changing the very unequal income distribution in the United States, which is one of the key social and economic problems of the market-liberal type of capitalism. An active minimum wage policy by the central government which can be supplemented by minimum wage policies in states and even cities would be very helpful.

The group with very high incomes, the substantial group of 'superstars' in the financial sphere and other areas, usually got their positions on the basis of luck.[4] High marginal income tax rates comparable with the ones existing before the Reagan tax reforms in the early 1980s are the way to go.

The European Monetary Union

The European Monetary Union (EMU) is facing a very complicated situation in the labour market. Wages should develop in accordance with trend productivity plus the central bank's target inflation rate. For the EMU as a whole this norm has been more or less realised. The national differences with regard to medium-term productivity development in EMU are enormous, however, and show no tendency to become smaller. The annual average percentage increase in productivity between 1999 and 2008 was around 1.3 per cent for the EU-15. Annual average productivity development in Italy is below 0.4 per cent and is also low in Portugal and even more so in Spain, while in Finland, Greece and Ireland, in contrast, trend productivity development is significantly above the EU-15 average. In Austria, France, Germany and the Netherlands, productivity development is around average.[5] In the light of such big differences, wage levels in each EMU country should be raised in accordance with specific trend productivity development, plus the European Central Bank's (ECB's) target inflation rate. If EMU countries follow this norm, the price competitiveness of different regions within the EMU would not change. However, wage development has not followed this norm. Wage increases in Germany have been far too low, whereas wages in Spain or Portugal in spite of their poor productivity development increased much faster than in Germany.

What is needed is a higher rate of wage increases in Germany first of all. Wages in Germany should rise more rapidly for a number of years than indicated by the wage norm. In EMU countries with high current account deficits, such as Greece, Portugal and Spain, nominal wages should rise more modestly for a while. To avoid deflation in part of the EMU, the adjustment of competitiveness should be achieved by relatively substantial wage increases in countries with high current account surpluses and not by reducing unit wage costs in countries with high deficits.

What is needed in Europe, and especially in the EMU, is institution building. Without further comprehensive integration in the EMU the existence of the currency union is at stake. Further integration has to include among many other things the development of an EMU fiscal policy and EMU wage coordination. Currently, there are no EMU-wide trade unions or employers' organisations. It is necessary to shift wage negotiations, at least in certain branches, to EMU level. There have been some developments in this direction, but they are not enough. This is a hazardous state of affairs and must be addressed by creating new institutions.

It is difficult to achieve the coordination of wage development within the EMU in the short term. As in the United States, this gives minimum wage policy an important role. A coordinated minimum wage policy could foster wage increases in countries like Germany. Germany has no general statutory minimum wage. In no other industrial country is the introduction of sufficiently high minimum wages as urgent as in Germany.

China

China needs to improve its labour market institutions. Wage negotiations at the firm level could start immediately and could give the existing unions a new function. A minimum wage policy could also be used more actively. Both policies could change the very unequal income distribution in China. In the medium term, employers' organisations should be supported in order to establish the conditions for industry wide negotiations. State-owned enterprises should use some of their retained and unused profits for bonus payments to their employees. An independent tripartite body of unions, employers' associations and government should provide nationwide wage guidelines.

9

GLOBAL FINANCES NEED GLOBAL MANAGEMENT

Reform of the financial system, including monetary policy, is an essential point for a decent capitalism. The dynamic power of capitalist production fuelled by the financial system is unparalleled. Yet it is also the major source of danger for economic stability, as is made abundantly clear by the recent subprime crisis, which – for all the huge media attention it has received – has been but the latest in a series of countless financial and monetary crises since the birth of capitalism. However, depending on specific conditions and approaches to regulation, there have been periods both of relatively high stability (as the two decades after the Second World War) and of high instability (as the market-liberal globalisation period from the 1980s onwards). Any debate on the future of capitalism must therefore necessarily find its point of departure in this sphere of the economy. Here, different aspects must be covered: the financial markets aspect covers issues such as the narrow oversights of banks and other financial institutions, but it is also necessary to consider elements such as exchange rates, global capital flows and finally the financial markets' influence on corporate governance. Finding the right calibration in these areas of the economy constitutes the first important step towards a decent capitalism and will be covered in this section.

RESTRUCTURING OF THE FINANCIAL SYSTEM

The reform of the financial system in a narrower sense is the issue which has been most hotly debated since the outbreak of the crisis – and this is the area where politics has made the biggest strides towards preventing future economic crises. While a number of economists, such as Hyman Minsky, Robert Shiller, Joseph Stiglitz and Nouriel Roubini, have long argued that the inadequate regulation of financial markets might lead to regularly recurring bubbles in stock and real-estate markets, destabilising credit expansions and – following that – credit crunches, gigantic current account imbalances and over-indebtedness on the part of countries and systemic worldwide financial market crises, these critics have long been perceived by their peers as mavericks. It took the US subprime crisis to bring the message of the problems of under-regulated financial markets home to the political, if not the academic, mainstream. The costs to the real economy of the financial market crises of the past few decades have been enormous and, with the subprime crisis, reached a new and mournful peak. Without fundamental reform of the financial system a decent capitalism is out of the question. A stable financial system, in this connection, can be regarded as a public good, which the state must supply in the public interest, by means of regulation.

With the passage of the Dodd–Frank Wall Street Reform and Consumer Protection Act in the United States in the summer of 2010 and the EU directives on hedge fund regulation and on financial market oversight passed later in the year, politicians have already made great efforts to restrain the financial sector. But before one can judge the details of the newly introduced and amended regulations, one first has to decide what is needed to achieve a sustained transformation of the financial system from a source of brutal shocks to a useful service provider for the rest of the economy.

Macroeconomic dimensions of financial market regulation

A fundamental problem with the reform of financial market regulation over the past few decades was that regulatory authorities, like the majority of economists, continued to believe in efficient markets. Regulation was regarded as mostly unnecessary. In the few instances where the market as an all-knowing, perfectly disciplining force was not completely accepted, the assumption underlying the remaining regulations was that the microeconomic stability of institutions would lead automatically to macroeconomic stability. As a result of these misjudgements, macroeconomic problems such as asset-market bubbles, the increasing fragility of the whole system due to rising debt ratios, the over-indebtedness of whole economic sectors and countries and similar problems were disregarded.

The first step towards a better financial system thus requires a change in the philosophy of regulation so that macroeconomic concerns are once more included. A macro-orientation also requires that the financial system should be regulated in such a way that it takes on a serving and supporting function for the enterprise sector. In order to assess the robustness of financial institutions, the supervisory authorities must review their business models. These must therefore be disclosed by the institutions in question. In the process, business models which rest predominantly or entirely on speculative activities must have much higher capital-adequacy requirements imposed on them by the authorities or, in extreme cases, simply be prohibited outright. Incentive systems which encourage management strategies that are too short term and carry excessively high risks should be banned or subjected to increased equity capital requirements.[1]

Supervisory authorities should in future be much better resourced, both financially and in terms of personnel. Qualified staff are indispensable in order to scrutinise complex events in the financial system adequately and, as the need arises, to present proposals for improvements. In this connection, the authorities should be given the freedom to query transactions not only when they infringe the letter of the law, but also – even if they meet the requirements in the strict sense – if they violate the spirit of the regulations. For this purpose, supervisory authorities should employ more macroeconomists alongside the microeconomically oriented inspectors.

Winding up of the shadow banking system

The second important step to more stable financial markets is the broad application of equal treatment and the comprehensive regulation of financial markets. Economic functions, regardless of which institution or locality they happen to be housed in, must be subject to the same regulations. If this does not apply, regulatory arbitrage emerges and regulation is undermined. Banks and other financial market actors would then naturally transfer their activities to legal regimes or locations in which regulation is lightest. This is exactly what we have seen over the past few decades with the development of a 'shadow banking system'. The shadow banking system has partly emerged within countries, and partly through the transfer of transactions to countries with a generally lower level of regulation. The relatively strictly regulated commercial banks simply outsourced their riskier activities to less regulated institutions, such as special-purpose vehicles or funds, some of which were established in offshore centres. The importance of traditional banks declined as a result and less or unregulated institutions, such as investment banks, investment funds and other non-bank financial intermediaries, gained ground. In this way, aided by the misjudgement that financial markets are inherently stable, an unregulated shadow banking system grew rapidly.

Given the problems that have arisen as a result of this, reforms of the financial market must aim, on the one hand, at winding up this shadow banking system and, on the other hand, at subjecting all financial institutions to comprehensive regulation which goes beyond their mere registration. Basically, as already emphasised, functions must be regulated rather than specific financial institutions. For example, prescribing capital-adequacy requirements for commercial banks, while special-purpose vehicles get off scot-free leads to regulation arbitrage with little positive effect. One way to achieve this end is the prohibition of special-purpose vehicles or other institutions which were established by the banking system in order to get around the regulations (preferably setting them up in more loosely regulated jurisdictions). An alternative to such a ban would involve including all the activities of a financial institution in one consolidated balance sheet and making that the basis of regulation. Also, all financial institutions – including investment banks and special-purpose vehicles – should be subject to specific equity capital provisions in order to limit the leveraging of these institutions through borrowing.

In parallel with this, the transparency provisions of hedge funds, private equity funds and similar non-bank financial intermediaries should be changed. Business models and day-to-day operations should be laid open to the public and the regulatory authorities, as well as ownership structures and investors in the funds.

The transactions of domestic institutions with offshore centres which are not subject to regulation should quite simply be banned. Such a ban can be imposed on a go-it-alone basis; for the United States and for the European Union or EMU, it would be neither administratively difficult nor economically harmful if transactions with offshore centres were prohibited. Only the political will is needed.[2]

Finally, one should try to insulate the commercial banking sector from potential problems in the more speculative part of the financial sector. From this point of view, the ideas of Barack Obama's advisor the former Federal Reserve Chairman Paul Volcker deserves merits: Volcker has proposed prohibiting commercial banks from certain activities such as proprietary derivative trading and sponsoring or investing in hedge funds, and a watered-down version of this has made it into the Wall Street Reform Act. However, even the original Volcker rule probably is not strict enough to prevent problems in the speculative part of the financial sector spreading to commercial banks. As long as commercial banks can still lend to speculative financial institutions, the insolvency of a large hedge fund or investment bank could bring the commercial banking sector down and create a financial crisis. Thus, close links between the commercial banking system and non-bank financial intermediaries should be broken. One option is to require commercial banks to hold much more equity capital for loans to less-regulated and high-risk institutions, such as investment funds, private equity funds or hedge funds. This would make loans to such institutions more expensive. A more radical solution would be to compel non-bank financial intermediaries to finance themselves exclusively from money they collect from individual investors and to prohibit commercial banks from lending to non-bank financial institutions. In any case it would be desirable not to allow commercial banks to own non-bank financial institutions and to split up financial institutions that do both commercial and investment banking. This also would be a step towards solving the problem of financial institutions that are too big to fail.

Prevention of pro-cyclical processes

Financial systems tend of their own accord towards cumulative pro-cyclical processes, since as a rule asset-market inflation goes hand in hand with the expansion of lending and, conversely, asset-market deflation with a credit crunch. This systemic pro-cyclicality leads to self-reinforcing tendencies in one direction or the other, and cannot be decisively broken by the use of today's rules and regulations.

Bank-specific risk models, which are necessarily based on historical data, operate pro-cyclically, since they indicate the risks to be low in an upturn and even during the development of an asset bubble. In such phases, in the nature of things, bad loans do not arise and typically banks markedly step up their lending, using their existing equity capital. In fact, however, with regard to the economy as a whole this would be the very time for a rather more measured credit expansion in order to avoid going too far. When the asset bubble eventually bursts and the risk models indicate greater danger, the banks scale down their lending at the very time the economy has already been weakened by the bursting asset bubble. This problem would be reduced by having a minimum equity capital holding independent of risk evaluations and/or by forcing banks to use risk models with anti-cyclical elements. But that would not be sufficient. We propose an equity capital deposit obligation which can be varied at the central bank's discretion for specific loans. In this way, loans for real estate, share speculation, the financing of private equity funds and so on could be made more expensive, as required. Other regulations are also conceivable, for example a discretionary variation of buyers' equity capital necessary for real-estate financing. The advantage of this regulation would be that it could be applied exclusively in regions experiencing a real-estate bubble.

Events in Spain show that such proposals can work. In 2000, the Spanish central bank, in response to the emerging real-estate bubble, forced the banks to build up their reserves with a view to compensating for possible losses. As a result, despite the bursting of the huge property bubble in the wake of the subprime crisis, the Spanish banking system remained relatively stable.

Such an approach would have an additional advantage: properly designed, it could solve the conflict monetary policy sometimes faces during the emergence of a bubble. One of the causes of the subprime crisis was undoubtedly the price bubbles in the US real-estate market. Both in the media and among economists the Federal Reserve and its former chairman, Alan Greenspan have been blamed. The argument is that Greenspan kept interest rates too low for too long in the period after the bursting of the dotcom bubble and the terrorist attacks of 11 September 2001, and that this was a key factor in the real-estate bubble.[3]

However, Greenspan was trapped between a rock and a hard place. Between 2002 and 2004, economic and wage development in the United States was persistently weak. There were serious indications that the US economy was even under threat of deflation. Until 2004, unemployment remained high. Furthermore, fixed capital investment by US companies at this time – measured as a proportion of GDP – was at an extremely low level. Raising interest rates sooner might have put the brakes on rising US real-estate prices, but it would also have further squeezed corporate investment activity, which would have kept unemployment high. Moreover, experience shows that hefty interest rate increases are necessary in order to bring asset price bubbles under control. If a house buyer counts on an annual rise in house prices of 10 per cent, a rise in financing costs of 5 to 6 per cent will have only a limited influence on demand for real estate. A large interest rate rise, which would certainly terminate speculation, would impose an enormous burden for the rest of the economy.

If one introduces the possibility of requiring differentiated capital requirements and allows the central bank to vary these requirements in the light of conditions both in the real-estate market and in the larger economy, this dilemma would be solved. Using these new instruments, the central bank could selectively limit credit expansion in those sectors in which asset price bubbles are developing.[4]

There is no hiding the fact that the introduction of such additional instruments would imply a sea-change in the monetary policy trends of recent decades. Within the framework of the debate on so-called 'financial repression', regulations on banks' lending and deposit operations were gradually reduced from the 1970s onwards. This trend also applied to monetary policy instruments such as the selective provision of central bank funds to commercial banks, or curbing their lending. The monetary policy of central banks in the advanced industrialised countries has been restricted, over recent decades, to a single instrument: the refinancing rate or the overnight interest rate in the market for reserves. The argument behind this development was that the market was in a better position than the central bank to decide in which sector capital would get the best return and so the largest welfare gains for the economy. The clear instances of fundamental market failure in financial markets indicate that this development has gone too far and that the central bank needs other instruments in order to achieve its goals. It should thus not be afraid to expand its toolbox.

Another element that would make the financial system less pro-cyclical would be a change in accounting principles. Accounting provisions in accordance with the US GAAP (Generally Accepted Accounting Principles) or the IFRS (International Financial Reporting Standards) put a strong emphasis on current market prices for the valuation of an asset.[5] According to 'mark-to-market' or 'fair-value' accounting, an asset's value is taken to be its current market price. This principle allows financial institutions to display large profits in times of a booming stock or real-estate market without having actually realised these gains, which leads to the extension of more loans in economic boom times. In a downturn, the opposite is true: falling market prices lead to unrealised losses which nevertheless have to be accounted for. This leads to a declining capital basis for the institution in question, which as a consequence has to cut back lending, thus exacerbating the downturn.

As the mark-to-market principle also leads to an extremely short-term orientation of managers, who will try to do everything to please financial markets and get their stock prices up in the short run while possibly neglecting long-term strategic goals, a further necessary reform would be to change this principle. It is not acceptable that private institutions, without any supervision or control, are able to decide such important things as international accounting standards. In this context, it would be good to prohibit financial institutions from booking unrealised gains as profits. If managers' pay is linked to profits, incentives should be given to corporations to link bonuses to long-term profit developments, not short-term gains in stock notations. A step in the right direction would be to end the tax deductibility of bonuses that are based on a company's stock valuation.

Standardisation and prohibition of financial products

Another fundamental issue is the reform of the way financial innovations are introduced into the market. Experience shows that financial products are every bit as hazardous as drugs. In the case of the latter, careful controls have become standard, and the same should apply to financial products. The highest levels of transparency, neutrality and control should therefore be observed in the evaluation of risk.

We propose that all financial products, like drugs, should be subject to licensing prior to introducing them into the market. Just as for drugs, a product would only be allowed into the market if the inventor can convince the regulator that the product in question provides added value to investors or borrowers and that the risks related with it, for the whole system as well as individual institutions, are worth taking given the additional benefits. If the government regulator deemed a new product to be too complex or too opaque to evaluate, the licence would be denied. Among other things, this would end the tendency of financial institutions to constantly create new financial products which have no economic added value. It would give rise to a bundle of standardised products, which would make the market more manageable. Such licensing controls would also prevent the multiple packaging of products, which has no intrinsic economic benefit, since investors are perfectly able to shuffle their portfolios as required.

The trading of financial products should be permitted only in organised markets which function as clearing houses. So-called over-the-counter (OTC) transactions, which can be conducted bilaterally, should be banned. This step is necessary, on the one hand, to guarantee adequate transparency in the markets. On the other hand, it would help to stabilise the financial system. Hitherto, large volumes of derivatives have been traded only via bilateral contracts between individual financial institutions. This applies, for example, to the gigantic market for credit default swaps (CDS). These contracts can be seen as some kind of credit insurance against the default of the borrower. One party in the contract pays the other a premium for receiving an agreed sum in the event of a credit default. Reliable sources indicate that in recent years this CDS market has grown to a value of more than US$60 trillion – around the same as annual global economic output. Other derivatives also account for immense sums.

The problem with OTC transactions is, first, that it is unclear which market participant holds which positions and whether or not these are likely to pose a systemic risk on an aggregate level. Second, in the event of the bankruptcy of one OTC trading partner, there is the risk that the other will lose its insurance coverage if derivatives have been used as a hedging instrument. In the past, market participants have just blindly assumed that OTC partners would always be able to step into the breach to the necessary extent. On this basis, business strategies were classified as secure if one had used derivatives to hedge against risks, although from a macroeconomic standpoint it must have been clear that this was not the case.

Dangers of this kind have become more evident in the wake of the nationalisation of US insurance company AIG. AIG had enormous sums in CDSs still outstanding, so that the US government feared a domino effect of bank failures if the insurance group went bankrupt, and it therefore nationalised the company. The fact is that the supervisory authorities were simply unable to foresee the consequences of insolvency and could not risk the collapse of AIG, given the already damaged financial system. A central clearing house could have provided the supervisory authorities with summarised information on existing risks.

Further issues

There are a number of other reforms necessary in the financial markets which nowadays are seen as no-brainers and which have already made their way into the legislative process. While these changes are important, they are very unlikely to solve the underlying riskiness and volatility of the financial sector by themselves. We therefore only discuss these issues here very briefly:[6]

- **Increasing capital-adequacy requirements:** In the years prior to the crisis, banks increasingly used mathematical risk models to run down their equity capital holdings. Limiting the extent to which these models can be used and checking these models more strictly as well as increasing the general capital-adequacy requirements would make the banking sector significantly more stable. If banks had to hold more capital, they would tend to be more careful in lending, as more of their own funds would be at stake. In addition, the risk of an individual bank failure would fall, as would the risk that the government would see itself forced to bail out insolvent institutions. A maximum leverage ratio could also be introduced as an additional element which would limit the amount of borrowing a financial institution could take on, regardless of the perceived riskiness of investments. Finally, in order to prevent banks from becoming too big to fail, one could increase the capital-adequacy ratio in line with the absolute size of a bank's balance sheet, thus making business for large banks more expensive than for small banks.

- **Removing incentives for reckless lending:** In the process of securitisation, banks and mortgage associations were sometimes able to sell the entire mortgage (or other loan) to other investors. In this case, there was no incentive left to screen borrowers properly. To prevent this, it would be necessary to force the original lender to keep a significant part of the default risk on its own balance sheet, either in the form of the first-loss tranche in the process of securitisation or in the case of some (randomly chosen) loans from the loan portfolio.
- **A new framework of credit rating agencies:** In the past, credit rating agencies, a small club of mostly private US companies, were usually paid by the issuer of a security. As there are several rating agencies which compete for business, this created a perverse incentive to look the other way. In the past, rating agencies used largely the same risk models as banks did, and therefore exacerbated the pro-cyclical behaviour of asset markets. The financing model for rating agencies should therefore be changed, and rating agencies should be more closely regulated and supervised and forced to publish how they come to their ratings.
- **Reform of the tax system:** The tax system in many countries has also created perverse incentives for excessive risk taking or leverage. For example, in many jurisdictions it is possible to deduct interest payments on loans as business expenses. When international holding structures are used, it is possible to circumvent tax payments by piling up large loans. Moreover, income from speculative activities is often treated more favourably than other types of income. A solution would be to cancel the tax deductibility of

interest payments and have a scale of capital gains tax depending on the period an asset was held, so that it starts with a very high rate on investments owned only for a few months and lower rates with investments held over a decade or so.

Levels of regulation

In the best case, the regulation of financial institutions and products with a transnational character should undoubtedly take place at international level. Regulation should occur at the same level as the transactions. On this basis, global financial market regulation is a classic international public good. There is an inherent danger that, in the absence of international coordination, this good will be in short supply.[7] A step in the right direction of better regulation in the wake of the outbreak of the subprime crisis was the establishment of the Financial Stability Board, agreed on by the G-20, and the upgrading of the International Monetary Fund. However, simply replenishing the funds of the IMF does nothing to resolve its legitimacy problems or those of other international organisations. Until their organisational structure reflects the current geo-economic importance of the different countries of the world, and as long as their traditional domination by the industrialised countries continues, this legitimacy deficit will persist. The IMF and other international organisations must also learn from their past mistakes. All too often these institutions served as drivers of the market-liberal globalisation model. They must now become the drivers of a new regulation at global level.[8]

In order to avoid a concentration of power at the global level, we propose the creation of a powerful global financial supervision authority, located at the Bank for International Settlements as a successor of the Financial Stability Board. Also at the global level, institutions should be established which carry out up-to-date and independent analyses of the development of international financial and capital markets, propose appropriate measures for worldwide regulation, and ensure ongoing and binding communication between international institutions. A Global Economic Council of Experts at the United Nations could be a third institution performing this function.

The creation of worldwide regulations, such as the establishment of international standards for financial institutions and products, is a political hot potato, however. It is not only in the United States that voters are reluctant to accept politicians handing over power to supra-national bodies. The governments of large emerging markets have also lately been asking why they should change their approach to regulating their financial institutions, given that the recent crisis originated in the United States and not in emerging markets.

Regional action, of course, is easier to achieve. For example, regulating the financial sector at the EU level would bring many of the benefits without the costs of unilateral action. If a European country tried to regulate its financial sector unilaterally and prohibit certain financial products or activities, they would most likely just be pushed to other European countries, given that both people and capital can flow freely between EU countries. Introducing some regulation at the European level, in contrast, might still allow financial institutions to move the activities in questions offshore, but those institutions would then forgo the easy access to customers allowed through Europe's single market. Within Europe, it would also be conceivable to move forward with a subgroup of countries, so long as they have sufficient size. For example, a tighter regulation for the countries of the EMU seems feasible even if this entails the danger that some business activity will be moved to the United Kingdom The loss of parts of the financial industry might be justified by the greater stability of the financial system.

For larger economies which are less integrated with their neighbours, such as the United States, India, or China, unilateral regulation is also an option. Here, the danger of pushing financial institutions abroad is less of a problem as the markets in question are too attractive to be abandoned. Moreover, successful regulation could then serve as a positive example and give rise to a bandwagon effect or put pressure on other regions and countries.

However, one must not forget that uncoordinated regional or even unilateral reform might create new problems. By the nature of such a reform process, each jurisdiction will in the end treat some activities more strictly than other countries and regulate some other activities more lightly. Moreover, the outcome will certainly lack a comprehensive global oversight structure. The result would be the creation for new regulatory arbitrage, with activities being shifted to the jurisdiction which regulates them the least.

The achievements so far

Even though the G-20 laid down general principles for financial market reform, the national economies have passed regulatory reform at their own pace and with their own focus. Among the large economies, the United States has so far moved the furthest. The Wall Street and Consumer Protection Act signed into law in July 2010 includes far-reaching changes in the oversight structure and the regulation of financial markets. For example, an office for consumer protection will be created that will educate consumers and guard against abusive loan practices by financial institutions. More importantly, there is a legal provision to put non-bank financial institutions under regulation of the Federal Reserve. Regulators in the future will have the power to break up large financial institutions so as to overcome the too-big-to-fail problem. In the realm of derivates and financial innovations, oversight bodies may now regulate OTC derivatives. Non-OTC derivatives which can be centrally cleared will be moved to clearing houses. Finally, the investment a commercial bank is allowed to make in hedge funds and private equity groups will be limited to 3 per cent of its capital.

While a number of provisions have been watered down in the reconciliation process between the US House of Representatives and the Senate, and others are formulated in rather vague terms that will be interpreted by the regulatory bodies themselves, one cannot dispute that this act is a huge step forward from the under-regulation and misregulation of financial markets during the years before the US subprime crisis.

Europe has not moved quite as far yet. Regulation has been proposed by the European Commission in a piecemeal way. Some tightening of hedge fund oversight for example was passed early in 2010. Other parts of financial market reform, however, got stuck in the complicated European law-making process. At the time when Barack Obama signed the Wall Street Reform Act into law, the European Commission had not even proposed a draft directive for regulating OTC derivatives in Europe. The proposed overhaul of the oversight structure, and especially the strengthening of the European level of supervision and oversight, had been deadlocked between the EU Council, in which the governments of the member states are represented, and the European Parliament, which is directly elected by the people. While the national governments were trying to limit the powers to be delegated to the European level, the European Parliament was trying to at least give the European supervisory body the oversight of large institutions which mainly operate across borders, and the power to effectively control supervisors at the national level. None of the draft directives for financial market reform brought forward so far make it possible to disentangle the shadow banking sector, hedge funds, private equity funds and the commercial banks.

While at the time of the writing the financial market reforms in the EU are far from finished, one can already see that the final result will fall significantly short of that in the United States. In the end, the supposedly more liberal United States has now proved to be much more committed to regulating financial markets and showing them their limits than the supposedly regulation-friendly European Union. Yet, one must not forget that even the tightened European regulation is a significant step in the right direction.

However, even if the new US law goes much further than the European equivalent, there are three more fundamental issues to be criticised in both reform packages. First, the macroeconomic perspective and the need for regulators to control the pro-cyclical lending of the financial system are still underdeveloped in all of the new laws and the currently discussed draft bills. It is true that both the US Wall Street Reform Act and the European proposals contain elements to monitor macroeconomic risks more closely. For example, European lawmakers have proposed a 'systemic risk board' which is also designed to look at macroeconomic risks, while in the United States, a 'stability oversight council' will be created. However, these bodies are not equipped with the necessary tools to counteract macroeconomic imbalances. Monetary policy in both regions will continue to run as before, with no provision for adjusting capital requirements in the economic cycle to prevent asset price bubbles or counteract the pro-cyclical tendencies inherent in the financial system.

Second, there is no a comprehensive approach to financial innovations. Some financial instruments such as securitised loans are now more tightly regulated, but the fundamental approach to financial innovation has not changed. Financial institutions are still allowed to introduce essentially whatever product or instrument they want into the financial markets. While regulators may now have more powers to limit trade in certain contracts or may make them more expensive for banks to enter into, the race between regulators and financial markets will most likely resemble the race between the animals in the Grimm brothers' story, 'The rabbit and the hedgehog'. In this tale, no matter how quickly the rabbit runs, the hedgehog always seems reach the goal before him. In the end, trying ever to run faster, the rabbit drops dead from heart failure. What the rabbit does not know, but what the brothers Grimm tell the reader, is that the hedgehog actually does not move at all during the race but uses his wife as a double to wait at the finish line. In the regulation of financial markets, by sheer weight of numbers, financial institutions will be able to churn out financial innovations and flood the market with them, and regulators will probably only be able to identify and limit the wildest excesses once a new crisis is imminent or has already happened.

Third, the link between the speculative part of the financial sector and the shadow banking system on the one hand and the commercial banking sector on the other hand has not been severed. In the United States, a first step has been made by limiting a commercial bank's investment in hedge funds and its proprietary trading. However, banks are still allowed to lend to speculative entities. In Europe, even the partial progress made in the United States is not matched yet. None of the draft directives currently in the process of becoming European law include comprehensive limits on banks' proprietary trading, loans to the shadow banking system or their investment in hedge funds and private equity funds.

The latest regulatory step has been taken under the so-called Basel III rules, which are supposed to increase capital requirements over the next decade in order to provide better protection against potential banking losses in the future. Such a move is to be welcomed in principle and should have a potential effect on the solidity of the financial system, but there are too many shortcomings in this new regulatory framework to make it an effective reform. The capital requirements are still too small, and Basel III neither gets a grip on the shadow banking system nor reforms the role of rating agencies in a significant way. And ultimately, it is not clear how Basel III is to be implemented on the national level, which proved to be a major cause for the dysfunction of Basel II. In the United States, Basel II was implemented later and with a different spin than in the European Union, for example, which rendered the whole idea of having a global banking standard ineffective. In the following section we sketch out our framework of a solid financial system.

REFORM OF THE GLOBAL MONETARY AND FINANCIAL SYSTEM

As we argued in Chapter 1, the financial and economic crisis of 2008–09 had deeper causes than just the inadequate regulation of financial markets. One important cause was the global imbalances created by unstable and huge international private capital flows along with attempts by emerging and developing countries to defend or create policy space by excessive undervaluation so as not to become dependent on volatile international capital flows. In order to solve these problems, it is important to reform the global financial system.

A new Bretton Woods system

A useful framework to start the debate is the so-called 'Impossible Trinity', which proposes stable exchange rates, free capital flows and autonomous monetary policy as three desired goals for a country. Only two of the three desired aims can be achieved, according to the argument. In terms of the Impossible Trinity, it is correctly argued that for almost all countries the combination of autonomous monetary policy, unregulated international capital flows and fixed exchange rates is not possible. The best option, it is proposed, is to renounce fixed exchange rates and to strive for a combination of unregulated capital flows, a nationally oriented monetary policy and flexible exchange rates. However, in many instances this combination is just not feasible, as countries often find currency devaluations hard to swallow and are forced to pursue a restrictive monetary policy in defence of the exchange rate, with negative consequences for domestic economic development. As was described in the first chapter of this book, devaluations can lead to inflationary developments and/or, if there are external debts in foreign currency, to an explosion of the real debt burden and the breakdown of the domestic financial system.

As mentioned, a system of fixed exchange rates with unregulated international capital flows likewise does not allow most countries in the world to operate a nationally oriented monetary policy. The problem is that, in such circumstances, monetary policy must be subordinated unconditionally to defending the exchange rate. Only the reserve currency country can pursue a national monetary policy in a system of fixed exchange rates, while the other countries are obliged to fall in line with it. Of course, such a reserve currency can experience temporary weaknesses which will also reduce the room of manoeuvre for domestic-oriented monetary policy.

And there is another problem. Flexible exchange rates and unregulated capital flows in no way guarantee current account imbalances will be sustainable. There are countless examples of countries which accumulated high current account deficits, even with flexible exchange rates, and were able to reduce their deficits only within the framework of a currency crisis. Nor do fixed exchange rates automatically lead to the limitation of current account imbalances to an acceptable level. As a result of different cost developments in two countries in a fixed rate system, for example, imbalances can build up which do not simply go away of their own accord. Although the country with current account deficits can pursue a restrictive monetary policy and trigger a stabilisation crisis in the face of financing difficulties to reduce the deficit, the losses in terms of domestic production and employment can be painful. Sometimes the fixed rate system crashes in such situations.

Thus, with unregulated international capital movements, neither a fixed nor a flexible exchange rate system, governed exclusively by market forces, will automatically lead to global economic stability and prosperity. Both systems require additional instruments if they are to fashion a stable framework for global economic development. The advantages of both systems should be used for that purpose.

We still regard John Maynard Keynes's proposal as a good foundation for global monetary system reform.[9] He proposed a system with exchange rates that were fixed in principle, but that could be adjusted in the face of emerging current account imbalances between countries. The permitted fluctuation margins around the central parity should be as small as possible. The adjustment mechanism which Keynes envisaged in the event of imbalances foresaw economic policy stimulus in a country with surpluses and a corresponding choking off in a country with deficits. Keynes therefore had a symmetrical adjustment process in mind.

As a rule, market processes lead to only the country with a deficit having to reduce imbalances by means of a restrictive economic policy. Not only is that excessively painful for the country affected, but it also has a negative effect on the development of the world economy. When deficit countries rein in their economies and surplus countries do not stimulate their own economies, a structural global demand shortfall arises, with correspondingly low world growth. In order to promote or even enforce a symmetrical adjustment process Keynes called for the introduction of punitive taxes both for countries with current account deficits and for those with surpluses.

Implicit in Keynes's proposal is close economic policy cooperation between the countries participating in the fixed exchange rate system. A joint committee would be needed for this purpose which, on the one hand, would make decisions on possible exchange rate adjustments, and on the other, would coordinate economic policy in the participating countries. In the Bretton Woods system, exchange rate adjustments were made within the framework of the IMF committee. However, the IMF had no specific coordination functions with regard to monetary policy or even other economic policies. A new global monetary system should rectify this.

Robert Mundell, by no means a radical economist, took up this problem. He proposed a fixed exchange rate system between the dollar, the euro and the yen. A joint independent governance committee would be set up to coordinate monetary policy, consisting of four US, three EMU and two Japanese representatives. They would coordinate and set monetary policy in the three currency areas.[10] Mundell's proposal, therefore, implies the transfer of the monetary policy competences of the participating countries to a supranational committee, while retaining the national currencies. Such a committee could also be set up at the IMF and have representatives of the world's most important central banks as members. This would obviously represent a quantum leap with regard to global economic governance. Even if current political structures make it unlikely, it is nevertheless important to get the discussion going once again.

Economic policy coordination would also include fiscal policy, alongside monetary policy. At least in global economic crises, fiscal policy must be coordinated among the most important countries. So far, this has occurred within the framework of the G-7, the G-8 or more recently the G-20. In principle, there are no objections to such a coordination mechanism, although consideration should be given, as already mentioned, to a Global Economic Council of Experts set up at the United Nations. Its task would also be to formulate recommendations on fiscal coordination, as well as in other areas such as the harmonisation of tax systems. Such a council might have more credibility than, for example, the G-8 or the G-20 summits, which have appointed themselves steering committees of the world economy.

How frequent should exchange rate adjustments be?

A number of other questions arise with regard to the establishment of a new Bretton Woods system. The first concerns the frequency of exchange rate adjustments. Harry Dexter White, the leader of the US delegation at the Bretton Woods negotiations, like Keynes, declared himself in favour of a system of fixed exchange rates. However, White wanted to apply the instrument of exchange rate adjustment more quickly. Evidently, Keynes had less faith in the exchange rate mechanism than White, which is understandable, given the many problems which might arise with regard to exchange rate adjustments. Our position is that symmetrical adjustment of the macroeconomic direction of economic policy in countries with unacceptable current account imbalances is preferable to an exchange rate adjustment. Needless to say, there are circumstances in which an exchange rate adjustment appears to be more appropriate.

Ultimately, the instruments which are most beneficial for the coordination of global economic development must be decided in light of the prevailing conditions.

Controls on capital movements and foreign currency market intervention

It is true that a new Bretton Woods system in accordance with the ideas presented here would help to stabilise international capital flows. However, there would be no guarantee that capital flows would not seriously disrupt or even destroy the system. For this reason, a number of precautions are necessary. First, all central banks, as is natural in a fixed rate system, should intervene vigorously in foreign exchange markets in order to compensate for destabilising capital flows. Developments in particular after the Asian crisis, and not only in China, showed that large-scale foreign exchange purchases by the central bank are possible and may well succeed.[11] At the same time, such a system requires a strong international institution for the financing of central banks which come under pressure due to capital outflows. The IMF is already in place and well suited to assume this function. There is already a legal provision to distribute Special Drawing Rights (SDR) to central banks which then can be used to intervene in foreign exchange markets. For a new Bretton Woods system, the only thing needing to be done would be to increase the issue of SDR and allocate a given amount to each central bank each year.

Finally, capital controls should once more become a normal instrument of monetary policy and economic stabilisation among the developed countries. Ideally, such an instrument would include coordinated inflow and outflow controls – in other words, there should be international coordination. Capital controls can be used flexibly, with varying intensity. There is no need to impede important capital flows, such as useful foreign direct investments, for long.

Capital controls can be implemented in many different ways. The so-called 'Tobin tax' is particularly well known and is the origin for the proposals now often debated of a 'financial transaction tax'. James Tobin (1978) suggested that all foreign exchange interventions should be subject to a modest tax. Important transactions, such as goods exports and imports or capital flows with a long-term orientation, would scarcely be affected by the tax, but it would put an end to very short-term speculation. Tobin hoped that the tax could be used to lengthen the time horizon of economic actors and so stabilise exchange rate developments, making them dependent on fundamentals. He hoped that the tax would 'throw sand in the works' of financial markets and slow them down a bit. For tax reasons – that is, for the sake of government revenues – the Tobin tax would make sense, but it is too weak to have much effect on international capital flows. Let us assume the tax rate would be well under 1 per cent – this would not be sufficient to significantly alter capital flows when returns from speculation might well reach 20 per cent or more. Of course, a Tobin tax could be differentiated according to the type of capital flow, but that was not Tobin's intention.

In drawing up regulations on capital movements it would make sense, first of all, to reduce specific international transactions or to force economic entities to cut them out of their repertoire. In this way, pension funds, insurance companies, special institutions (such as building societies) or banks in public or cooperative ownership (for example, savings banks) would be obliged to transact their business exclusively in the domestic market. Specific foreign institutions could be prohibited from engaging in business domestically. Of course, in regions where countries are already closely economically integrated with each other, the relevant border need not be a national border but can be the border of a regional integration agreement. In Europe for example, it would not make sense to limit transactions to the domestic markets of the Netherlands or Luxemburg, but it would make sense to limit transactions to within the European Union or within the EMU. The proposed regulations would both simplify and strengthen banking and financial market oversight in relation to these institutions.

International portfolio investments and bank loans which leave a currency area or flow into a currency area would be relatively easy to control. Such transactions are carried out by financial institutions which are overseen by the supervisory authorities anyway. These capital flows could either be subject to a high transaction tax or, in specific circumstances, even banned. Transaction taxes or bans could be carefully targeted. For example, short-term international loans, international share transactions and international purchases of interest-bearing securities could be treated separately.

Also conceivable is an obligation in cases of capital transactions to make an interest-free deposit for a certain period at the central bank, an instrument which has been implemented in Chile. The effect of this is that the costs of capital flows depend on how short term transactions are. If credit transactions between currency areas were subject to an interest-free deposit of the loan sum at the central bank for four weeks, loans of under four weeks would clearly make no sense and loans over a period of two months would become relatively expensive, but a ten-year loan would be only marginally more expensive than at present.[12] In any case, the same applies to these controls as to taxes or bans: if the political will is there, they can be imposed.

For emerging markets which have not yet completely opened up their capital accounts, this approach would mean that they should proceed much more slowly and carefully and should think twice before they liberalise further. This applies above all to China, but also to countries such as India or Brazil.

Governments could, as mentioned above, just prohibit outright all transactions with offshore centres. Again, such a policy could be pursued by some big countries alone (such as the United States or Japan) or by a group of countries as the European Union or the Euro area.

An international reserve medium for central banks

Under the Gold Standard before the First World War, the British pound took on the role of a global currency; in the 1950s and 1960s, it was the US dollar; and in the current global economic constellation, the US dollar and the euro perform this function together, with the US dollar playing the leading role. The coincidence of national and international monetary functions has considerable advantages for those countries whose currencies take on an international role. They are able to borrow abroad in their own currency, transact a large portion of their foreign trade in their own currency and realise particularly high so-called 'seignorage' profits, since their notes and coins circulate worldwide and, in countries with weak currencies, even drive out the national currency. But there are also disadvantages. One of these is the fact that central banks and private economic actors hold money assets largely in international currencies. As a rule, these investments are short-term, so that, in particular in a monetary system characterised by several internationally important reserve currencies, asset restructurings from one reserve currency into another are probable. Such restructurings can bring external economic turbulence, with negative effects for reserve currency countries and the world economy in their wake. Furthermore, a reserve currency country also faces the danger that high demand for its currency will lead to constant inward capital flows, sustained revaluation and, accordingly, incessant and high current account deficits, which in turn choke off domestic growth.

There is also no guarantee that a country whose currency carries out international functions will pursue an appropriate monetary policy.

US economist Robert Triffin (1961) warned as long ago as the 1960s, in testimony to the US Congress, that the dollar cannot assume the double role of national and international currency without crisis tendencies emerging for the global economy. What would be feasible is an international currency created by the IMF which can be used only by central banks for holding international reserves and for transactions between them. Although such a currency would solve only some of the current problems facing the world economy, it would constitute a step towards its stabilisation. Central banks would no longer hold any foreign currency reserves in national currencies such as the dollar or the euro, but only in the currency unit which they themselves have created. The advantage of such a system would be that the world's central banks would acquire a stable reserve medium. As a consequence, they would no longer be forced to choose between, for example, the dollar and the euro. Currency restructuring by central banks would therefore be a thing of the past.

This proposal of a currency for central banks is nothing new. The problem was addressed during the discussions on a global monetary system after the Second World War, at Bretton Woods in 1944. John Maynard Keynes proposed the 'bancor'.[13] Later Robert Triffin supported this idea. In 1969, for the first time, the creation of an international currency for central banks in the form of Special Drawing Rights (SDRs) was agreed on. SDRs are created by allocating a special sum of them to the accounts of national central banks by the IMF. The value of special drawing rights was tied on creation exclusively to the dollar, with one unit corresponding to US$1. Since the collapse of the Bretton Woods system in 1973, special drawing rights have been defined on the basis of a basket of currencies. Special drawing rights were created in two waves in the 1970s and by the end of 2006 had accumulated 21.4 billion units or a little more than US$30 billion. In spring 2009, shortly before the G-20 summit in London, Zhou Xiaochuan (2009), president of the Chinese central bank, called for a reduction in the role of the dollar as an international reserve medium for central banks and an intensification of the provision of SDRs At the G-20 summit in London in 2009 a new issue of SDRs was agreed, to the value of around US$250 billion.

We support a bigger role for SDRs and a reduction of the role of the dollar and the euro in the reserve holdings of central banks. An annual increase corresponding to the needs of the global economy would make sense, as well as an obligation on the part of central banks to hold SDRs. A controlled transition of existing reserves from national currencies into special drawing rights could be assayed. Central banks will be willing to hold all their reserves in SDRs only if they have confidence in the institution which creates it. This means that such an institution must have high credibility, which entails a new level of global cooperation legitimacy of such an institution.

Supranational organisations related to the global financial system

In order to ensure a stable framework for the globalisation process, old institutions must be reformed and new ones established. In general, these organisations have to be democratised, since hitherto the industrialised countries have played a dominant role and all other states have been under-represented. This is a problem, not only because, it means that these institutions lack legitimacy, but also because the rise of emerging and developing countries, such as China and India, means that they are less inclined to accept existing structures and to grant these institutions new powers. By way of example, we shall look briefly at some of the necessary reforms.

First, the IMF is in need of far-reaching reform, in particular in relation to existing voting rights and the allocation of SDRs. The industrialised countries, and especially the European states, have far too much weight, while in particular countries like Brazil, Russia, India or China are under-represented. The Netherlands has more voting power than, for example, India; Switzerland has more than Brazil; and the United Kingdom, Germany and France have greater weight than China. The United States has more than twice the voting power of China, India and Brazil combined, even though measured in purchasing power, the latter three have a GDP similar to the United States. If the IMF wishes to be universally recognised and legitimised, these weightings must be adapted to the actual significance of the participating countries. Cosmetic changes will not suffice. One vote for the EMU for example would be reasonable.

Second, in the past the IMF has interfered in the internal affairs of countries in an illegitimate manner. In this respect, the IMF did not show itself particularly open to different models of capitalism. Its principles, referred to as the 'Washington Consensus', were long based on neoclassical ideas about the deregulation of goods and financial markets, as well as the rolling back of the state. The IMF repeatedly tried to impose these ideas on countries that had got into trouble by attaching conditions to its loans. Since the market-liberal globalisation strategy has produced so much instability and shortcomings, it can no longer serve as the basis for future credit allocation. Naturally, the IMF cannot be expected to grant loans arbitrarily; they must be subject to conditions of some kind. With a shift in power relations inside the IMF, however, the basic principles for loan allocation would change, especially given that most of the emerging and developing countries are critical of the Washington Consensus.

At last, with the subprime crisis and its systemic effects, it has become clear that the supervision of the world financial system is of central importance. Of course, it is not possible to create a single central global institution capable of effectively supervising the complex global financial system, including regulating events in individual countries. Nevertheless, an institution should be set up to constantly observe the global financial system, develop reform proposals and organise a committee for the intensive exchange of information between national authorities about the supervision of multinational banks and other financial institutions. For this purpose, we recommend a World Economic Committee on Financial Market Supervision. This would not be located at the IMF, because otherwise the Fund would take on too many functions, which it would not do any harm to separate. The Bank for International Settlements in Basel is the right place for international financial market supervision. The Basel Committee on Banking Supervision, founded in 1974 by the banking supervisory authorities and central banks of the ten leading industrialised nations at that time, can be converted into such an institution, as proposed by former UN official Professor José Antonio Ocampo.[14]

In the past, excessive foreign debt has led to major upheavals and often prolonged stagnation in the affected countries. Individual creditors, from private institutions to states, have taken advantage of the situation of debtor countries to extract concessions for their own economic and political benefit, and not infrequently simply to exploit the countries concerned. It would therefore be a good idea to establish an institution which, in the event of a country becoming over-indebted, arranges orderly debt relief and facilitates a compromise between debtors and creditors. At the national level, such procedures have already been established. At the international level, however, no such institution exists. We therefore recommend an international debt arbitration panel which goes into action, on the basis of general principles, when a country incurs excessive debts, and arranges fair burden-sharing between creditors and debtors in a crisis.[15]

The relationship between industrialised and developing countries

Large current account imbalances in industrialised and developing countries have been a constant source of instability in recent years and therefore should be prevented. Generally speaking, these imbalances should remain low in comparison to a country's GDP. For a long time, the general textbook prescription has been that developing countries should allow current account deficits, which means that they import capital. The rationale was that they could thus buy more equipment and increase their capital stock more rapidly than otherwise. However, empirically, the problem was that a number of developing countries following this advice piled up enormous amounts of external debts which led to problems once financial markets stopped to provide fresh loans, as has happened in so many crises in the countries of the South. As a consequence, especially after the Asian crisis in 1997, many Asian countries, led by China, started to amass large surpluses. The reverse side of the coin was that the United States accumulated excessive current account deficits. This combination also does not prove stable, as has been explained above.

In order to stabilise the global economy and allow developing countries faster growth, the optimum solution would be for the developing countries to pursue moderate surpluses, while the industrialised countries go for moderate deficits. However, this means that the United States in particular would have to reduce its current account deficit, the EMU and Japan must accept moderate deficits, while some of the emerging markets, particularly China and other Asian states, have to curb their high surpluses. For the developing countries, the proposed constellation of current account balances has the advantage of enabling them to integrate their economies into the global economy via exports. At the same time, in this way the danger of currency crises and excessive foreign debts would recede. For the industrialised countries, which as a rule can borrow abroad in their own currency, moderate deficits do not pose a financial problem.

The proposed structure of current account balances between the countries on the periphery and in the centre is certainly compatible with inflows of foreign direct investments into the peripheral countries. Such inflows would simply have to be balanced by capital exports by the private sector, the public sector or in the form of foreign exchange interventions, as has happened, for example, in China.[16] In any case, other forms of capital inflows, apart from foreign direct investments, have done little for developing countries, merely increasing their current account deficits. And not all foreign direct investment is good or well designed to improve technologies or organisational skills in host countries. In many developing countries, for example, it fuelled real-estate bubbles which were later difficult for those countries to deal with. Developing countries which have deregulated international capital movements have not experienced successful growth when compared with countries which have controlled international capital movements, as Joseph Stiglitz (2004), among others, emphasises.

To be sure, there is a small group of developing countries, especially in Africa, which would find it difficult to run export and current account surpluses. But even these countries could have generally balanced current accounts if development aid was granted in the form of transfers, not loans. This group of countries may in any case not expect high private capital inflows. Partial debt relief for some of the most debt-ridden countries on the periphery can smooth the way to a new permanent balance for the world economy. In support of this, goods markets in advanced industrialised countries should be opened up to products from developing countries in an asymmetric way; that means allowing these countries trade protection and at the same time opening up markets in developed countries.

Monetary and exchange rate policy without global cooperation

Although a global solution is desirable, there is also room for unilateral steps at the national or the regional level. Any of the world's central banks can pursue a monetary and exchange rate policy which seeks to shield their own economy from external economic shocks. This would also contribute to global economic stability.

A central element would be to keep the exchange rate as stable as possible, since sharp revaluations and devaluations have negative effects on economies. But desirable as exchange rate stability undoubtedly is, it must be balanced against other economic policy objectives. As has been argued above, moderate current account deficits for the advanced economies and moderate surpluses for developing countries should not pose a problem. If high current account deficits build up, this leads to the accumulation of foreign debt, the danger of a sudden reversal of capital flows and so of violent swings in the exchange rate which wreak havoc with the real economy. A prolonged period of high deficits must, therefore, end in a devaluation of the exchange rate. However, this should take place in a controlled manner, avoiding overreaction. In the case of current account surpluses, conversely, a revaluation of the currency should be attempted.

From this perspective, the Chinese renminbi should be allowed to appreciate against the US dollar. In fact, a gentle correction would be beneficial for both countries. In the United States, it would help to boost exports and limit imports, and hence create jobs. For China, such a policy would bring the advantage of making the world economy more stable. The recent crisis has been a stark reminder for countries depending heavily on exports such as China, Japan or Germany that the stability of the world economy and the absence of crises in any of the other large economies is a matter of common concern.

However, gentle corrections in the exchange rate rarely happen in today's world with its free capital flows. If a country tries to manage a gradual appreciation or depreciation of its currency today, the danger is always that speculative international capital flows will amplify the movement and lead to overshooting.

Thus, in contrast to the fashion of recent decades, but well in line with proposals from Nobel Laureate Joseph Stiglitz among others, regulations on capital movements are necessary to prevent destabilising capital flows, unsustainable current account imbalances and exchange rate turbulence. Capital import controls can reduce periods of currency revaluation and rising current account deficits, while capital export controls can combat cumulative and uncontrolled devaluations. Countries can also stabilise exchange rates through intervention in foreign exchange markets. Together, these instruments can be deployed unilaterally, and wisely used they provide a defence against current account imbalances and exchange rate turbulence.

Even if many countries used this approach without coordination, globalisation would not necessarily suffer, but merely be guided onto a stable path. While certain types of capital flows would be dampened, international trade would not suffer as stable exchange rates reduce risks in the trade of goods and services.

REFORM OF CORPORATE GOVERNANCE

Criticism of a corporate governance that is narrowly concerned with shareholder value alone has grown considerably since the subprime crisis. Models of enterprise management must be reintegrated into some sort of societal context. The interaction of a number of stakeholders in an enterprise – in particular, employees but also, of course, shareholders – offers a starting point for efficient, but also stable enterprise management. Corporate governance, in these terms, is based on the notion that the economic success of a company depends on a range of participants, who should also play a role in enterprise management. According to the stakeholder approach, the circle of those who participate in enterprise management goes beyond the investors around whom the shareholder-value model revolves. The stakeholder model is based, among other things, on the observation that the core element of the shareholder approach – namely, the management's focus on raising the short-term share price – is harmful. Share prices fluctuate erratically and unpredictably, and are driven by expectations which have no anchor and are often exclusively short-termist. Given this lack of an anchor for share prices, enterprise management based on shareholder value is really a form of casino economics.

The short-term orientation which has developed in corporate governance in recent decades has had fatal consequences for economic development. If, for example, investment in a production plant or in employee training is not sufficiently profitable in the short term, in terms of financial market demands for a short-term return, then they will simply be dropped. Within the framework of the shareholder-value ideology, innovation tends to take place above all in the realm of process optimisation for the purpose of cutting costs. The consequences manifest themselves in the medium to long term, namely when demand, production and innovation fail to materialise. The investment ratio in the economy as a whole may remain low due to the short-term orientation of enterprise management and this can lead to unemployment. There is, therefore, no evidence of more dynamic investment or growth as a result of the unfettering of financial markets and their dominance over firms' management.

The points of departure to overcome the shareholder principles of corporate governance may be sought, on the one hand, within the company, and on the other, in changing the rules for corporate control, which is increasingly being shaped by institutional investors, large investors and finance-oriented managements. Improved corporate governance in the sense of a longer-term orientation with regard to enterprise management would, in this context, require first turning away from the current trend towards the 'financialisation of the economy', as the increasing dominance of the financial over the real economy and employees is generally described. It goes without saying that the shareholder-value approach does not sufficiently reflect the interests of the employees. For example, restructuring programmes in enterprises, such as outsourcing in order to increase profitability even if the enterprise already makes high profits, have grave consequences for employees. These tendencies can be curbed by bolstering employees' rights in the enterprise.

But the negative aspects of the shareholder-value approach are not confined to its short-termism and neglect of employee interests. Dividend payments to shareholders become a central issue. Of course, there is no reason on earth why dividends should not be paid when profits resulting from high turnovers are high; however, high dividends are paid out even when profits are only the result of increases of asset prices on the books of companies (mark-to-market accounting) or enterprises have no profits at all. Another problem is rooted in share buy-back programmes used to artificially inflate the share price (and so the part of management remuneration related to the share price) and sometimes to fend off hostile takeovers.

Companies should be permitted to purchase their own shares only in exceptional circumstances. The payment of dividends in the absence of profits should also be prohibited. These proposals would boost enterprises' equity capital base and have a stabilising effect on the economy overall.

The shareholder-value approach has led to obscenely high management salaries. In the United States, where the dominance of the financial sector has gone furthest, management pay in relation to that of the average worker has risen from 30:1 in the 1970s to as much as 500:1 today. These figures show that the original aim of shareholder value, which was to subject the management solely to the interests of the owners, has had only limited success. Instead, management has been able to assert its own interests and enrich itself at the expense of the shareholders. Managers' remuneration systems should be changed. Arguments in favour of alternative remuneration and bonus systems for managers are based not only on appropriateness, but also on enterprise success itself. In the medium term, the success of a company results from prudent strategic decision-making and not from short-term actionism on the capital markets.

One important element of a new form of corporate governance would be the limiting of management's problematic short-term orientation, as well as its one-sided alignment with the interests of investors. For this purpose, all stakeholders in an undertaking, as well as their expectations, must be identified and given greater weight. What we should strive for is an increase in 'social' productivity, in respect of which improving the quality of work and environmental considerations should play an important role. Social productivity is a prerequisite of a real increase in prosperity, beyond monetary and numerical considerations. The goal should be to maintain innovation in the economy by means of competition between enterprises and to make this compatible with a socially and environmentally sustainable model of society.

Giving workers more influence over corporate decisions might actually help to make the companies more successful as workers tend to identify more with their company if they have a larger say. Germany is a good example of this. In Germany, there has traditionally been a strong role for workers' participation in company decision-making, with employee representatives on supervisory boards, and in the metal industry even on management boards. Yet, this tradition has by no means hindered German companies from becoming world leaders in their markets – just the opposite: German manufacturing companies are among the most productive and most competitive in the world.

In the case of private equity companies, which are often set up solely to 'plunder' other enterprises, specific regulations are required. Corporate governance standards – for example, those worked out by the OECD – do not apply to private equity companies, which are exempt from numerous regulations. This needs to change and enterprises need to be protected from predatory private equity companies. One possibility would be to give employees of a company some kind of say in proposals about profit transfers to private equity holding companies or to borrowing and lending funds when a private equity company has stakes in the enterprise. Private equity companies could also be forced to keep the equity of companies for a minimum time.

Even in the 'homeland' of shareholder value, corporate governance is undergoing something of a rethink. For example, more than half of US states have recently begun to adopt stakeholder laws which oblige managements to provide an impact assessment of their decisions on other stakeholders, including employees, customers, suppliers and communities. In this way, the United States is already, to a considerable extent, turning away from a one-sided focus on financial markets in enterprise management. Together with extensive regulation of financial markets, their actors and instruments, a revival of the stakeholder orientation can lead to a new corporate culture, one that is no longer subordinate to the financial markets. Whether or not this will happen is a political matter.

10

A NEW GROWTH PARADIGM

When discussing our concept of a better capitalism since the publication of our German book at the end of 2009, we are often confronted with the questions 'Why growth?' and 'Is further growth possible', and also 'If growth, then what growth?' These are important questions and we share the scepticism of many about the existing growth model. We want to discuss three very legitimate and important questions. First, why should we want further economic growth, given the level of production we have already achieved? Second, is it possible to have permanent economic growth without destroying the environmental fundamentals on which we all depend? And third, is it conceivable that we can actually find someone to buy and consume all the services and goods produced?

WHY MORE GDP IS STILL A WORTHWHILE GOAL

Let us address these questions one by one. Given the vast amounts of material goods we have at present available in rich societies, the sheer number of toys in the average child's room, the appliances in a middle-class household or just the number of cars in our streets, a legitimate question is: Why do we want (or need) more? In addition, we know from happiness research, which uses questionnaires to determine life satisfaction, that higher per-capita incomes does not necessarily make us happier. Empirically, from a level of average annual per-capita GDP of about US$27,500, increases do not seem to have a significant impact on reported well-being.[1] Obviously, there are some material wants whose fulfilment really does increase perceived well-being: housing, food, clothing, some appliances and participation in cultural events, for example. Beyond these basic needs, however, accumulating further goods does not add much further utility. Societies with an average GDP per capita of about

US$27,500 seem to be able to provide most of their populations with the goods and services necessary to satisfy their basic needs. Additional income beyond this threshold seems to be used for additional consumption which does not increase perceived well-being.

All this is true and is easily understood by most of us. If you already own a family house with 3,000 square feet, doubling this space will probably not increase your well-being much.

It is also well known that GDP is a poor indicator of welfare. If production and consumption harm the environment and the damage is repaired by governments, the repair work increases measured GDP without increasing welfare at all. Billions of dollars are spent, to take one more example out of many, on marketing activities – not all of which seem to increase our welfare. And GDP measures tell us nothing about the distribution of income or wealth. In this context, it is very sensible to consider different ways of measuring economic progress beyond the traditional measurement of GDP. For this reason, French President Nicolas Sarkozy has established a 'Commission on the Measurement of Economic Performance and Social Progress', headed by Nobel Prize winners Joseph Stiglitz and Amartya Sen and the French economist Jean-Paul Fitoussi. In their final report, the economists propose a number of additions to the traditional method of measuring GDP. For example, they propose that data should be provided on environmental degradation and there should be less focus on the production of goods and services in the economy as a whole (which might include the production of cruise missiles deployed in Iraq), and more on the amount of goods and services a typical household can consume. However, even these new measurement methods do not invalidate the quest for economic growth – they just help politicians to see when the growth path that society is embarking on really increases overall welfare and when it does not. Economic growth, properly measured, will still be the most efficient way to improve the well-being of many people.

There are a number of reasons why, despite these observations, increasing economic output still remains a worthwhile goal. Of course the quality of output should always be kept in mind. First, evidently, the world is not only made up of rich nations. While per-capita incomes are high in a handful of industrialised countries, a large number of countries still have per-capita incomes below the level at which we would assume that basic necessities are provided for. While these countries are often outside our main range of attention, the greatest part of humankind actually lives in such places. In large areas of Africa, India, China, Guatemala or even

Brazil, poverty is still widespread and there is a large-scale lack of basic necessities. Even if there is no outright starvation, the lack of these necessities has a permanent and significant negative impact on human well-being. In many developing and emerging countries, income and wealth distribution is very unequal. While parts of the Brazilian financial capital Sao Paolo may have living standards similar or superior to those in Europe, in the north of Brazil, there are hundreds of small communities where many people do not even own a pair of shoes of their own. The lack of decent footwear then translates into infestations with parasites which badly affect people's health, life expectancy and ultimately their quality of life.

In these countries (which by the way have not yet reached the US$27,500 threshold by quite some distance), redistributing income between the rich and the poor might help to fight poverty. However, given that the number of very rich in these countries is very small and the number of very poor is still extremely large, redistribution will not be sufficient to guarantee a decent standard of living to everyone. The standard of living would still be far below that of the rich countries and real material needs would still remain unsatisfied. Take the example of India: even taking into account the income of the super-rich and the fact that prices in India are below those of the United States, the overall GDP there is insufficient to provide a decent living. According to IMF data, in 2009 the average per-capita-GDP (including the income of the super-rich Indians as well as those living in dire poverty) was a little more than US$1,000 *a year* (or US$83 a month). Taking into account the low level of prices in India, this translates to a purchasing power of around US$3,000 a year or US$250 a month. Moreover, this sum is not what is actually available to the individual, as it includes the spending of the government sector and the military; this means that in fact there is perhaps US$150 per person per month to spend on food, housing, health, heating, energy, transportation, clothing and entertainment.

Here, increased economic output is clearly necessary to achieve a decent living for the broad population. Denying the populace the goods and services needed to satisfy their basic wants would be cruel and unfair. Hence, at least in these cases, economic growth seems to be the obvious solution.

The second reason supporting the quest for economic growth is that even in our rich and affluent societies, there are still pockets of poverty and want. Even in Germany, which is considered a rich country with a good social safety net, it makes one cry to walk into certain public housing projects and to see the kind of deprivation that children are living in. Of course, there are always the stories of welfare kings and queens, parents with a lot of children who live on welfare and who have their homes filled with the latest electronic equipment and the latest version of Sony's Playstation or Nintendo Wii. However, this is only part of the picture. Even in households where there are plenty of electronic gadgets, there might be a lack of good quality food (junk food is cheaper than fresh fruit and vegetables) or of books or other toys that are important for children's development. Moreover, not all parents on welfare know how to play the welfare system. In many of these cases, an improvement in the provision of goods and services might make the families concerned better off. In this context, one needs to keep in mind that economic output does not mean only the production of an additional DVD player or an additional car. Economic output can also be used for the provision of more social services, such as an additional support worker looking after the neglected children in a housing project.

One could of course argue that all this could be achieved with the average per-capita GDP of US$27,500, just by redistributing parts of the income: that is, by increasing taxes on the middle class and paying the support workers with the proceeds. This might even be true. However, redistribution on the scale required is probably impossible to achieve in a democratic society.

From behavioural economics and the happiness research quoted above, we know that people are more sensitive to the potential loss of something than to the possible gain of the same good or service, and hence put more weight on the former than on the latter. When it comes to financing social workers or other socially desirable projects, this means that paying for them by taxing additional income from economic growth is politically much more feasible than just taxing existing income or wealth. Thus, while more GDP might not automatically make us happier, it might help a good government to implement policies which do so for the poor.

These arguments acquire even more weight on a global scale. Clearly, large-scale redistribution from the United States and other developed countries to countries such as India and Bangladesh might help to eradicate poverty there (though not necessarily helping development, which does not automatically result from transfers). However, considering the huge scale of transfers necessary for this – taking into account the questionable effects on development and given the fact that even the tiny amount of Official Development Assistance the United States is providing today is already hugely unpopular – the prospect of such redistribution seems hopelessly unrealistic.

Productivity gains can be distributed between less working time and more production and consumption. Who should decide which of the two options or which combination of the two should be chosen? There is no 'good dictator' available who can enforce one of the options upon society. If people prefer to consume more and if the population is growing, the economy has to grow to satisfy these preferences. This leads us to the question whether sustainable growth is possible or not.

RECONCILING ECONOMIC GROWTH AND ECOLOGICAL SUSTAINABILITY

The second important question is whether our ecological surroundings can sustain a continued economic growth process. There is no doubt that growth rates in developed industrial countries must go down. If our per-capita incomes continue to grow at a rate of 2 per cent, this would mean a seven-fold rise in per-capita incomes over the coming century.[2] However, the question is whether we should and can have growth at all. Sceptics argue that economic growth inevitably brings with it an increase in the use of natural resources, be it fossil fuels, metals or just the use of our atmosphere as a sink for carbon dioxide and other pollutants. To make this clear: for ecological reasons it is simply not possible to continue with the existing type of growth for another century or so without disastrous consequences. Even if from now on there were no GDP growth in the world, the existing structure of production and consumption would not be sustainable. There are two key areas of importance: global warming and a scarcity of natural resources.

The world's temperature is getting warmer. There is no doubt that the world temperature has increased very rapidly in the past century and the warming process has accelerated in recent decades. And there can also be no doubt that this development will become very costly for humankind and the world economy. In a UK government review of climate change from the year 2006, a former Chief Economist of the World Bank, Nicholas Stern, summarised the results of a large research team. The general message of the Stern Review is that an increase in global temperature of more than 2°C will create huge and even incalculable costs. If no actions are taken, the report argues, 5 per cent of global GDP will be lost every year, now and forever. If a wider range of risks and impacts are taken into account, the costs could increase by up to 20 per cent of GDP or more. The problem is that the extent of future warming and its repercussions are highly uncertain. The negative effect may be more dramatic than what is thought today to be the most likely outcome. Recent years have deepened the understanding that a number of effects that have historically not been predicted can lead to a cumulative non-linear increase of world temperature. For example, higher temperature will drive more carbon dioxide in the atmosphere as drying soils, dying forests and warmer oceans release more gas.[3]

Most of the increase in greenhouse gas emissions comes from an increased global population and output growth in developing countries. Between 1976 and 2004, annual carbon dioxide (CO_2) emissions per capita in developed countries stagnated and fell even from slightly above 12 tons of CO_2 per capita to below 12 tons of CO_2 per capita. The group of developing countries still have a very low level of CO_2 emission, increasing between 1976 and 2004 from below 2 tons per capita to 4 tons per capita, with emissions increasing most markedly after the 1980s. This means that, under present conditions, any catching up in GDP per capita by developing countries leads to an unsustainable, strongly accelerating trend in CO_2 emissions.[4] In addition, population growth in developing countries is still substantial. We should also note that most of the 'dirty' industrial production is concentrated in developing countries. According to the International Energy Agency, annual energy-related CO_2 emissions in developed countries have increased between 1980 and 2010 only modestly from a level of 10 billion tons, and will probably reach 15 billion tons in 2030. The CO_2 emissions of transition countries stagnated at a level of around 4 billion tons, and this trend will probably continue over the next 20 years. However, it is estimated that developing countries have increased their CO_2 emissions from 4 billion tons in 1980 to over 10 billion tons in 2010, and this will grow to 20 billion tons in 2030.[5]

Today, the concentration of CO_2 in the atmosphere is around 430 parts per million (ppm), and in 2015 it will be around 450 ppm. In the Stern Review it was argued that a concentration of 500 ppm would already be dangerous. With a 95 per cent probability, the temperature then will be more than 2°C higher than in 1850, with a 3 per cent chance that warming will be above 5°C. In comparison, from 1850 until today, global average temperature has increased by only 0.8°C, a rise which was itself extremely fast in historical perspective. Many scientists argue that an atmospheric concentration of 500 ppm of CO_2 would in fact be much too dangerous and recommend bringing the level down to 400 ppm; this would reduce the likelihood of a temperature increase of more than 2°C to 50 per cent. Waiting another 30 years before taking effective action would lead to concentration levels of 525 to 550 ppm and would make it very difficult to avoid an increase to 600 ppm. As Stern puts it: 'That is extremely dangerous territory.'[6]

The vast majority of climate scientists argue that the greenhouse effect is due to human activity and is responsible for global warming. Emissions of greenhouse gases are too large to be absorbed by natural processes. As rain forests are cut down, the absorption of greenhouse gases is even further reduced. Only a small minority believes that global warming has natural explanations connected with certain activities of the sun. In spite of these small doubts about the reasons for climate change and uncertainties about how fast and to what extent the climate is changing, there is really no rational option except to assume that the majority of scientists – who are indeed not merely a group of do-gooders – are correct. Not to act would be to play Russian roulette, with the difference that there is more than one bullet in the pistol and we cannot even be sure that every chamber in the magazine is not fully charged. We might be very lucky, but the risk and the consequences of failure are extremely high.

The problem with global warming is not only higher temperature as such. Water has the biggest effect. The expected events are not only extreme weather conditions like droughts and floods, but also the melting of the polar ice and a rise in the sea level (in some scenarios by seven metres). Natural disasters, lost land by rising sea level and desertification of large areas will unavoidably lead to a new wave of migrations and to economic and political disturbances.

From 1950 until today, around 70 per cent of greenhouse gas emissions have come from developed countries (where only about 1 billion of the roughly 6.7 billion people in the world live). As emissions in OECD countries will increase only slowly in the future, most further emission growth will, as mentioned, come from developing countries.[7] The figures show that developing countries are central to the debate on global warming for several reasons. First, developing countries correctly argue that in the past developed countries were responsible for most of the emissions and that it would be unjust to burden the poorer countries with the whole burden of adjustment. Second, developing countries are the ones most affected by global warming. Often, they are geographically very vulnerable. Bangladesh, for example, will be severely hit by increasing sea levels. Parts of Africa are the regions that suffer most from droughts and parts of Asia are threatened by heavy monsoons. At the same time, these countries lack the resources to protect themselves against the effects of climate change. Even a modest climate change will substantially reduce the chances of smooth and swift development in many of the poorer countries. Third, without cooperation between developed and developing countries there will be no solution to the threat of global warming.

The second big problem is the limited reserves of natural resources. For example, the present world oil consumption is not sustainable as it will soon deplete all available reserves. And the world demand for oil is increasing. To reach the maximum point of cheap oil production – peak oil – is not a matter of many decades, the problem is more urgent. The International Energy Agency (2006) argued that non-OPEC oil production will peak within a few years. It pointed out that the world's growing demand will depend on oil production in Saudi Arabia, Iran and Iraq. For the future political stability of this region this is not good news. But in OPEC too the big and cheap oil fields are limited and will not be able to satisfy increasing demand quickly. There is still a lot of oil available, for example in oil sand and deep below the ocean. However, getting the oil out of the sand is costly and deep-sea extraction is not only costly but also risky. This also applies to the production of gas.[8] Without drastic changes even in optimistic scenarios, shortages and enormous price hikes are very likely in the coming decades. As with global warming, it would be irresponsible not to react quickly and then leave a much higher burden to future generations. One could hope that the likely onset of peak oil will slow down global warming. However, that would probably lead to the use of coal, with even bigger CO_2 emissions as a result.

Does the world have to stop growing to reduce, avoid or even solve these immense problems? We think that the answer to this question is clearly no. Under certain conditions, economic growth can be combined with meeting ecological needs. To solve the problems mentioned earlier, economic growth may in fact be necessary for the foreseeable future. As long as the economy creates growth while maintaining sustainable levels of greenhouse gas emissions and uses resource-saving technological innovations, economic growth is possible over an extended period of time even with limited resources. However, it is clear that infinite growth is not possible as long as growth needs a minimum constant amount of non-reproducible resources.[9] It is only if resources used become reproducible that permanent growth will be possible. This highlights the need for production and consumption that do not rely upon the use of non-reproducible inputs, at least in the long run. The physical input of materials such as steel, oil or minerals into the consumption and production process has to be replaced by the input of more knowledge about the best use of these resources and the use of reproducible inputs. As the production of knowledge is less resource-intensive than the production of physical goods, growth with sufficiently low greenhouse gas emissions and natural resource consumption is achievable.

Empirically, there is evidence that such an innovative process is possible. In fact, there are some countries that have cut back their CO_2 emission significantly despite having robust economic growth. Take the example of Sweden. In 1970, Sweden was emitting about 90 million tons of CO_2 per year by burning fossil fuels. By 2007, emissions had fallen to less than 50 million tons. During the same period, after correcting for inflation, Swedish GDP more than doubled. Sweden thus managed solid economic growth while significantly decreasing its carbon footprint. While Sweden might be an extreme case, as it used a lot of wind, hydropower and nuclear energy to bring down CO_2 emissions, this example shows that there are huge possibilities for saving of resources if policy-makers set the right framework and provide appropriate incentives. The Swedish example also shows how much room for efficiency gains exists in other countries: while the US GDP per capita measured in purchasing power in 2007 was only about 25 per cent above the Swedish level, the average resident of the United States emitted an annual 19.1 tons of CO_2, or almost four times as much as the average Swede. Or to put it differently: if the United States managed to get its CO_2 emission per unit of GDP down to the Swedish level, the country could cut emissions by almost three-quarters without any loss in economic output. The Swedish example also puts the issue of growing carbon dioxide emissions of China and other emerging markets in a different light: China in 2007 emitted 4.6 tons of CO_2 per capita, not even 10 per cent less than Sweden. Yet Chinese GDP per capita was not even a fifth of the Swedish GDP. Thus, if China used the same technology as Sweden, it could approach the Swedish level of per-capita economic output with a mere 10 per cent increase in CO_2 emissions.

Sceptics might now argue that maybe Sweden has just outsourced the production of goods which require a lot of CO_2 emission to China and is now importing these goods instead of producing them itself. This might be partly true. However, Sweden is not a deindustrialised country as one would expect if this were the main reason for the fall in emissions. It still has a sizable steel and car industry, both industries that are usually not regarded as being low in CO_2 emissions. This suggests that Sweden has managed to bring down CO_2 emissions by real efficiency increases rather than just by exporting the emission problem.

Of course, Sweden is a special case as in 2008 it produced 42 per cent of its electricity in nuclear power stations and around 47 per cent came from hydroelectric power.[10] Nuclear power is another example of Russian roulette. Accidents have a relatively low probability – if probabilities really can be calculated – but a major accident creates a huge disaster. In spite of these reservations the Swedish example shows that potential technological solutions can be found and natural conditions exploited. The same can be done by radically increased use of wind and solar energy. For example, in 2010, the German Federal Environment Agency published a thorough feasibility study of how far Germany could switch its electricity production to renewable sources. The surprising result: even assuming a constantly growing economy (with per-capita incomes growing by 65 per cent over the coming 40 years) and even with a growing manufacturing sector, it is feasible for Germany to produce 100 per cent of its electricity needs by 2050 from renewable sources. Of course, this shift would require huge efforts as Germany – with its dark winters, cloudy weather and relative lack of opportunities to produce hydroelectric power – does not have an environment particularly conducive to the production of renewable energy. However, according to the German Federal Environment Agency, this shift would be cheaper than the expected costs of the alternative path of continuing to emit CO_2 at the present rate. If Germany, a global manufacturing powerhouse, can shift to 100 per cent renewable energies, other countries with more favourable environmental conditions should be able to do so as well.

The crucial question is whether it is possible over a sustained period of time to maintain the process of permanent technological innovation which would be necessary to enable continuous economic growth with a decreasing use of resources and a sufficient reduction of dangerous emissions. This is a tough question to answer. No one can predict the future with certainty. We will thus never know whether this process can go on for all eternity. What is more important at the moment, though, is not whether this process is possible in the distant future, but for the next 10, 20 or 30 years.

And for a timeframe of only a few decades, one can be quite optimistic about the possibilities of technological innovation. We believe that with quick and radical changes in the quality of production and consumption, this is possible. If we can sustain the process of increasing energy efficiency and reducing use of resources, and can achieve low-carbon growth over this period, our grandchildren can in due course return to the debate about whether further economic growth is still feasible; but we might by then have managed to improve the lot of billions of people around the world who now live in poverty.

A 'GREEN NEW DEAL'

Markets do not only fail in the workings of financial systems and in creating sufficient employment and acceptable income distribution; they also fail fundamentally in their impacts on the natural world. Markets suffer from so-called external effects, which means that the price system does not accurately identify scarcities or costs, and that some goods can be used for free in spite of the fact that they are precious. Firms and households can pollute the atmosphere without any direct consequence for themselves. For example, greenhouse gas is emitted by driving cars and producing electricity without alerting the consumer or producer to the high costs involved in terms of global warming. The felling of trees in rain forests which absorb CO_2 inflicts costs that are greater than the price which can be achieved by selling the timber. Wherever such external effects come into play, a systemic gap is created between the cost paid by the individual buyer and the actual cost to society as a whole.

Moreover, the scarcity of natural resources is only reflected in an imperfect way. Future generations have no chance to bid for oil today. These effects result in extreme inefficiency and waste in market economies. An unregulated market mechanism is not even able to guarantee the continued existence of societies, a fact that Karl Polanyi pointed out as long ago as 1944. As prices give misleading signals, the capitalist machine has been developing technologies in the wrong direction. If nature had set the correct price, the technologies we use today and the physical world around us would look completely different. At this point, we do not even have to convince mainstream economists to become radical ecologists. If they take their own models seriously they must accept this fundamental and fatal failure of markets. The greenhouse effect is only one of the many examples of this type of market failure. Most countries have – while increasing their energy efficiency impressively over the past half century or so – continued to use more resources as they grew. Hence the speed and direction of innovation or at least of implementing innovations in this field has not been enough.

What is needed is an explicit economic policy that sets the framework to increase the direction and speed of innovation towards greater resource-efficiency and a method of production and consumption which combines economic growth with ecological sustainability for future generations. What is needed to stop global warming and avoid the negative effects of peak oil and shortage of other resources is a Green New Deal.[11] The old New Deal is associated with US President Franklin D. Roosevelt, who put forward a fundamentally new economic policy after the economic meltdown during the Great Depression in the 1930s, including the creation of new institutions and government interventions. A Green New Deal must confront even bigger problems than Roosevelt did. The present crisis is not only an economic and social one. There are also still unknown challenges in terms of global warming and resource shortages. And today it is much more a global crisis. For example the ecological challenges simply cannot be solved just on a national level or even within the group of developed countries.

Five elements for a Green New Deal seem to be crucial. The use of energy and other non-renewable resources has to come with a higher price tag. If oil remains as cheap as it was during most of the 1990s or even until the mid-2000s, the incentives for energy savings will remain low. Second, inventors and investors need to know that the price of energy and other non-renewable resources will remain high. Only if they can count on a certain minimum price for oil or other resources will they be sure that a successful resource-saving innovation will really pay in the future. The solution of these two points is relatively easy: introduce a heavy tax on the use of non-renewable resources and let it increase over time. The tax then becomes a kind of price floor for the use of these resources as even if the pre-tax price of oil, for example, falls to lower levels, the final sales price will remain high thanks to higher taxes. As we said earlier, the current fashion for using tradable emission permits, which is followed in the European Union among others, is not desirable as this approach causes large fluctuations in the price of resource use, depriving companies of a stable and predictable price floor – just one reason why we are against markets for carbon trading. In addition to changing the structure of prices towards their real costs, bans, rules and regulations are indispensable.

The third element is that governments need to create markets for new, environmentally friendly products. Companies are often deterred from developing new, energy-efficient products because they are not sure whether consumers will actually buy the new goods once they hit the markets. Some technologies only become viable if enough people are using them. A hydrogen-powered car will only be bought if people can rely on a sufficient network of refilling stations. At the same time, the private sector will not build a network of such stations before enough customers are likely to use it to make it profitable. Certain technologies might carry a stigma which prevents their quick dissemination. Hydrogen-powered cars for example, might be thought to be too dangerous by many people. In these cases, the government can take a leading role by procuring certain specific products. The announcement of the government's intention to have zero CO_2 emission standards for new public buildings from a certain date in the near future, or to only buy police cars with a certain maximum CO_2 emission, would help companies to be able to trust a stable demand for new products will develop, and so resolve the Catch-22 dilemma described above.

Fourth, governments need to promote innovation more directly. Some research projects might be too big or their outcome too uncertain for the private sector to undertake. Moreover, a particular innovation might not lead to a patented item that is commercially usable in itself, but might nonetheless provide some additional knowledge on resource efficiency which benefits the whole economy. In these cases, governments might have to increase direct funding for research institutions concerned with renewable energies and the increase of resource productivity.

Fifth, governments have to undertake comprehensive and long-term-oriented infrastructure projects which allow and enforce more ecologically friendly production and consumption. Energy production, public and private transport, public utilities and urban planning are examples where governments can change structures fundamentally. In many of these areas privatisation has gone too far and has not brought any positive effect except high profits for companies. A large public enterprise sector, especially in the field of basic infrastructure, can be used to drive radical changes towards more ecological consumption. Changes in the infrastructure, a changing structure of prices, and government support for green research and innovations can stimulate a long-term public and private investment dynamic which allows growth compatible with the solution of ecological challenges. In the medium term, without growth fundamental changes may even not be possible.

All of these things can in principle be brought forward by any of the leading economic blocs such as the United States, Europe or even some of the emerging market economies. Of course, if policies such as taxes on the use of resources are implemented unilaterally, there is the danger that resource-intensive industries will be relocated to areas where taxes are lower. Thus, some kind of coordination at the G-20 level is necessary. On the other hand, countries moving unilaterally towards higher pollution taxes might benefit from a higher pace of innovation in resource-saving technologies among their local companies. As a last resort, one could consider new policy instruments such as tariffs which vary according to the CO_2 intensity of a certain import.

Some economists have been arguing for a long time that inventions that increase resource efficiency might have a 'rebound effect' which in the end leads to more, not less, pollution and resource consumption. They argue that for example as cars get more fuel-efficient, the costs of travelling one mile will fall and thus the demand for miles travelled by automobile will increase. In the end, nothing has been gained. These economists usually cite a host of historical anecdotes to support their claim. For example, even though the efficiency of street lamps increased about 20-fold in the United Kingdom between 1920 and 1995, this was more than counteracted by an increase of the number and strength of lamps installed for street lighting. In the end, electricity consumption per mile of roads actually increased by a factor of 25.

Despite these vivid anecdotes, we think this argument is problematic, at least if one wants to draw lessons for the future. While the increased use of resources through economic growth might have outrun efficiency gains in the past, there is no reason in principle why this should always be the case, especially if governments intervene in order to prevent the excessive use of resources. One reason why energy consumption has grown so much over the past 150 years or so is that energy prices have not risen much in real terms. While the oil price might have increased quite strongly in dollar terms since the 1950s, the increase relative to the price of other goods and services has been muted. In fact, measured against the purchasing power of the dollar, a barrel of crude oil in the mid-1990s was not more expensive than in the year 1900. Only after 2005 did the oil price rise on a sustained basis to levels unknown before. In general, over the very long period of strong economic growth after the

Second World War (with the exceptions of the years just after the oil shocks) energy has remained disproportionately cheap. With oil remaining a bargain over such an extended period, it is no wonder that the demand for energy has outpaced the increases in energy efficiency. Yet, low oil prices are not a natural law. Governments could intervene in the energy markets as explained above, by putting a tax on energy consumption that increases every year. If the rate of increase is high enough, the use of services which consume a lot of energy such as air travel, heating or air conditioning will not become cheaper (but might even become more expensive) in spite of technological advances. If prices for these services do not fall or even increase, there is no reason to expect the demand for these services to increase more quickly than the savings from improved energy efficiency. Hence, a wise government policy should always be able to prevent the rebound effect.

WHAT WE CAN PRODUCE IN THE FUTURE

Some readers might now claim that we are contradicting ourselves: If we want to have economic growth, yet the demand for services that use a lot of energy such as air travel should not increase, *what* can then be additionally produced and sold? After all, the production of most everyday goods such as cars, houses, refrigerators or TV sets uses up non-renewable resources.

A part of the answer lies in the way GDP (and thus economic growth) is measured and computed. A surprisingly large number of people believe that economic output is only measured in the number of cars, DVD players or T-shirts our factories pour out each year. This impression is wrong for two reasons. First, GDP should take into account quality improvements. Second, a large (and growing) share of GDP is made up of services, parts of which are not very resource-intensive.

The first point is important as it means that shifting from the present bundle of consumer goods to more environmentally friendly goods and services might actually imply an increase in GDP and thus economic growth. An article that is more durable and more environmentally friendly is usually also more expensive than a traditional one, and also more valuable. If you want to buy a car today that consumes 6 litres of petrol every 100 kilometres (47 miles per gallon), you usually pay more than for a car that uses 10 litres every 100 kilometres (28 miles per gallon). For example, the Volkswagen Golf, a best-selling German car, is marketed in two versions; with a traditional engine consuming 6.4 litres (44 miles per gallon) it costs (at the time of writing; September 2010) 30 per cent less than the version that consumes only 3.8 litres (74 miles per gallon). Hence, the more fuel-efficient Golf adds 30 per cent more to measurements of GDP. Thus, if all cars produced in the future were of the fuel-efficient kind instead of the standard variety, value added in the car sector (and thus GDP for this part of the economy) would increase by 30 per cent, with no increase in the actual number of cars produced (and, if the new cars just replaced old ones, without any increase in the number of cars on the roads).

The second point is that new services are included in GDP in the same way as an additional TV set or an additional car produced. If we can get a person who is long-term unemployed (and has no realistic chance of entering the labour market) to go to our grandparents and read to them for two hours a day or take them out for a walk, GDP has increased (as long as the service is paid for). GDP is the sum of all goods and services produced and sold in a country. If a market is created for a certain service or its provision is increased in the realm of health, education, childcare, entertainment or care for the elderly, GDP increases. Of course, we need to find a way to pay for these services, but we have to pay for any additional kind of production or provision of services. As the service providers earn money which they can spend on other goods and services, and which also increases tax revenue, this should not be a problem from a macroeconomic perspective. Also if you look at it from a welfare point of view, the aggregate well-being in the society might actually be increased even more by the provision of such a new service than by the production of an additional TV.

Thus, a society in which your car would last for 30 years and uses 3 litres of petrol for 100 kilometres travelled, and where the elderly get a lot of personalised help and the average family eats organically grown food prepared by first-class cooks in fancy local restaurants three times a week, might have a higher GDP than our present-day society in which your car needs to be replaced after ten years, the elderly are only looked after for 30 minutes a week by their families, and most people eat a cheap pre-cooked meal just defrosted and heated in their old, energy-guzzling microwave. Moving from the latter to the former thus provides years of economic growth.

Market forces alone will most likely not lead to this kind of resource-conserving society. Again, governments need here to point the right direction, set incentives, adjust taxes and organise payment for certain services where for various reasons the private sector is not willing to fund these activities directly.

MORE LEISURE TIME

Closely related to the question of increasing resource efficiency is the ever-growing efficiency of labour. Technological progress not only makes energy and resources go further, but also leads to a continuous decline in the number of work hours needed to produce a car or a pair of shoes. Consequently, the amount of goods and services that can be produced in our society constantly increases.

As we have seen above, in principle this is a good development. We are still quite far away from a situation where all basic needs and wants even in the rich societies are satisfied, not to speak of the billions of people who live in poorer countries. A more equal distribution of income and a government with a stable and sufficient revenue basis can create the demand for this continuously increasing supply of goods and services.

However, even if a more balanced income growth can support a more balanced – and less crisis-prone – growth of consumption demand than the one we have observed over the past decades, it is far from clear that it will always suffice to keep demand up with a supply in a way that would result in the employment of all of the workforce with a standard 40-hour working week. It is important to recognise that the market does not automatically convert increasing productivity into higher economic output, as mainstream economists tend to claim, but can also lead to unemployment. The problem becomes more acute if the working-age population grows and, as a result, the labour supply increases. Capitalism is also devoid of any automatic mechanism for providing the additional population with more job opportunities. If, with growing prosperity, people really do not know what to spend their additional income on and they increase their savings for lack of spending opportunities, while at the same time the government cannot think of sensible ways to tax and spend the unused private income, there might be a long-term shortfall of aggregate demand below supply.

In this book, as a medium-term strategy we have proposed, first of all, boosting overall economic demand as a solution; among other options, this could be done by redistribution from richer households, with their lower tendency to consume, to poorer ones, whose tendency to consume is higher. However, there should be no dogma that production always has to increase, even taking into account the qualifications made above. In the long run, in mature societies increasing output per capita may cease to be an aim.

Rising productivity of course can also be used to provide more leisure time. This could also manifest itself in slower consumption growth and gradual reductions in working time. Working time reductions of various kinds must be considered by mature industrialised societies, and indeed have been many times since the beginning of industrialisation. Under the pressure of the subprime crisis and the sovereign debt crisis in Europe, there has been a tendency to increase working time within the framework of cost reduction strategies. This policy is senseless and merely serves to intensify unemployment problems. If in the long run growth is not preferred or not needed to increase welfare, working time has to be adjusted in such a way that unemployment does not become a problem.

Having said that, rapid reductions in working time are difficult. This has less to do with the system itself, which can function adequately with less growth, than with general social attitudes which are fixated on growth and the desire of many people who, despite fulfilling their basic material needs, wish to keep on consuming more – as Keynes observed in the 1930s.

The current debate on a new development model must not neglect such fundamental considerations. In particular, working time reductions should be part and parcel of any future economic and social model. Productivity increases can partly be used for working time reductions, to some extent at the expense of rises in real wages. People's willingness to go along with working time reductions will, of course, depend on income distribution. Those at the lower end of the income distribution in particular will be unwilling to cut their working time as they feel that they still have material needs to be satisfied. Only if distributional issues are addressed will they opt for shorter working hours.

CONCLUSION

A NEW TALE TO TELL

Many readers might now think that a 'decent capitalism' which combines the powerful dynamic innovative forces of capitalism with justice, equality, sustainability, human progress and stability is (still) wishful thinking. It might sound good, but is it not completely unrealistic? Change the rules of the game and shift the roles of governments, society and the market at the local, national and global level – and the powerful few who have been benefiting greatly from the current brand of capitalism might actually lose out.

However, we believe that the outlook for change is not that bleak, and we thus continue to argue very strongly for this kind of capitalism and change. First of all, economic history is full of deep shifts in opinion, followed by deep shifts in the structure of economic institutions. For example, it was long considered inconceivable that money should not be backed by precious metals. Today, no major currency is redeemable in gold or silver at the bank of issue any more. At the beginning of the Great Depression in the 1930s, it was believed that governments could and should do nothing to counteract economic swings. The New Deal in the 1930s in the United States under President Franklin Roosevelt fundamentally changed power relations in society, taming the financial system, strengthening unions and labour market institutions and changing income distribution. At about the same time, John Maynard Keynes turned such thinking upside down with his *General Theory*. Up until 2007, virtually no one would have believed that the UK and US governments would become shareholders in their biggest private banks. Today, large parts of the financial systems of both countries are dependent on the state or in public ownership. If such developments are accompanied by lasting changes in the relationship between market and state, major changes may also ensue in the economy as we know it. Naturally such swings are not only a result of a new (economic) idea or 'objective necessities' for a particular regulation or form of economic architecture. Just like political action, ideas rather follow the interests of those who are most powerful to articulate and enforce their notion of reality. For example, nationalising a bank – as we have seen a number of times during the latest crisis – does not mean that socialism is dawning somewhere on the horizon. One could even argue that the opposite is true. A bank might be nationalised or a banking system as a whole might be publicly bailed out *in order to preserve* a status quo relationship between government and the market.

Nonetheless, crises can be windows of opportunities for more radical change. They allow us to call into question all doctrines and interests which have been disseminated virtually unquestioned. They offer an opportunity to step back and reflect on what has gone wrong in the economy over the past few decades and why our economic system was overly flawed in too many respects. For many, market-liberal globalisation changed their lives for the worse. Many people's lives became more precarious and many more were socially excluded. Employment and social security systems were increasingly exposed to financial market tempests, while crises and new management methods threw career plans and thus people's lives into disarray from one day to the next. This is not only morally deeply offensive but also economically counterproductive, as we have shown in this book. A large and growing part of society feels itself to be at the mercy of ever more violent and uncontrollable markets. Social cohesion is jeopardised by apathy or even social unrest. In the face of such dangers, better regulation of globalisation at all levels is imperative. A crisis such as the latest one allows political and civil society actors to make a connection between the closure of a public library and the billion dollar bail-out for a mismanaged money institute. There is again rhetorical space for political antagonisms in our societies that were long silenced by the omnipresent noise of market liberalism.

One thing is very clear, however: a 'decent capitalism' will not be created by the profiteers of the current system of non-regulation. Their profits are built too heavily on certain prerogatives, which they will not just hand over to public control. Quite the opposite is true: it is mostly mere placebos that have been rubber-stamped by the global financial elite so far. For deeper reform, as we have argued in this book, the underlying power relations of current finance capitalism will have to change, which means that the relationship between states and markets will have to be radically rebalanced.

A necessary precondition for such change is new seismic insights into the functions and *dys*functions of markets and their actors, and telling the story of what has happened so that it gets heard and understood. Deep economic disruptions and crises vividly illuminate such a tale, since they open up the opportunity to shed a light on the fault lines of capitalism. Such breaking points have been the most notable symptoms of the excessive behaviour of deregulated domestic and international financial market actors on an unimaginable scale. Their specific incentive structure (bonus payments) combined with the structural necessity to outperform (benchmarking) and systemic lack of prudent oversight and regulation created a vicious circle which led in the late 2000s to one of the deepest crises of capitalism ever. However, as we have tried to show, to focus on a single aspect of such dysfunction in the system (like limiting bonus payments) would not be enough to break this vicious circle. This is why we have taken this deep look into our abysmal economic system. Isolating single destructive dynamics will not cure the system of its structural deficiencies. Fixes like the Dodd–Frank Wall Street Reform and the Consumer Protection Act in the United States or the German ban on some types of short-selling of financial products are steps in the right direction, but they do not tackle all or even the major roots of current capitalism's flaws.

It is a matter of arguments, political will and in the end political power, whether such first steps will be the start of a long struggle towards more far-reaching proposals and concrete measures which go beyond the cosmetic corrections so often seen. It is therefore very important to implement initial reforms in order to push forward for longer-term changes. However, such minor steps might have the effect of a placebo, giving false comfort to people and politicians while actually having no effect, or only minor impacts, on the functioning of the system. In that case, the reform momentum for a 'decent capitalism' might well lose steam and run out sooner rather than later. As the great thinker Theodor W. Adorno said in one of his last radio shows in the summer of 1969, there is a wondrous mechanism at work against any form of empowerment and emancipation. He reasoned that any serious attempt to bring society or the individual (ourselves!) to greater maturity is exposed to indescribable antagonisms, since all the selfish and greedy behaviour in the world immediately finds silver-tongued advocates, who will prove to you that everything you want is unnecessary or utopian. The political attempt to move forward has to build on the new tale to tell, fight the old fight against suppressive moments working for vested interests, and refrain from its own self-castration by handing over agenda-setting to those whose power is to be considerably reduced.

We proposed a reform agenda which can keep up the reform momentum as it goes beyond the narrow debate on financial regulation, which is a highly technical discourse led by experts in the finance ministries and finance faculties. And it is *because* we see the dysfunctions of many markets that we still argue for markets.

We have developed a set of proposals which would embed the market in such a way that it would be sufficiently free to unfold its essential and inimitable dynamism for the good of all, but at the same time to fail as infrequently as possible. Markets in a decent capitalism should release their full potential for innovation and efficiency. They are – alongside government regulations – a crucial instrument for a Green New Deal for a sustainable and just society.

Markets need private ownership, but they are also compatible with other forms of ownership. The best mixture of different forms of ownership cannot be decided theoretically; it depends on tradition and many other factors. Economic democracy is a key concept in this context. All stakeholders – especially the employees – should have a voice in enterprise decision-making. The debate on forms of corporate ownership needs to become more objective. The question of what form of ownership is chosen, for example for the provision of public services, such as water, electricity or refuse collection, should be decided on the grounds of expediency. Private enterprises are not more efficient if they focus mainly on paying lower wages and impose precarious working conditions.

Markets can be instruments of emancipation. Compared with market societies, all other types of societies that we have known so far, including planned economies, were characterised much more by direct relations of superiority and subordination between people, as well as by far less scope for individual choice, than market societies. In principle, markets offer a better framework for self-realisation than societies without them. They allow individual decisions about what goods to consume, how much to work or whether to start a business. It is true, however, that those who have no income or are unable to sell their labour are excluded from the market. By and large, it is usually the weakest in society who suffer this fate, whereas many of the rich receive income that is not earned by their own efforts. Many of those with high incomes live off interest and dividends from inherited wealth. Unregulated markets result in ever-greater differences in income distribution and social participation.

As we have shown, financial markets in particular tend towards excesses. Because these markets – in contrast to, say, the market for shirt buttons – have an effect on the economic system as a whole, the state must step in when correction is needed. Other markets, such as the labour market, also tend towards socially undesirable outcomes. And there cannot be any doubt that the market has been leading to a gigantic failure in the area of ecological problems. In a nutshell: the market is a good servant, but a bad master. It must be given clear tasks, clear rules and clear limits.

In addition to limiting market forces, however, our proposals also have another very important dimension: the intention to make the international open market economy more robust and durable. The current market-liberal project carries with it the risk that globalisation will be called into question and discredited, giving rise to a dramatic political backlash against the globally interconnected economy and societies. Already during the latest crisis there have been renewed tendencies to pursue national interests at the expense of other countries. Some of the stimulus packages adopted around the world contained elements which stimulated the purchase of domestic products. In almost all of them, care was taken that the bulk of the funds did not end up being spent on imports and so benefiting neighbouring countries. We see a real danger that if the consequences of the subprime crisis are not overcome and politicians do not manage to bring ecologically and socially sustainable prosperity to the people, political forces will lead to a disintegration of the world economy into its separate parts.

The development of protectionism or competitive devaluations, not to mention denial of credit to countries experiencing major currency crises, cannot be ruled out. This would plunge us back to the period between the two world wars when economic recovery was repeatedly scuppered and the world economy plunged deeper and deeper into crisis. It would serve only to impede the positive elements of globalisation, which in recent decades have helped to free millions of people from poverty, particularly in Asia. There is nothing wrong with international trade in itself, which today bestows upon us an abundance of goods and services unimagined in the past, although of course such trade must be fair and take into account the ecological effects of transportation. A collapse of globalisation, such as occurred after the First World War, would also make it difficult to solve many of the urgent problems facing humanity, not least the environmental crisis and the shortage of natural resources such as oil or water. By their very nature, these problems require a global approach.

The argument that one's own reform proposals are the only way of averting a catastrophe should naturally be made with some caution. It is quite possible that the worst will be a long time coming. But even if the crisis does not result in the collapse of the globally integrated economy, action is urgently needed. As we have just experienced, a global economic crisis can come upon us at any time with little warning, and throw millions of people into unemployment and poverty. If we fail to act after such a crisis of capitalism, despite having the technology that enables us to do so, we will be responsible for future deterioration of the economy and society.

NOTES

CHAPTER 1

1. On this, see the influential contributions by Friedman (1953) and Johnson (1972).
2. OPEC (the Organization of Petroleum Exporting Countries) was founded in 1960 and includes most Arab and some African and Latin American states. In the 1970s it produced more than 50 per cent of the world's oil, falling to around 40 per cent today. In reaction to the Arab-Israeli Yom Kippur war in 1973, the oil price rose rapidly. In 1979, the Islamic revolution in Iran triggered a second oil shock.

CHAPTER 2

1. Cf. Shiller (2008).
2. Cf. Dodd (2007).
3. Cf. Dodd (2007).
4. Cf. IMF (2008). The 'savings & loan' crisis in the United States in the 1980s, which was also a real-estate crisis, was of similar dimensions (cf. Hellwig 2008: 3ff). However, it proved possible to contain the latter's negative repercussions.
5. Cf. Cardarelli, Igan and Rebucci (2008).
6. Cf. Rajan (2005).
7. Cf. Williamson (2005).
8. Cf. Rodrik (1998) and Stiglitz (2004).
9. Cf. Shiller (2008a).
10. Cf. on this and also on what follows Lazonick (2008).
11. See Lucas (1981), Sargent (1979) and Sargent and Wallace (1976).
12. See Shackle (1958).
13. Cf. Black and Scholes (1973).
14. Cf. Hellwig (2008), p. 31.
15. IMF (2010).
16. Cf. Stiglitz (2004).

CHAPTER 3

1. See for example Friedman (1953); Johnson (1972).
2. Cf. Dornbusch (1976).
3. Paul Krugman and Maurice Obstfeld (2006: 488) show clearly that every version of the purchasing power parity theory fares badly.
4. Cf. Schulmeister (2008).
5. Cf. Williamson (2005).
6. Cf. Eichengreen and Hausmann (2005).
7. Cf. Kaminsky and Reinhart (1999).
8. Fed (2010).
9. As sources see IMF COFER (2010) and IMF (2010).
10.   Cf. Dooley, Folkerts-Landau and Garber (2003).
11. Cf. UN (2009) and Stiglitz (2006).
12. Cf. Krugman (2007).
13. For a comprehensive debate see Helleiner and Kirshner (2009).
14. Cf. Herr (1997).
15. Cf. Naughton (2007) and Herr (2008, 2010).
16. CIA (2010).
17. Cf. Dullien and Fritsche (2009) and Herr and Kazandziska (2007).

CHAPTER 4

1. Cf. Friedman (1968).
2. Cf. Lucas 1981.
3. Cf., in particular, Layard, Nickell and Jackman (1991).
4. Cf. Keynes (1930); Herr (2009).
5. Cf. Soskice (1990).
6. Cf. OECD (2009b).
7. Cf. AMECO (2010); European Commission (2007).
8. On this argument, see in particular Kalecki (1969); for a reformulation, see Hein (2008).
9. Sraffa (1960) made clear that the functional distribution of income can be explained in a Keynesian way by giving the profit rate or in a classical way by giving wages.
10. See ILO (2008).
11. We use here the Gini coefficient (see OECD Glance 2009).
12. Cf. Piketty and Saez (2006).
13. Cf. OECD Glance (2009).
14. Cf. Levy and Temin (2010).
15. Cf. Reich (2010).
16. See Blinder and Yellen (2001: 35ff).
17. Cf. Streeck (2009).
18. Bispinck and Schulten (2009: 203).
19. Cf. Bosch, Kalina and Weinkopf (2008: 425).

20. Cf. Naughton (2007) and Zenglein (2008).

CHAPTER 5

1. *Guardian*, Thursday 22nd July
2. For a survey of individual measures, see OECD (2009a).
3. Together, Brazil and China have only about half of the GDP of the US economy. In addition, consumption, especially in China, is a much smaller share of GDP than in the United States.
4. For the Japanese case see Herr and Kazandziska (2010).

CHAPTER 6

1. In a growing economy, this is entirely compatible with significant surpluses or deficits. With growth in nominal GDP of 5 per cent (3 per cent real and 2 per cent inflation), a sector can show a financing deficit of 3 per cent of GDP forever, without its net indebtedness ever rising above 60 per cent of GDP.
2. For a more detailed description of this and other functions of the financial system, see Priewe and Herr (2005: 140ff).
3. This was stressed by Keynes (1936).
4. The economic historian Charles Kindleberger (1986) provides a convincing account of this.
5. For an analysis of the inner life of the Washington Consensus, see Kellermann (2006).
6. Keynes (1926: 116).

CHAPTER 7

1. Funnell, Jupe and Andrew (2009).
2. See OECD (2001).
3. One example of this is the furniture store IKEA. IKEA stores usually pay a license fee to a foreign parent company for permission to use the IKEA name and business model. In this way, IKEA's profits and so tax liabilities are reduced.
4. Cf. Büttner and Ruf (2007) and Oestreicher and Spengel (2003).
5. Cf. Weichenrieder (2007).
6. Cf. Kellermann, Rixen and Uhl (2007).
7. Cf. Kellermann and Kammer (2009).
8. Cf. Dullien (2008).
9. For the following paragraphs also see Herr and Kazandziska (2011).
10. Cf. IMF (2010); AMECO (2010).
11. Cf. AMECO (2010), IMF (2010).
12. 'Furthermore, it seems unlikely that the influence of banking policy on

the rate of interest will be sufficient by itself to determine an optimum rate of investment. I conceive, therefore, that a somewhat comprehensive socialisation of investment will prove the only means of securing an approximation to full employment; though this need not exclude all manners of compromises and of devices by which public authority will cooperate with private initiative' (Keynes 1936: 378).

13. Cf. Blinder and Yellen (2001).

CHAPTER 8

1. Cf. Soskice (1990).
2. Cf. Pollin, Brenner and Wicks-Lim (2008).
3. Cf. Card and Krüger (1995) who give an overview about the theoretical and empirical debate on minimum wages; also see Herr, Kazandziska and Mahnkopf-Preprotnik (2009).
4. Cf. Taleb (2005).
5. Cf. OECD: Stat (2009).

CHAPTER 9

1. Bonus payments to managers should not be tax deductible as operating expenses. Share options should be taxed as income when they are exercised in accordance with their current value.
2. The former German Chancellor Helmut Schmidt, himself an economist and by no means a radical, agrees with the feasibility and sense of this proposal, when he writes: 'Financial investments and financial credits in favour of such enterprises and persons legally registered in tax and regulatory shelters [should be] forbidden' (Schmidt 2009).
3. Cf. for example, Larosière et al. (2009).
4. A similar proposal is made by the British economist Charles Goodhart (2009: 30ff).
5. Cf. FSF (2008).
6. For a more comprehensive debate of reform proposals for the financial system, see Dullien and Herr (2010) which can be downloaded at http://library.fes.de/pdf-files/id/ipa/07242.pdf.
7. Cf. Kindleberger (1986).
8. Cf. Kellermann (2006; 2009).
9. Compare in this connection the proposals which Keynes presented at the negotiations on the Bretton Woods system (Keynes 1969).
10. 'The assignment for the Bank of Japan and ECB would be to keep exchange rates fixed while that for the expanded Federal Reserve would be to stabilize the price level. The Policy Committee of the Federal Reserve (now the Open Market Committee) would incorporate Japanese and European as well as American experts. A nine-member

Committee might include four Americans, three Europeans and two Japanese. Members of the Committee should be independent of their governments (as are, theoretically, members of the Governing Council of the ESCB). The expanded Fed would make the decisions about tightening or loosening credit. There would be a common target for monetary policy. ... Members would then cast votes for tightening or loosening credit just as the three central banks do today. There would also be a formula for redistributing seignorage, just as in the ECB' (Mundell 2000).

11. Interventions were combined with sterilisation policy. In this case the central bank issues own securities to decrease the liquidity created by its foreign exchange interventions.

12. It is beyond the scope of this book to describe capital controls in detail. For those who want to read more, good accounts can be found in articles by Akira Ariyoshi et al. (2000) and John Williamson (2005).

13. See Keynes (1969); see also Stiglitz (2006: Chapter 9).

14. Cf. Ocampo (2009: 10).

15. Cf. on these proposals Stiglitz (2006: Chapter 8) or Kellermann (2006).

16. For a description of this mechanism, see Herr (2008, 2010).

CHAPTER 10

1. The income level reported in the literature on happiness suggest that the level at which it does not increase any more is usually around $20,000 in 1995 prices. As prices have risen significantly in the past 15 years, we have translated this into the new value of $27,500 in 2010 prices, using inflation data. For an accessible introduction to happiness research, see Layard (2006).

2. The reason that GDP would increase more than sevenfold over the coming century is compound growth, by which the growth does not only apply on the original level, but on the accumulated level.

3. Cf. Stern (2007: XVff); Green New Deal Group (2008).

4. Cf. Stern (2009: 19ff).

5. Cf. International Energy Agency (2006).

6. Stern (2009: 40), for the data see Stern (2009: 38ff).

7. Cf. Stern (2009: 23).

8. Cf. Green New Deal Group (2008).

9. Actually, even an existing level of production is not possible for eternity, if non-reproducible resources are needed.

10 Cf. World Nuclear Association (2010)

11. For the basic ideas of a Green New Deal see for example Green New Deal Group (2008); Stern (2009); Pollin, Brenner and Wicks-Lim (2008); Friedman (2009).

BIBLIOGRAPHY

Akerlof, G.A. and Shiller, R.J. (2010) *Animal Spirits*, Princeton University Press, Princeton, NJ.

AMECO (2010) *Annual Macroeconomic Database*, European Commission, Brussels.

Ariyoshi, A., Habermeier, K., Laurens, B., Otker-Robe, I., Canales-Kriljenko, J.I. and Kirilenko, A. (2000) *Capital Controls: Country experiences with their use and liberalisation*, IMF, Washington D.C.

Bispinck, R. and Schulten, T. (2009) Re-Stabilisierung des deutschen Flächentarifvertragssystems, *WSI Mitteilungen*, Vol. 62, pp. 201–17.

Black, F. and Scholes, M. (1973) The pricing of options and corporate liabilities, *Journal of Political Economy*, Vol. 81, pp. 637–54.

Blinder, A. and Yellen, J.L. (2001) *The Fabulous Decade: Macroeconomic lessons from the 1990s*, Century Foundation Press, New York.

Bosch, G., Kalina, T. and Weinkopf, C. (2008) Niedriglohnbeschäftigte auf der Verliererseite, *WSI Mitteilungen*, Vol. 61, pp. 423–29.

Büttner, T. and Ruf, M. (2007) Tax incentives and the location of FDI: evidence from a panel of German multinationals, *International Tax and Public Finance*, Vol. 14, pp. 151–64.

Card, D. and Krüger A.B. (1995) *Myth and Measurement: The new economics of the minimum wage*, Princeton University Press, Princeton.

Cardarelli, R., Igan, D. and Rebucci, A. (2008) The changing housing cycle and the implications for monetary policy, *International Monetary Fund, World Economic Outlook*, April, pp. 103–32.

CIA (2010) *The World Factbook*, CIA, Washington DC.

Cohen, B.J. (2009) Towards a leaderless currency system, in E, Helleiner and J. Kirshner (eds), *The Future of the Dollar*, Cornell University Press, Ithaca.

Dodd, R. (2007) Subprime: tentacles of a crisis, *Finance and Development*, IMF, Vol. 44, No. 4, pp. 15–19.

Dooley, M., Folkerts-Landau, D. and Garber, P. (2003) *An Essay on the Revived Bretton Woods System*, NBER (National Bureau of Economic Research) Working Paper No. 9971.

Dornbusch, R. (1976) Exchange rate expectations and monetary policy, *Journal of International Economics*, Vol. 6, pp. 231–44.

Dornbusch, R. (1990) *From Stabilisation to Growth*, National Bureau of Economic Research Working Paper, No. W3302, Cambridge, Mass.

Dornbusch, R. and Frankel, J. (1988) The flexible exchange rate system: experience and alternatives, in S. Borner (ed.), *International Finance and Trade in a Polycentric World*, London.

Dullien, S. (2008) Eine Arbeitslosenversicherung für die Eurozone: Ein Vorschlag zur Stabilisierung divergierender Wirtschaftsentwicklungen, in *der Europäischen Währungsunion*, SWP-Studie 2008/S01, Berlin.

Dullien, S. and Fritsche, U. (2009) How bad is divergence in the euro zone? Lessons from the United States and Germany, *Journal of Post Keynesian Economics*, Vol. 31(3), pp. 431–57.

Eichengreen, B. and Hausmann, R. (eds) (2005) *Other People's Money: Debt domination and financial instability in emerging market economies*, University of Chicago Press, Chicago.

European Commission (2007) *The Labour Income Share in the European Union*, European Commission, Brussels.

Fama, E. (1970) Efficient capital markets: a review of theory and empirical work, *Journal of Finance*, Vol. 25, pp. 383–417.

Fed (2010) *Fedstats: Economic and Financial Data for the United States*, Federal Reserve Bank of St Louis, http://www.stlouisfed.org/

Fisher, I. (1933) The debt-deflation theory of great depressions, *Econometrica*, Vol. 1, pp. 337–57.

Friedman, M. (1953) The case for flexible exchange rates, in M. Friedman, *Essays in Positive Economics*, University of Chicago Press, Chicago.

Friedman, M. (1968) The role of monetary policy, *American Economic Review*, Vol. 58, pp. 1–17.

Friedman, T. (2009) *Hot, Flat and Crowded*, London, Penguin.

FSF (Financial Stability Forum) (2008) Ongoing and recent work relevant to sound financial systems, Cover note by the Secretariat for the FSF meeting on 29–30 September 2008, www.financialstabilityboard.org/publications/on_0809.pdf.

Funnell, W., Jupe, R. and Andrew J. (2009) *In Government We Trust: Market failure and the delusions of privatisation*, Pluto Press, London.

Galbraith, J.K. (1967) *The New Industrial State*, Houghton Mifflin, Boston.

Goodhart, C.A.E. (2009) *The Regulatory Response to the Financial Crisis*, Edward Elgar, Cheltenham, UK.

Green New Deal Group (2008) A Green New Deal: joined-up policies to solve the triple crunch of the credit crisis, climate change and high oil prices, http://www.neweconomics.org/publications/green-new-deal.

Hein, E. (2008) *Money, Distribution, Conflict and Capital Accumulation*, Palgrave Macmillan, Houndmills.

Helleiner, E. and Kirshner, J. (eds) (2009) *The Future of the Dollar*, Cornell University Press, Ithaca.

Hellwig, M. (2008) *Systemic Risk in the Financial Sector: An analysis of the subprime-mortgage crisis*, Max Planck Institute for Research on Collective Goods, Bonn.

Herr, H. (1997) The international monetary system and domestic policy, in D.J. Forsyth and T. Notermans (eds), *Regime Changes: Macroeconomic policy and financial regulations in Europe from the 1930s to the 1990s*, Berghahn Books, Providence, RI.

Herr, H. (2008) Capital controls and economic development in China, in P. Arestis and L.F. De Paule (eds), *Financial Liberalisation and Economic Performance in Emerging Markets*, Edward Elgar, Cheltenham.

Herr, H. (2009) The labour market in a Keynesian economic regime: theoretical debate and empirical findings, *Cambridge Journal of Economics*, Vol. 33, pp. 949–65.

Herr, H. (2010) Credit expansion and development: a Schumpeterian and Keynesian View of the Chinese miracle, *Intervention: European Journal of Economics and Economic Policy*, Vol. 7, pp. 71–90.

Herr, H. (in press) Money, expectations, physics and financial markets: paradigmatic alternatives in economic thinking, in H. Ganssmann (ed.), New *Approaches to Monetary Theory: Interdisciplinary perspectives*, Routledge, Abingdon.

Herr, H. and Kazandziska, M. (2007) Wages and regional coherence in the European Monetary Union, in E, Hein, J. Priewe and A. Truger (eds), *European Integration*, Metropolis Verlag, Marburg.

Herr, H. and Kazandziska, M. (2010) Asset price bubble, financial crisis and deflation in Japan, in S. Dullien, E. Hein, A. Truger and T. van Treek (eds), *The World Economy in Crisis: The return of Keynesianism?*, Metropolis, Marburg.

Herr, H. and Kazandziska, M. (in press) *Macroeconomic Policy Regimes in Western Industrial Countries: Theoretical foundation, reform options, case studies*, Routledge, Abingdon.

Herr, H., Kazandziska, M. and Mahnkopf-Praprotnik, S. (2009) The theoretical debate about minimum wages, Global Labour University Working Paper, No. 6, February 2009, Berlin.

ILO (International Labour Organisation) (2008) *Global Wage Report 2008/09*, ILO, Geneva.

IMF (International Monetary Fund) (2008) *Financial Stress and Deleveraging: Macro-financial implications and policy*, Global Financial Stability Report, October, Washington, D.C.

IMF (2010) World Economic Outlook, data, Washington, D.C. http://www.imf.org/external/pubs/ft/weo/2010/02/index.htm.

IMF COFER (2010) database, Washington D.C. www.imf.org/external/np/sta/cofer/eng/index.htm.

Inflationdata.com (2010) http://www.inflationdata.com/inflation/.

International Energy Agency (2006) *World Energy Outlook 2006*, IEA, Paris.

Johnson, H.G. (1972) The case for flexible exchange rates, 1969, in H.G.

Johnson, *Further Essays in Monetary Economics*, Allen & Unwin, Winchester.

Kalecki, M. (1969) *Theory of Economic Dynamics*, A.M. Kelley, New York.

Kaminsky, G.L. and Reinhart, C. (1999) The twin crises: the causes of banking and balance-of-payments problems, *American Economic Review*, Vol. 89, pp. 473–512.

Kellermann, C. (2006) *Die Organisation des Washington Consensus: Der Internationale Währungsfonds und seine Rolle in der internationalen Finanzarchitektur*, transcript Verlag, Bielefeld.

Kellermann, C. (2009) *Der IWF als Hüter des Weltgelds? Zum chinesischen Vorschlag einer globalen Währung*, Friedrich-Ebert-Stiftung, Internationale Politikanalyse, Berlin.

Kellermann, C. and Kammer, A. (2009) Deadlocked European tax policy: which way out of the competition for the lowest taxes?, *Internationale Politik und Gesellschaft* and *International Politics and Society*, No. 2, pp. 127–41.

Kellermann, C., Rixen, T. and Uhl, S. (2007) *Unternehmensbesteuerung europäisch gestalten*, *Internationale Politikanalyse*, Friedrich-Ebert-Stiftung. http://library.fes.de/pdf-files/id/04761.pdf.

Keynes, J.M. (1926) *The End of Laissez-Faire*, Hogarth Press, London.

Keynes, J.M. (1930) *Treatise on Money, Vol. I: The pure theory of money*, in *Collected Writings*, Vol. V, London and Basingstoke 1979.

Keynes, J.M. (1933) [1973] *Towards the General Theory, Collected Writings, Vol. 8*, Macmillan, London.

Keynes, J.M. (1936) [2007] *The General Theory of Employment, Interest and Money*, Macmillan, London.

Keynes, J.M. (1937) The general theory of employment, *Quarterly Journal of Economics*, No. 51, pp. 209–23.

Keynes, J.M. (1969) Proposals for an international clearing union, in J.K. Horsfield (ed.), *The International Monetary Fund 1946–1965, Vol. 3, Documents*, Washington DC.

Kindleberger, C.P. (1986) *The World in Depression, 1929–1939*, 2nd enlarged edn, University of California Press, Berkeley.

Kindleberger, C.P. (1996) *Manias, Panics, and Crashes: A history of financial crises*, 3rd edn, Basic Books, New York.

Krugman, P. (2007) *The Conscience of a Liberal*, W.W. Norton & Co., New York.

Krugman, P. (2009) *The Return of Depression Economics and the Crisis of 2008*, Norton, New York.

Krugman, P. and Obstfeld, M. (2006) *Internationale Wirtschaft*, 7, Auflage, München.

Larosière, J. et al. (2009) *Larosière Report for the European Commission, High Level Group on Financial Supervision in the EU*, European Commission, Brussels.

Layard, R. (2006) *Happiness: Lessons from a new science*, Penguin, London.

Layard, R., Nickell, S. and Jackman, R. (1991) *Unemployment:*

Macro-economic performance and the labour market, Oxford University Press, Oxford.

Lazonick, W. (2008) The quest for shareholder value: stock repurchases in the US economy, www.uml.edu/centers/CIC/Lazonick_Quest_for_Shareholder_Value_20081206.pdf.

Levy, F. and Temin, P. (2010) Institutions and wages in post-World War II America, in C. Braun and B. Eichengreen (eds), *Labour in the Era of Globalisation*, Cambridge University Press, Cambridge.

Lind, D. (2010) *Between Dream and Reality*, Working Paper for FES Nordic Countries, Friedrich Ebert Foundation, Stockholm, http://www.fesnord.org/media/pdf/100308_Daniel%20Lind%20english.pdf.

Lucas, R.E., Jr. (1981) *Studies in Business Cycle Theory*, MIT Press, Cambridge, Mass.

Marx, K. (1867) *Das Kapital: Kritik der politischen Ökonomie, Band I*, Marx-Engels-Gesamtausgabe, Zweite Abteilung, Bd. 5, Berlin.

Minsky, H.P. (1975) *John Maynard Keynes*, Columbia University Press, New York.

Mundell, R. (2000) Currency areas, exchange rate systems and international monetary reform, Paper delivered at Universidad del CEMA, Buenos Aires, Argentina, 17 April 2000, www.columbia.edu/~ram15/cema2000.html.

Naughton, B. (2007) *The Chinese Economy: Transition and growth*, MIT Press, Cambridge, Mass.

Ocampo, J.A. (2009) A 7-Point Plan for Development Friendly Reform, in *Re-Defining the Global Economy*, Dialogue on Globalisation, Occasional Papers, Friedrich Ebert Foundation, New York.

OECD (2001) *Transfer Pricing Guidelines for Multinational Enterprises and Tax Administrations*, OECD, Paris.

OECD (2009), The effectiveness and scope of fiscal stimulus, *Economic Outlook Interim Report*, Chapter 3, March, OECD, Paris.

OECD (2009a), Addressing the labour market challenges of the economic downturn: a summary of country responses to the OECD-EC questionnaire, Background paper for the OECD Employment Outlook 2009, Paris.

OECD (2009b) *Economic Outlook*, No. 85, Paris.

OECD (2009c) Trade union density in OECD countries, 1960–2007, www.oecd.org/dataoecd/25/42/39891561.xls.

OECD Glance (2009) *OECD: Society at a Glance 2009*, OECD Social Indicators, http://www.oecd.org/document/24/0,3343,en_2649_34637_2671576_1_1_1_1,00.html.

OECD Stat (2009) OECD, Paris.

Oestreicher, A. and Spengel, C. (2003) Steuerliche Abschreibung und Standortattraktivitat, in *ZEW Wirtschaftsanalysen Band 66*, ZEW, Mannheim.

Piketty, T. and Saez, E. (2006) How progressive is the U.S. federal tax system? A historical and international perspective, NBER Working Papers 12404.

Polanyi, K. (1944) [2001] *The Great Transformation*, Beacon Press, Boston.

Pollin, R., Brenner, M. and Wicks-Lim, J. (2008) *A Measure of Fairness: The economics of living wages and minimum wages in the United States*, Cornell University Press, Ithaca, NY.

Pollin, R., Garret-Peltier, H., Heintz, J. and Scharber, H. (2008) *Green Recovery: A program to create good jobs and start building a low-carbon economy*, CAP, Washington DC.

Posner, R.A. (2009) *A Failure of Capitalism: The crisis of '08 and the descent into depression*, Harvard University Press, Cambridge and London.

Priewe, J. and Herr, H. (2005) *The Macroeconomics of Development and Poverty Reduction: Strategies beyond the Washington Consensus*, Nomos Verlag, Baden-Baden.

Rajan, R.G. (2005) Has financial development made the world riskier? National Bureau of Economic Research Working Paper, No. W11728, Cambridge, Mass.

Rajan, R.G. (2010) *Fault Lines: How hidden fractures still threaten the world economy*, Princeton University Press, Princeton and Oxford.

Rappaport, A. (1986) *Creating Shareholder Value: The new standard for business performance*, Free Press, New York.

Rappaport, A. (2005) The economics of short-term performance obsession, *Financial Analysis Journal*, No. 61, pp. 65–79.

Reich, M. (2010) Minimum wages in the United States, politics, economics, and econometrics, in C. Braun and B. Eichengreen (eds), *Labour in the Era of Globalisation*, Cambridge University Press, Cambridge.

Rodrik, D. (1998) Who needs capital-account convertibility? *Essays in International Finance*, No. 207.

Roubini, N. and Mihm, S. (2010) *Crisis Economics: A crash course in the future of finance*, Penguin, New York.

S&P and Case-Shiller (n.d.) Home price indices (Composite-10 CSXR), www.homeprice.standardandpoors.com.

Sargent, T.J. (1979) *Macroeconomic Theory*, Academic Press, New York.

Sargent, T.J. and Wallace, N. (1976) Rational expectations and the theory of economic policy, *Journal of Monetary Economics*, Vol. 87, pp. 169–83.

Schmidt, H. (2009) Wie entkommen wir der Depressionsfalle?, *Die Zeit*, 15 January 2009.

Schulmeister, S. (2008) Profitability of technical currency speculation: the case of yen–dollar trading 1976–2007, WIFO Working Papers, 325/2008, Vienna.

Schumpeter, J.A. (1926) *Theorie der wirtschaftlichen Entwicklung, 2*, Auflage, München u.a.

Sen, A. (1999) *Development as Freedom*, Oxford University Press, Oxford.

Shackle, G. (1958) *Time in Economics*, North Holland, Amsterdam.

Shiller, R. (2008) *The Subprime Solution*, Princeton University Press, Princeton.

Soskice, D. (1990) Wage determination: the changing role of institutions in advanced industrial countries, *Oxford Review of Economic Policy*, Vol. 6, pp. 36–61.

Sraffa, P. (1960) *Production of Commodities by Means of Commodities: Prelude to a critique of economic theory*, Cambridge University Press, Cambridge.

Stern, N. (2007) *The Economics of Climate Change: The Stern review*, Cambridge University Press, Cambridge.

Stern, N. (2009) *The Global Deal: Climate change and the creation of a new era of progressive prosperity*, Public Affairs, New York.

Stiglitz, J.E. (2004) Capital-market liberalisation, globalisation, and the IMF, *Oxford Review of Economic Policy*, Vol. 20, pp. 47–71.

Stiglitz, J.E. (2006) *Making Globalisation Work*, Penguin, London.

Stiglitz, J.E. (2010) *Freefall: Free markets and the sinking of the global economy*, Allen Lane, London.

Stiglitz, J.E. and Greenwald, B. (2003) *Towards a New Paradigm in Monetary Economics*, Cambridge University Press, Cambridge.

Streeck, W. (2009) *Re-Forming Capitalism: Institutional change in the German political economy*, Oxford University Press, Oxford.

Taleb, N.N. (2005) [2007] *Fooled by Randomness: The hidden role of chance in life and markets*, 2nd edn, New York/London, Penguin.

Tobin, J. (1978) A proposal for international monetary reform, *Eastern Economic Journal*, Vol. 4, pp. 153–59.

Triffin, R. (1961) *Gold and the Dollar Crisis: The future of convertibility*, Yale, New Haven, Conn.

United Nations (2009) *Recommendations by the Commission of Experts of the President of the General Assembly on Reforms of the International Monetary and Financial System, 19*, United Nations, März, www.un.org/ga/president/63/commission/financial_commission.shtml.

Weichenrieder, A.J. (2007) Profit shifting in the EU: evidence from Germany, CESifo Working Paper No. 2043, Munich.

Williamson, J. (2005) *Curbing the Boom–Bust Cycle: Stabilizing capital flows to emerging markets*, Institute for International Economics, Washington D.C.

Wilkinson, R. and Pickett, K. (2009) *The Spirit Level*, Allen Lane, London.

Wolf, M. (2008) *Fixing Global Finance*, Johns Hopkins University Press, Baltimore.

World Nuclear Association (2010) Nuclear power in Sweden, http://www.world-nuclear.org/info/inf42.html.

Zenglein, M. (2008) Marketization of the Chinese labor market and the role of unions, Global Labour University Working Paper No 4, Berlin.

Zhou Xiaochuan (2009) Reform of the International Monetary System, People's Bank of China, www.pbc.gov.cn/english/detail.asp?col=6500&id=178.

INDEX

This book has been published with the support of the
Friedrich Ebert Foundation.